Praise for

• T H E •
GOURMET
L • I • G • H • T
MENU COOKBOOK

"'Never to make do, but to do well' is the goal of Greer Under-wood in her health cookbooks. . . . Here are more than 150 dishes for the health-conscious, taste-conscious cook."
—*Diet & Nutrition Letter,* Tufts University

". . . Tailor-made for our times, satisfying America's demand for sophisticated tastes in addition to our desire to stay trim and healthy."
—*The Gourmet Retailer*

". . . Provides menus and recipes for meals ranging from quick weekday suppers to special-occasion dinner parties. Menus are interspersed with kitchen tips and short pieces on nutrition topics."
—*Working Mother* magazine

"Savor the natural flavors of foods—without the fat! Easy, elegant dishes every calorie-conscious chef should try."
—*Woman's World, The Woman's Weekly*

"The book lives up to its subtitle: 'Exciting New Recipes for the Health-Conscious Cook.' The menus given are full of wonder-fully appetizing dishes . . . that are low in calories, sodium and saturated fats."
—*Los Angeles Magazine*

"Try some of these recipes for yourself and see how delicious 'good' eating can be."
—*Ideas For Better Living*

"Greer Underwood knows how to cook food that is good and good for you, too. . . . Each of the book's recipes is a study in good nutrition."
—*Beverly* (MA) *Times*

". . . Interesting and usable recipes, elegant menu suggestions, helpful kitchen aids and techniques, plus sound nutritional guidance; all combined through interesting and skillful writing into a most valuable cookbook . . ."
—Jelia C. Witschi, lecturer on nutrition, Harvard University

·T H E·
GOURMET
L·I·G·H·T
MENU COOKBOOK

Exciting New Recipes
for the
Health-Conscious Cook

By Greer Underwood

illustrations by Frank Westerberg

The
Globe
Pequot
Press

CHESTER, CONNECTICUT

Library of Congress Cataloging-in-Publication Data

Underwood, Greer.
  The gourmet light menu cookbook.

  Reprint. Originally published: The enlightened gourmet.
Chester, Conn.: Globe Pequot Press, © 1986.
  Includes index.
  1. Cookery. 2. Nutrition. I. Title
TX652.U534 1988   641.5   88-19962
ISBN 0-87106-805-2

Manufactured in the United States of America
First Edition/Third Printing

❖ Contents ❖

❖ Acknowledgments ❖

Many thanks to all the people who have helped to make this book possible: To Cary Hull, an expert editor, who unerringly corrected my slip-ups, made the copy consistent, and suggested many changes for the better; this is a better book for you the reader. To Kate Bandos for her persuasive campaigns to get *The Enlightened Gourmet* noticed. To Kevin Lynch and Linda Kennedy for producing a lovely and readable book. To Lissa Tully, who gave me her last bag of black beans when the local store was out. To Nina Simonds and the staff of Al Forno for allowing me to adapt their recipes. To Carolyn Van Dam, who volunteered to take the photos for Frank Westerberg, who drew the clear, simplifying illustrations. To Jelia Witschi, Jane Lavine, Evette Hackman, and Laurie Burrows Grad for taking time from their busy schedules to review this book. To those at the Frances Stern Nutrition Center who figured all the nutrient values. And special thanks to Tripp and Tyler for sharing the computer with Mom, and to Teddy, who took us out when I couldn't cook another thing.

❖ Introduction: ❖
The Leaning of America

Less is more, physically speaking that is—more healthful, more attractive, more energizing. Consequently, American tastes are changing. The evidence is as ubiquitous as the salad bar, as prevalent as the backyard vegetable garden, as overwhelming as the selection of frozen low-calorie dinners. The leaning of America is changing the way we think about food, as more and more we are asking that daily fare not only be "thinning," but healthy, too. Nutrition is on the tip of everyone's tongue, and it's getting more than lip service. Yogurt sales are up; whole milk and egg sales are down. And though we still eat comparatively more red meat, poultry consumption hit a record 67.5 pounds per person in 1984. The fishing industry is reeling in profits, too, as nutrition-minded consumers turn to the sea in search of low-cholesterol, low-calorie alternatives to red meats.

Once the ethic primarily of the sandaled, head-banded young, nutrition has outgrown its organic roots, mushrooming into a mighty, healthy trend. From unassuming yet slightly sanctimonious brown rice and wheat germ have evolved sophisticates like Timbale of Dover Sole with Green Sauce. Such a dish is offered at New York's Four Seasons, one of a growing number of restaurants where a calorie-, cholesterol-, fat-, and sodium-controlled menu has become popular.

People of all ages and minds are asking not only that food satisfy, but also that it contribute to, not undermine, their well-being. Age is not—or shouldn't be—a factor in America's new abstinence. Epidemiological studies have pointed out a connection between childhood diet, adult cardiovascular disease, and some cancers, suggesting that it's never too soon to develop healthy, lifelong eating habits.

Led by fitness-centered "baby boomers," many Americans are doing just that. Whether the catalyst is a heart attack, a bout with cancer, or a simply a commitment to health, Americans have a new reverence for the workout and the knife and fork. It seems that what goes in is as important as what comes off. This belief in what's been called "The Right Foodstuff" may prove to be health science's most effective tool yet.

Research Suggests a Link between Diet and Disease

More people die in this country of coronary heart disease than any other illness. The second largest killer is cancer; the third, stroke. While diet does not cause these diseases, certain dietary patterns have been identified as risk factors in their high incidence. By contrast, in certain Third World countries where a low-fat, high-carbohydrate diet is the rule, heart disease is virtually unknown. In the past decade, as Americans have cut back on cholesterol and/or calorie-heavy foods such as eggs, red meat, whole milk, and butter, deaths from heart disease have dropped by more than 25 percent. Undoubtedly, though improved surgical techniques and quitting smoking have contributed to the decline, some health experts believe that up to 40 percent of the reduction can be attributed to America's changing diet.

Evidence is also mounting that some forms of cancer, the second leading cause of death, are influenced by diet as well. In Japan, for example, where the typical diet is less than 20 percent fat (ours is about 30 percent), the rate of breast cancer is significantly lower than it is here. Japanese women who have moved to the United States in adolescence and added more meat and dairy products to their diet have increased their rate of breast cancer. This suggests that childhood as well as adult diet plays an important factor in lifelong disease prevention.

A nine-member panel of doctors, biochemists, and nutritionists brought together in 1983 by a government agency as the Dietary Guidelines Advisory Committee has written a prescription for healthy eating. Fortunately, heart disease and some cancers can be combatted with the same forkful. Their recommendations:

- Cut down on foods high in saturated fats and choles-terol in favor of whole grains, vegetables, and fruit. (In 1984 a panel convened as part of the National Institutes of Health concluded "beyond a reasonable doubt" that lowering elevated blood cholesterol levels would re-duce the risk of heart attacks, though some special-interest groups will still argue the connection between elevated blood cholesterol levels and heart disease.)
- Eat a variety of foods. (While most foods have more than one nutrient, no single food provides all the es-sential nutrients.)
- Eat foods high in fiber. (Studies of population groups that eat lots of fiber show lower incidences of colon cancer.)
- Avoid too much sugar; maintain ideal weight. (People who weigh within 10 percent of the desirable ranges have the lowest cancer rates.)
- Avoid too much sodium. (This is of particular concern to those susceptible to or with hypertension.)

Nutrition Know-how

Given America's changing diet, it seems that we can look forward to a healthy future. Encouraging as the prognosis is, however, there are still discouraging signs. Sales of cheese—a high-fat, high-calorie, high-cholesterol prod-uct—have soared, tripling in the past thirty years. More-over, thanks to the persistence of the American sweet tooth, the candy business has never been sweeter. We are eating more protein foods than ever before, almost three-quarters of a pound a person per day; this is way more than we need or is even recommended, as a high-protein diet is also often a high-fat diet. Soft drink, beer, and wine sales are spirited, with the soft drink business growing 300 percent in the past thirty years.

This is not to question the earnestness of America's eaters; a Harris Poll showed that 90 percent of those sur-veyed were "very concerned" or "somewhat concerned" about nutrition. Rather, it points up the complexity of knowing what's good for us. After all, there's more to nutrition than that adage about carrots and eyesight.

Test your nutrition awareness with this quiz.

The Questions

1. Veal is lower in cholesterol than other red meats.
2. Not all vegetable oils are high in unsaturated fats (the good kind) and low in saturated fats (the bad kind).
3. Shellfish is high in cholesterol.
4. Granola bars are a better nutritional value than a candy bar.
5. If a product is labeled "sugar free" it has no calories from sweeteners.
6. Chicken McNuggets (six to a serving) are higher in calories, sodium, and cholesterol than a McDonald's hamburger.
7. A carob candy bar, the kind you buy at the health food store, is better for you than a chocolate candy bar.
8. Whole wheat bread is lower in calories than white bread.
9. Dietary cholesterol is an important concern when feeding youngsters.
10. Protein foods give us strength.
11. Today, Americans are eating more chicken and fish per person than red meat.
12. "Natural" foods, such as "pure" spring water, raw (unpasteurized) milk, and "organic" vegetables, are healthier because they contain fewer harmful and foreign substances.
13. Which is most important to good health: cutting the amount of fat in the diet or getting enough vitamins and minerals?
14. Removing the skin from poultry lowers its cholesterol value.
15. If the label says "no cholesterol," the product can still be high in saturated fats.

The Answers

1. **False.** While veal is generally lower in calories than other red meats, it is slightly higher in cholesterol values.
2. **True.** Some vegetable oils, specifically palm and coconut oils, which are widely used in commercially prepared foods and mixes, are high in saturated fats, which can raise blood cholesterol levels.
3. **False.** Until recently it was thought that shellfish was high in cholesterol. That's because traditional methods of food analysis identified certain fats in shellfish that are similar to cholesterol as true cholesterol. Newer methods have shown shellfish to generally have lower readings than meat. Shrimp carries about 150 milligrams of cholesterol per serving, crab and lobster about the same as meat, and oysters, clams, and scallops a rather low 50 milligrams per serving. And shellfish is decidedly lower in calories than meat.
4. **True.** But, ever so slight. Once 50 to 60 percent of the calories in a granola bar came from sweeteners and fats. But as the proportion of oils, modified food starches, emulsifiers, and candylike ingredients has grown, the proportion of oats and wheat that gave the bar a slight nutritional edge has shrunk. Most granola bars now attribute 70 to 80 percent of their calories to sweeteners and fat, thus providing a minimal advantage over candy bars.
5. **False.** A product sweetened with sorbitol, xylitol, mannitol, or fructose supplies calories from those sweeteners.
6. **True.** Although McNuggets are made from chicken, a lower-calorie alternative to beef, they are processed with bits of skin throughout the meat and fried, predominantly, in animal fat, making them a higher-calorie choice (80 more, in fact) than the single hamburger. The sodium is roughly the same (505 milligrams, about 1/5 teaspoon of salt), but the amount of cholesterol more than doubles. How a food is

cooked is often as important as the raw ingredient.

7. **False.** Both the carob and candy bar are high in saturated fats. In the chocolate bar the fat comes from cocoa butter; in the carob bar, the fat comes from palm oil.

8. **False.** They are identical in calories.

9. **True.** Studies have shown that childhood diet does have an influence on health later in life. And we don't need professional studies to know that if nutrition awareness starts young, education and retraining won't be needed later on.

10. **False.** Strength comes from exercising a healthy body—a body made healthy by carbohydrates, fats, protein, vitamins, and minerals.

11. **False.** Although we are eating more poultry than in early times, we still eat more red meat.

12. **False.** "Natural" products are not necessarily purer. Raw milk has accounted for 95 percent of the milk-borne diseases reported to the Centers for Disease Control in the past thirty years. Bottled water is not always as healthful as we might like to think; it can came from a source that is high in sodium, for example. Up to three-quarters of the bottled water sold in the United States is *processed* from local taps. And "organically" grown vegetables are not higher in vitamin or mineral content than other vegetables.

13. Most health experts concur that the average American diet supplies enough vitamins and minerals. What is needed for a healthy diet is not more but less—less fat, that is. Fat should account for no more than from 25 percent to at most 30 percent of the diet.

14. **False.** Oddly, removing the fat from chicken doesn't lower its cholesterol value, but it does reduce calories and saturated fats.

15. **True.** Foods such as margarines can be low in cholesterol but still be made with oils high in saturated fats, which in turn can elevate blood cholesterol levels.

Public awareness of nutrition has come a long way from the notion that certain foods were mysteriously "good for us." Though now accepted by the mainstream, good nutrition is still fraught with myths. It's possible that these misconceptions may have serious consequences if you are in a high-risk group for either heart disease or cancer. Making nutritionally sound choices requires being guided by fact as well as taste. It's my hope that this book will provide the reader with both.

Who Is the Enlightened Gourmet?

The enlightened gourmet believes that good food needn't be loaded with calories, sodium, or saturated fats. The enlightened gourmet is someone who wants it all, good taste plus nutritional benefits. The enlightened gourmet is not looking for the secret of everlasting life nor expecting "miracle" cures from foods but views eating as a social pleasure. The enlightened gourmet believes that while eating foods can't provide a cure, overindulgence in some foods can contribute to ill health and/or overweight. The enlightened gourmet takes pleasure in eating delicious but health-conscious foods.

The Recipes

Taste, coupled with an eye for nutritive values, was always my guiding light for recipe writing. That means there's compromise between the purely medical stance and the culinary one. Butter, for example, which is high in saturated fats but superior in flavor compared with other shortenings, is cautiously used here. When flavor is paramount, such as for the saucing of vegetables or as a spread, the judicious use of butter is recommended; but when a recipe requires only the properties of a fat, unsaturated vegetable oils are specified. Foods high in cholesterol and saturated fats have been avoided, but that doesn't mean that there are no red meats. Lean cuts are used exclusively; the reader is advised on techniques that can render these tougher cuts more tender. As in my previous book, *Gourmet Light*, the aim was never to make do, but to do well. For that reason there are no sugar substitutes, no attempts to whip dry milk powder into a palatable dessert topping, and no hocus-pocus to transform chopped chuck into porterhouse in *The Enlightened Gourmet*—only an honest effort to serve up food with a bit of panache, yet sensibly seasoned and complemented (read no blueberry-sauced chicken breasts). These are recipes that aim to highlight the natural goodness of food through calorie-, cholesterol-, and sodium-conservative selection and preparation.

Among the more traditional meals are a few vegetarian menus. When possible, legumes, oats, barley, and other high-fiber, cholesterol-fighting food items are used. Trendy ingredients—porcini, for example—are not much used because they're not available in all sections of the country. Whenever possible, alternatives are suggested. The majority of the recipes are easy to prepare but others will allow the devoted cook to indulge in a creative pastime.

Each recipe has been analyzed by the Frances Stern Nutrition Center of the New England Medical Center Hospitals for calories and protein, fat, carbohydrate, sodium, cholesterol, and dietary fiber values per serving. The recipes have been denoted ✦ to identify those particularly low in calories, low in cholesterol (100 milligrams or less per serving), low in sodium, and containing a good amount of dietary fiber. These designations were determined in light of recommended daily allowances (for healthy persons) of cholesterol (300 milligrams), sodium (1,000 to 3,000 milligrams), and fiber (25 grams), and by comparing the *Enlightened Gourmet* versions with traditional recipes. Also considered was the prominence of the food in the daily diet. An entree supplying 75 milligrams of cholesterol, for example, would be considered low, but a dessert or salad with a similar count would not. Readers interested in weight loss should think twice before indulging in a dessert of 175 calories or so. While the *Enlightened Gourmet* recipe may be lower in calories than the standard version, it may not fit into a sensible reduction scheme but is more suitable for those maintaining a healthy weight.

The Enlightened Gourmet is divided into four sections. The first, "Festive Occasion Menus," are three-course meals for entertaining or for a quiet but elegant dinner for two. The second, "Menus for Informal Entertaining or Family Dinners," includes main-dish recipes with vegetable accompaniments, sometimes with a dessert. In "Pasta Passions," the third section, commercial or homemade pastas are offered with appropriate salads and an occasional dessert. The fourth section, "Dinner in the Kitchen," is a collection of simply-prepared meals, some followed by a sweet. The menus were selected to provide balance, nutritionally and visually. Unlike eighteenth-century Russia where dinners were planned around a monochromatic scheme—all red, for example, or all green—we look for contrasts of color and texture in our meals. The menus were also planned with the cook's organization in mind; last-minute cooking chores are kept to a minimum. Anything that can be done ahead is noted, with tips on reheating conventionally or in a microwave oven when possible. In all menus, any unusual ingredient is pointed out in the brief introduction, and any complicated steps are illustrated.

I do not give recipes for boiled rice, steamed asparagus, and a few other basic dishes included in the menus. These are marked with an asterisk.

Although the recipes are presented in menu form, any may be used singly. The recipes in "Festive Occasion Menus" are not necessarily for the fancy table, nor are recipes from "Dinner in the Kitchen" solely for casual meals. To help locate recipes without going through each menu, there is the Recipe Index, by food category, beginning on page 354. This is followed by the conventional back-of-the-book index.

Throughout the book are "Focus" items. Anywhere from a few short sentences to several paragraphs in length, these are topics of concern to cooks and those interested in the foods they eat. Some of these topics are culinary in nature, some involve kitchen chemistry, and some deal with nutritional points of interest. All are meant to entertain and inform—as is *The Enlightened Gourmet.*

To your good health and eating pleasure!

FESTIVE
OCCASION
MENUS

❖ Festive Occasion Menus ❖

In this section are menus for those special occasions that command commemoration. From a cocktail party for fourteen to a cozy fireside dinner for four, these are meals designed to pamper your guests. Yet no one need feel guilty with every forkful. These are fresh foods prepared without excessive calories. Every effort has been made to trim the nutritional "bad guys" while enhancing the healthy; to deliver flavor unhitched to fat.

Throughout the recipes are instructions on what may be accomplished ahead of serving time. These are generally outlined in the menu introduction, then noted specifically within the recipe. Last-minute chores have been kept to a minimum.

The reader is encouraged to play with the menu suggestions as whim and availability direct, substituting here, deleting there. Although these recipes are labeled "special occasion," taken out of context, many are casual enough for family meals.

❖A study of Masai warriors, who walk and exercise a lot each day, proved them to be in excellent physical condition. Despite a diet high in saturated fat and cholesterol, heart disease is virtually unknown in their culture. While exercise alone can't be completely credited (factors such as stress, smoking, and genetics were not taken into account), the benefits of exercise can't be overlooked either.❖

A COCKTAIL PARTY

Shiitake and Pine Nut Tartlets

Steamed Crabmeat Wontons

Sweet and Sour Onions

Chili-Coriander Dip

Grilled Beef Sticks with Horseradish Sauce

Roasted Cherrystones Oregano

Garlic Shrimp

Because social occasions most often revolve around eating and drinking, the diet-conscious must either practice enormous self-restraint or pay the price with unwanted weight. Typical cocktail nibbles of cheese, pâtés, and sour cream dips are loaded caloric bombshells guaranteed to explode right on your hips. Never mind that a carrot stick carries the dip to your mouth or the cheese rests on a nice whole wheat cracker; your mind may be fooled but the scale won't lie. The temptations are even harder to resist after a mind-weakening drink or two.

Here then is a cocktail party, for as many as fourteen, where you don't have to be on your guard. From the rich-tasting wild mushroom tarts with a flaky phyllo crust (much lower in calories than traditional pastry) to the finger-licking spicy shrimp, this is cocktail fare that's missing nothing but calories.

Organizing your work for the party will greatly simplify it. You may start your preparation as much as a month ahead, if you like, with the Shiitake and Pine Nut Tartlets, freezing them (great to have on hand for drop-in company), leaving just a quick reheat at party time. The Steamed Crabmeat Wontons also may be frozen for as much as a week; just steam them at party time. Plan to whip up the Sweet and Sour Onions and the Chili-Coriander Dip up to three days ahead. The day before the party, marinate and skewer the beef for the Grilled Beef Sticks with Horseradish Sauce, make the topping for the Roasted Cherrystones Oregano, and prepare the vegetables to accompany the Chili-Coriander Dip. That will leave the Garlic Shrimp to prepare the day of the party.

Before the party arrange and garnish the serving trays. Copy all the heating and any cooking instructions on pieces of note paper and tape them to the stove. If possible hire someone (possibly two teenagers) to man the ovens and pass the trays.

Enjoy! You won't have to work it off tomorrow!

❖ Focus: Imported ❖ Mushrooms

At about the same time we Americans became fiercely chauvinistic about food, we also discovered a whole world of hitherto strange and once mostly imported mushrooms. Many supermarkets now sell fresh shiitake (shi-tauk-e) and oyster mushrooms, and enokis have popped up occasionally too. Make use of these often, for such exotic mushrooms deliver great flavor for few calories and minimal fat. Here are some of the more common, uncommon mushrooms:

Chanterelles: Very mild in flavor with a yellow to orange color, chanterelles are sold both fresh and dried.
Cepes: (Rhymes with steps.) Cinnamon colored cap, sold fresh in some sections of the country and available all year in dried form. Also known as porcini. Fabulous flavor, strong and earthy.
Shiitake mushrooms: Also known as Chinese black mushroom or Doubloon. Cinnamon brown to light beige. Very compatible with Oriental seasonings and garlic. Excellent, meaty flavor.

Shiitake and
Pine Nut Tartlets

❖

These delicious little tartlets taste deceivingly rich, yet are light and easy to make. They may be made a day ahead, then chilled and reheated, or frozen up to a month. Don't be tempted to reheat them in a microwave oven though, or they'll suffer from a soggy crust.

> 6 ounces mushrooms
> 2 small onions, chopped (about ¾ cup)
> 1 garlic clove, minced
> 2 tablespoons homemade chicken stock or
>   canned broth
> 1 tablespoon corn oil
> 3½ ounces fresh shiitake mushrooms, sliced
> 4 tablespoons minced fresh parsley
> 2 tablespoons freshly grated Parmesan cheese
> a few gratings fresh nutmeg
> freshly ground black pepper to taste
> 3 tablespoons pine nuts
> 1½ sheets (14 by 18 inches) phyllo dough
> 1 tablespoon butter, melted
> ¾ cup whole milk
> 1 egg
> 1 egg white
> freshly ground black pepper to taste

To Prepare the Filling

1. Finely chop the mushrooms (but not the shiitakes) in a food processor or by hand. Mound the mushrooms on an absorbent kitchen towel, gather the ends together, and squeeze the mushroom "ball" over the sink to extract the liquid.
2. "Saute" the onions and garlic in the chicken broth in a

covered 12-inch nonstick skillet over medium-low heat until the onions are transparent, not browned.

3. Add the squeezed mushrooms to the skillet. Raise the heat to medium-high and cook the mushrooms, stirring frequently, until they have turned grayish and the liquid has evaporated. Scrape the mushroom-onion mixture into a 1-quart bowl.

4. Heat the corn oil in the empty skillet. Add the shiitake mushrooms and saute for 3 to 4 minutes over medium-high heat. Add to the mushroom-onion mixture along with the parsley, cheese, nutmeg, and pepper.

5. Coat the same skillet with cooking spray. Over high heat toast the pine nuts until browned, about 2 minutes, shaking the pan by the handle frequently. Be careful they do not burn. Stir them into mushroom mixture.

To Prepare the Tartlet Pans

1. Coat 18 2-inch tartlet pans with cooking spray. Arrange in rows of three on a baking sheet.

2. Preheat the oven to 350 degrees. Fold a sheet of phyllo dough in half the short way. (The dough will now measure 9 inches by 14 inches.) With scissors cut the dough lengthwise into fourths. (Each strip will measure approximately 9 inches by 3½ inches.) Lay each strip over a row of 3 tartlet pans; snip the dough between the pans. Trim the dough to the rim of the pan with scissors; brush the dough with melted butter as you complete a row. Repeat until all the pans are lined with dough. Don't worry that the edges are messy now. You will have half a sheet of phyllo left over; just throw it away.

To Assemble and Bake

1. Whisk together the milk, egg, egg white, and pepper in a 2-cup or larger measuring cup. Place a rounded teaspoon of mushroom mixture in each lined tartlet pan. Fill the tartlet with the milk mixture, smooth the top,

and gently submerge the dough edges in the liquid.

2. Bake in the lower third of the oven for 25 to 30 minutes or until puffed slightly and golden brown. If you are planning to reheat the tartlets before serving them, undercook them slightly. Cool them for ½ hour on the counter, then refrigerate or freeze them in the pans. Reheat the frozen tartlets in a 325-degree oven for 20 to 25 minutes or until they are browned and hot. Do not thaw before reheating.

Yield: 18 2-inch tartlets
✦ **Calories per tartlet: 55**
   Carbohydrate per tartlet: 4g
✦ **Cholesterol per tartlet: 19mg**

Dietary fiber per tartlet: 0g
Fat per tartlet: 4g
Protein per tartlet: 2g
✦ **Sodium per tartlet: 25mg**

Steamed Crabmeat Wontons

❖

Bundles of crabmeat in a wonton wrapper, steamed not fried, provide an Oriental touch without all the fat calories of the more typical deep-fat-fried crispy wonton. These may be prepared and frozen for as long as a week—not much longer, though, or they begin to lose flavor. If they're to be held more than 3 hours before steaming, pop them into the freezer to prevent the wrappers from getting soggy. If you don't have a wok and bamboo steamer, fashion one by placing a rack on inverted custard cups in a deep electric skillet.

As there are more than 24 wonton wrappers in a package, you might like a few extra to garnish a hot and spicy soup: Add 4 to 5 wontons and ½ cup bean sprouts to a 10½-ounce can of beef broth, and season it to taste with reduced sodium soy sauce, sesame oil, and hot oil. Sesame oil and hot oil are Oriental seasonings available in some markets and specialty food shops.

For the Dipping Sauce

⅓ cup reduced-sodium soy sauce
2 tablespoons rice wine or dry sherry
¼ teaspoon sesame oil

For the Crabmeat Wontons

½ cup canned water chestnuts (if fresh, peel and
    blanch)
2 scallions, minced
1 piece (¾ ounce) bacon
2 teaspoons minced fresh ginger
½ teaspoon sesame oil
2 egg whites
1 teaspoon rice wine or dry sherry
4–5 drops hot oil
1 tablespoon cornstarch
1 cup flaked, uncooked crabmeat (available
    frozen) or seafood flakes
1 tablespoon water
24 wonton wrappers

To Prepare the Dipping Sauce

1. Combine the soy sauce, rice wine, and sesame oil in a small bowl. Stir to combine. Set aside (refrigerate if holding more than ½ hour).

To Prepare the Wontons

1. In a food processor combine the water chestnuts, half the scallions, bacon, half the ginger, sesame oil, 1 egg white, rice wine, hot oil, and cornstarch. Process a few seconds until well mixed. Add the crabmeat; pulse the machine just to mix, don't puree.
2. With a fork beat the remaining egg white with the

MAKING WONTON CANAPES

After folding the filled wonton wrapper in half into a triangle, pinch the three corners of the triangle tightly together to form a "topknot."

water. Place 4 wonton wrappers on a work surface. Brush edges with the egg wash. Place a rounded teaspoon of the crabmeat filling in the center. Fold the wrapper in half to form a triangle. Then bring all three corners together, pinching tightly to form a "top knot." (Refer to the illustration as you do this.) Repeat with remaining wonton wrappers.

3. If you are holding the wontons more than 3 hours before steaming, freeze (up to 1 week) to prevent the wrapper from becoming soggy. They may be cooked frozen or thawed.

4. To steam, bring 2 cups water to a boil in a wok with the remaining ginger and scallion. Cover the bottom of a bamboo steamer with cheesecloth to prevent wontons from sticking. Arrange wontons in the steamer in a single layer so they don't touch (stack two bamboo steamers if possible). Fit bamboo steamer into wok and cook 12 to 15 minutes, moving the top steamer to the bottom after 6 minutes. If wontons are done in two or

more batches, add more water to wok. Serve with dipping sauce.

Wontons

Yield: 24–25 wontons
✦ Calories per wonton: 36
Carbohydrate per wonton: 4g
✦ Cholesterol per wonton: 13mg

Dietary fiber per wonton: 0g
Fat per wonton: 1g
Protein per wonton: 2g
Sodium per wonton: 94mg

Sauce

Yield: 8 tablespoons
Calories per teaspoon: 5
Carbohydrate per teaspoon: 0g
Cholesterol per teaspoon: 0mg

Dietary fiber per teaspoon: 0g
Fat per teaspoon: 0g
Protein per teaspoon: 0g
Sodium per teaspoon: 128mg

Sweet and Sour Onions

❖

Because these cocktail onions will only improve with a few days' soak in the sweet-sour sauce, they may be made several days in advance. Try any leftovers (an unlikely event) as a delicious hot vegetable; they are particularly good with beef or game.

½ pound pearl onions
2 teaspoons arrowroot
1 cup homemade chicken stock or canned
    chicken broth
1 tablespoon minced red bell pepper
1 tablespoon minced green bell pepper
2 tablespoons brown sugar
1 tablespoon balsamic vinegar
4 whole cloves
1 teaspoon minced fresh ginger
¼ teaspoon salt
dash of cayenne pepper

1. Trim the root end from the onions. Cut a small cross into the bottom of the onions so they won't explode when cooking. Bring a quart of water to a boil, add onions, and boil 3 to 4 minutes. Drain, and when cool enough to handle, slip off the skins. Place the onions in a bowl.
2. Moisten the arrowroot in 2 tablespoons of the broth. Heat the remaining chicken broth and the peppers in a 1-quart pan until just boiling.
3. Remove the pan from the heat and whisk in arrowroot. Return to medium heat, whisking until thickened, about 2 to 3 minutes. Off the heat whisk in brown sugar, vinegar, cloves, ginger, salt, and cayenne.
4. Pour the sauce over the onions and chill at least 8 hours, covered. Serve with toothpicks.

Yield: about 48 onions
✦ Calories per 3 onions: 13
Carbohydrate per 3 onions: 17g
✦ Cholesterol per 3 onions: 0mg
Dietary fiber per 3 onions: 0g
Fat per 3 onions: 1g
Protein per 3 onions: 3g
Sodium per 3 onions: 347mg

Chili-Coriander Dip
❖

This marvelously zesty dip is a healthy alternative to the sour cream and mayonnaise dips so frequently offered up with crudités. Very reminiscent of a basil pesto, it may be served as is or mixed to taste with plain yogurt. It will keep under refrigeration for up to 2 weeks, so you might want to double the recipe; it'll make a mid-afternoon snack of carrot sticks infinitely more appealing.

1 cup fresh coriander, snipped
1 cup fresh parsley, snipped
½ fresh jalapeño pepper, or to taste

1 tablespoon dry bread crumbs
2 garlic cloves, peeled
1 tablespoon olive oil
2 tablespoons slivered almonds
2 tablespoons freshly grated Romano or Parmesan
    cheese (optional)
1 teaspoon lemon juice
½ teaspoon salt
1 teaspoon white wine or herb vinegar
½ cup homemade chicken stock or canned broth

1. Combine all ingredients except the chicken broth in a
   food processor. Gradually add the broth while the machine continues to run. Stop to scrape down the sides,
   then continue to process until herbs are well minced,
   but dip is not pureed. Chill until serving time.

Yield: 1 cup
✦ Calories per tablespoon: 22
Carbohydrate per tablespoon: 1g
✦ Cholesterol per tablespoon: 1mg

Dietary fiber per tablespoon: 0g
Fat per tablespoon: 2g
Protein per tablespoon: 1g
Sodium per tablespoon: 114mg

Grilled Beef Sticks with Horseradish Sauce

❖

Meat lovers don't get the short stick when these tangy
hors d'oeuvres are served. Easy to prepare, and easy to eat,
they're a natural anytime you need to serve "stand-up
food." Horseradish and beef are natural partners, but if
you prefer, the amount of horseradish may be halved. The
beef may marinate, skewered or not, for up to 24 hours
before grilling or broiling. You will need 30 9- or 10-inch
skewers.

2 pounds boneless top loin beef steak, trimmed
2 cups plain yogurt
⅔ cup prepared horseradish
⅛ teaspoon ground cloves

1. The meat can be sliced more easily if it is partially frozen. Slice it on the bias in ¼-inch-thick, 2-inch-wide strips. The thick piece at the end of the steak may be flattened before slicing by placing it between 2 sheets of waxed paper and pounding with a mallet.
2. Combine the yogurt, horseradish, and cloves. Marinate the meat either threaded on the skewers or not, as you like. If skewers are not marinated with the meat, soak them in water for a half hour before threading on the meat for grilling.
3. Grill or broil the meat 3 to 5 minutes a side, depending on how well done you like it. Baste meat with marinade as it cooks.

Yield: 30 skewers
✦ **Calories per skewer: 52**
Carbohydrate per skewer: 1g
✦ **Cholesterol per skewer: 17mg**

Dietary fiber per skewer: 0g
Fat per skewer: 1g
Protein per skewer: 5g
✦ **Sodium per skewer: 25 mg**

Roasted Cherrystones Oregano

❖

For shellfish lovers here's an easy-to-eat taste of the sea, embellished a bit with a crisp herb topping. The cook will be happy not having to pry open stubborn shells, for a hot oven does the work quickly. The topping may be made as much as 24 hours in advance and the clams opened and chopped as much as 8 hours before party time. Don't combine the two until just before baking, however, or the topping will be soggy, not crispy. And be sure to make fresh crumbs from authentic French bread for the best flavor and texture.

2 tablespoons unsalted butter
2 tablespoons olive oil, extra-virgin recommended
1 garlic clove, minced
1 shallot, minced
2 cups loosely packed crumbs from fresh French bread
16–20 leaves raw spinach, stems removed
⅓ cup minced fresh parsley
1 teaspoon dried oregano
⅛ teaspoon salt
freshly ground black pepper to taste
24 cherrystone clams, scrubbed
1 tablespoon lemon juice

1. Melt butter and oil in a 9-inch skillet over high heat until foamy. Saute garlic and shallot over medium heat until tender, but not browned. Add bread crumbs and cook over medium-high heat until lightly browned.
2. Meanwhile, stack the spinach leaves and roll up jellyroll fashion. Slice crosswise into thin strips. Toss with the crumbs over medium-high heat 1 to 2 minutes or until slightly wilted.
3. Remove the pan from the stove. Add the parsley, oregano, salt, and pepper. Set topping aside (it may be refrigerated up to 24 hours).
4. Preheat oven to 450 degrees. Cook clams on a baking sheet in the upper third of the oven until they open, about 2 to 3 minutes. Cool clams, but leave the oven on if you're completing recipe now. Shuck clams, reserving juice as a base for fish stock or to enjoy, strained, as a beverage. Discard one half of shell, and free the meat from the remaining shell. Rinse meat, then chop it roughly either by hand or in a food processor.
5. Divide the chopped clams among the 24 shells. Sprin-

kle with the lemon juice. (Refrigerate up to 8 hours, if you wish.)

6. Just before baking divide the topping mixture over the clams. Bake in top third of 450-degree oven for 15 minutes or until lightly browned and heated through.

Note: If you prefer, cook clams ahead and reheat on medium power in a microwave oven.

Yield: 24 clams	**Dietary fiber per clam: 0g**
Calories per clam: 70	**Fat per clam: 3g**
Carbohydrate per clam: 8g	**Protein per clam: 3g**
✦ **Cholesterol per clam: 12mg**	**Sodium per clam: 128mg**

Garlic Shrimp
❖

This is my variation of a popular Chinese dish. While oenophiles might blanch, we love to make a meal of these with a bottle of champagne as often as we can drum up some event that needs celebration. While it is a last-minute dish, the few items needed may be readied at stove side in preparation for the 4 or so minutes of cooking time.

> 2 tablespoons peanut oil
> 2 garlic cloves, minced
> ½ pound unshelled raw shrimp (26–32 to the pound)
> 1¼ teaspoons chili paste with garlic, available at Oriental markets, some supermarkets, and specialty food shops
> 1 teaspoon sweet paprika
> 1 tablespoon pine nuts

3 tablespoons Chinese cooking wine or
  medium-dry sherry
a few drops lemon juice
2 tablespoons minced fresh parsley (optional)

1. In a 12-inch skillet heat the oil over high heat until it is
   hot. Add the garlic and cook, stirring, until pale golden.
   Reduce the heat to prevent burning, if necessary.
2. Add the shrimp and chili paste. Cook over high heat for
   1 minute, shaking the pan by the handle, until shellfish
   are pink. Add paprika and pine nuts; cook, continuing
   to shake the pan, for 30 seconds.
3. Add the cooking wine and boil for 30 seconds. Season
   with the lemon juice. Transfer to a serving platter and
   sprinkle with parsley.

Yield: 32 shrimp

✦ Calories per shrimp: 28	Dietary fiber per shrimp: 0g
Carbohydrate per shrimp: 1g	Fat per shrimp: 2g
✦ Cholesterol per shrimp: 14mg	Protein per shrimp: 3g
	✦ Sodium per shrimp: 9mg

❖ Focus: Dieting ❖

A good diet:

- establishes a reasonable weight loss goal.
- reduces the daily intake of calories while
  increasing the physical expenditure of calories to
  ensure a steady and continuous loss.
- retrains the person's eating behaviors forever, not
  just for the duration of the diet.
- provides a variety of foods, interestingly prepared
  and presented so boredom and/or inadequate
  nutrition are never a factor.
- allows for adequate time for the desired weight
  loss. No one gets heavy in a week or two, yet we
  all want to get skinny quickly.

The successful dieter:

- is mentally prepared for the hard work of losing weight.
- has a working knowledge of basic nutrition and the general caloric content of common foods.
- knows one day's discretion will not ruin a week's weight loss, but also doesn't use that thought as an excuse to overeat regularly.
- provides him- or herself with rewards for good eating behavior. The reward may just be the self-satisfaction gained from success or something more material.
- is prepared to be totally honest about the amount and kinds of foods eaten.
- above all, is self-motivated to lose.

❖Meat, and particularly liver, provides the most abundant source of usable iron. Although iron is also found in legumes, grains, and green vegetables, it is not always readily available to the body. For example, although a cup of cooked spinach contains 4.3 milligrams (women of childbearing age need about 18 milligrams daily) of iron, the body can only use about 1 to 2 percent of that. If you don't eat meat (including poultry and eggs) you'd be wise to include soybeans, dried fruits such as raisins, enriched grain products, broccoli, and collard and mustard greens in your diet. Include orange juice or some other acid (sprinkle broccoli with raspberry vinegar, for example) in the meal to boost iron absorption.❖

SPRING FLING

"Cream" of Asparagus Soup

Hot Mushroom Salad with Red Pepper Jelly Dressing

Lamb Medallions in Phyllo with Green Peppercorn Stuffing

Minted Peas

Lemon Mousse Cake with Raspberry Sauce

What better reason to celebrate than the fragrant return of spring and some special seasonal foods—asparagus, new peas, and tender lamb. This is an ambitious menu, although much can be done ahead. It is planned for just four, or possibly five.

At the center of the menu is a leg of lamb that is boned, trimmed of all fat, and sliced into medallions. Smeared with a green peppercorn dressing and wrapped in phyllo, it makes a lovely (yet economical) presentation. It can be prepared and frozen days—even weeks—in advance of baking.

Some days before the dinner, prepare and freeze (if holding more than two days) the lamb medallions. The day before, complete the soup (gently reheat in a double boiler), vegetables for the salad (the mushrooms reheat nicely conventionally or by microwave), the salad dressing, the cake, and the raspberry sauce. The morning of the dinner prepare the lemon mousse and assemble the cake. This completes the cooking chores except for reheating a few items and cooking the peas. If the time is not an issue, prepare the soup the day of the dinner.

Because there is no starch in this menu due to the phyllo, peas, and cake, you might think your plate looks a bit empty. Put the salad directly on the dinner plate, or perhaps use a smaller dinner plate.

"Cream" of Asparagus Soup
❖

It's hard to believe one would ever tire of asparagus simply steamed and buttered, but the thick-stalked tougher types might do better as a soup. Here's a bowl of flavor without the fat of a typically prepared cream soup. If the soup is made ahead, reheat it in a double boiler over barely simmering water.

> 1 pound fresh asparagus
> 1 small onion, chopped (about ¾ cup)
> 3 cups homemade chicken stock or canned broth
> 1 egg
> ⅔ cup whole milk
> 3 teaspoons arrowroot
> ¼ teaspoon salt
> freshly ground black pepper to taste
> a few gratings fresh nutmeg

1. Trim the whitened, tough ends from the stalks. Thick asparagus are best peeled: Grasp the asparagus at the tip; pull a vegetable peeler down the length of the stalk, rotating the spear as each length is finished. Set ½ pound aside; chop the remaining ½ pound.
2. Combine chopped asparagus, onion, and chicken stock in a 2½-quart saucepan. Cover, bring to a boil, reduce heat, and simmer 30 minutes.
3. Pour soup base into a food processor, blender, or food mill, and puree. Return the soup to the saucepan.
4. Blanch the remaining ½ pound of asparagus in a 10-inch skillet three-quarters full of water until just tender

(about 3 minutes for very thin stalks, as long as 6 to 7 minutes for thicker ones). Drain, chop, and add to the soup base.

5. Beat the egg with the milk and arrowroot. Whisk into the soup over low heat. Season with salt, pepper, and nutmeg. Continue to whisk over low heat until soup thickens, about 4 to 5 minutes. Serve immediately, or refrigerate and reheat in a double boiler.

Yield: 5 1-cup servings
✦ Calories per serving: 84
Carbohydrate per serving: 9g
✦ Cholesterol per serving: 60mg

Dietary fiber per serving: 1g
Fat per serving: 3g
Protein per serving: 8g
✦ Sodium per serving: 155mg

Hot Mushroom Salad with Red Pepper Jelly Dressing

❖

Red pepper jelly was the hostess gift of choice the year it made the cocktail circuit with cream cheese and crackers (before the "eat light" era!); perhaps a stray jar or two is now gathering dust next to your fondue pot. Here it makes a comeback as a zesty salad dressing. If the cupboard's bare, most gourmet shops sell jalapeño pepper jellies, which will do very nicely. Check the label; some are *very* hot. The mushrooms, peppers, and dressing may be prepared a day ahead; before serving toss the vegetables in a nonstick skillet over medium-high heat until warmed through, and leave the dressing at room temperature for 30 minutes to liquefy or heat briefly in a microwave oven.

1 red bell pepper
12 ounces mushrooms, sliced

2½ tablespoons red pepper or jalapeño pepper
   jelly
5 tablespoons canned beef consomme or
   homemade beef stock
2½ tablespoons balsamic vinegar
4 tablespoons olive oil, extra-virgin recommended
a dash of cayenne pepper if jelly isn't hot
1 small head Boston or other soft-leafed lettuce,
   rinsed and spun dry

1. To roast the pepper, cut it in half the long way, and remove the seeds. Flatten each half with the heel of your
   hand. Broil on a baking sheet, skin side up, until blackened and charred, about 5 minutes. Cool in freezer or
   on the counter in a tightly closed paper bag. Pull off
   the skin and discard; julienne the flesh.
2. Coat a 10-inch nonstick skillet with cooking spray.
   "Saute" the mushrooms over high heat until lightly
   browned, about 4 to 5 minutes, stirring often. Add
   pepper strips and toss until they are heated through.
3. Meanwhile, melt the jelly in a small, heavy saucepan
   over low heat or in a microwave oven. Remove the pan
   from the heat, and stir in the consomme, vinegar, olive
   oil, and cayenne.
4. Line salad plates with lettuce. Divide mushroom-pep-
   per mixture over the lettuce. Dress each serving with 2
   to 3 tablespoons hot or room-temperature dressing.

Note: You might like to sprinkle each serving with a teaspoon or so of freshly grated Parmesan cheese.

Yield: 5 servings
+ **Calories per serving: 138**
  Carbohydrate per serving: 8g
+ **Cholesterol per serving: 2mg**

+ **Dietary fiber per serving: 2g**
  Fat per serving: 12g
  Protein per serving: 3g
+ **Sodium per serving: 14mg**

Lamb Medallions
in Phyllo with
Green Peppercorn Stuffing

❖

A do-ahead dazzler. Be sure you get the sirloin half of the lamb leg, as the shank half has more bone. Save the lamb bone in the freezer for the Barley and Mushrooms recipe (see page 39).

> 3½ pounds sirloin half leg of lamb
> 6 ounces mushrooms
> 1 shallot, minced (2 tablespoons)
> 3 tablespoons homemade chicken stock or
>   canned broth
> ¼ cup minced fresh parsley
> ½ teaspoon salt
> 1 tablespoon green peppercorns, drained
> freshly ground black pepper to taste
> a few gratings fresh nutmeg
> 6 to 7 sheets phyllo dough
> Dijon mustard
> 2 teaspoons unsalted butter, melted

1. Have the butcher bone the lamb. Trim off all fat and gristle. Lay the meat flat on the work surface, with what was the fat side down. Remove the small triangular flap of meat that is covered with a white membrane; save it with the bone to cook with the barley. Pull the meat with your fingers; it will naturally separate into two (sometimes three) pieces. One section of meat will have a thin "tail"; tuck it under to form a uniformly thick cylinder of meat. Cutting across the grain, cut the two pieces into medallions, about ¾-inch to 1-inch thick and about 4 ounces each. Don't worry if one or two of the medallions is less than gorgeous, perhaps

MAKING PHYLLO FLOWERS

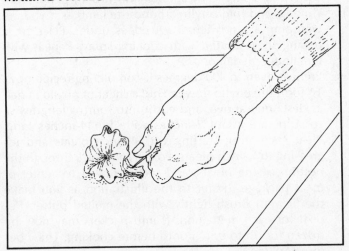

Fold a 2-inch by 14-inch phyllo strip into ½-inch pleats. Secure the pleats at the base with a toothpick, and fan the phyllo into a flower.

even made up of smaller pieces; it will cook the same and look as good when done. Set meat aside. (May be done several hours ahead.)

2. Mince the mushrooms by hand or in a food processor. Scrape them into a thick kitchen towel, gather into a ball by twisting the towel ends, and wring out over the sink to extract excess moisture.

3. "Saute" the shallot in the chicken stock in an 8-inch skillet over high heat until tender and the stock has evaporated, about 3 to 4 minutes.

4. Add mushrooms, saute 5 minutes, stirring often. Add parsley, salt, peppercorns, pepper, and nutmeg. Set aside. (This stuffing may be prepared several hours ahead.)

5. Lay a sheet of phyllo in front of you so the long side is perpendicular to the edge of the counter. Fold the top to the bottom. Brush lightly with a pastry brush dipped in mustard. Center a lamb medallion on the phyllo, top

with 2 heaping tablespoons mushroom-peppercorn stuffing, and fold phyllo around the lamb as if you are wrapping a sandwich. Tuck edges under. Place on a baking sheet coated with cooking spray. Repeat with remaining medallions.

6. Preheat oven to 400 degrees if completing recipe now. To form the phyllo flower: Fold a sheet of phyllo in half as described above, and cut it into fourths lengthwise so strips are about 2-inches wide by 14-inches long. Pleat each strip, starting with ¼-inch pleats and increasing to ½-inch pleats. Poke a toothpick through the bottom of the pleats, and secure flower to center of meat package. (Refer to the illustration as you make the flower.) Brush lightly with the melted butter. Repeat for each medallion. (Lamb packets may now be frozen for up to one month before cooking. Thaw before cooking.)

7. Place the baking sheet in the upper third of a preheated 400-degree oven, and roast 15 minutes for pinky, rare meat. An instant-reading meat thermometer will register 120 degrees when the lamb is quite rare, more red than pink, and 130–135 degrees for pinky meat. The thermometer will register 145 degrees for well-done meat, which will take about 25 minutes cooking time.

Yield: 5 servings
✦ Calories per serving: 273
Carbohydrate per serving: 2g
Cholesterol per serving: 509mg

Dietary fiber per serving: 0g
Fat per serving: 14g
Protein per serving: 28g
Sodium per serving: 509mg

❖For label readers: **Enriched:** means nutrients originally in the food and lost during processing are added back to the refined food at a government prescribed level. **Fortified:** means nutrients are added to a refined food that weren't there (or present only in very small quantity) before processing.❖

Minted Peas

❖

A hint of mint spices up an old standby.

2 pounds fresh peas (before shelling)
3 tablespoons snipped fresh mint
1 tablespoon unsalted butter
½ teaspoon salt
freshly ground black pepper to taste

1. Shell the peas. Place in a 1-quart saucepan with the mint. Cover with water. Cover the pan and bring the peas to a boil. Remove cover, and boil 8 to 12 minutes or until tender. Drain, then season with butter, salt, and pepper.

Yield: 5 servings
✦ Calories per serving: 47
Carbohydrate per serving: 4g
✦ Cholesterol per serving: 6mg

Dietary fiber per serving: 1g
Fat per serving: 2g
Protein per serving: 2g
Sodium per serving: 237mg

Lemon Mousse Cake
with Raspberry Sauce

❖

While the cake and raspberry sauce can well stand a day's delay before serving, the lemon mousse is a bit more demanding and will lose its froth if prepared more than 24 hours in advance. Don't toss out any leftovers, though. While they may not be as pretty as freshly made mousse, they're just as delicious.

For the Lemon Mousse

⅓ cup sugar
1 tablespoon plus 2 teaspoons cornstarch
½ cup boiling water
1 egg, separated
2 tablespoons lemon juice
finely grated rind (zest) of one lemon

1. Combine sugar and cornstarch in a double boiler. Gradually add the boiling water while stirring. Cook over hot water until the mixture thickens, about 3 to 4 minutes.
2. Beat the egg yolk in a small bowl with a fork. Pour a couple tablespoons of the sugar mixture into the yolk while beating. Then whisk yolk into the remaining sugar mixture in the double boiler. Cook, whisking, 2 minutes longer. Remove from heat and add lemon juice and zest.
3. Beat the egg white until soft peaks form, then fold it into the lemon mixture. Chill 4 hours before assembling the cake roll.

For the Raspberry Sauce

1 10-ounce package frozen raspberries, without sugar if possible
2 tablespoons Crème de Cassis or other black currant liqueur

1. Puree the fruit in a food processor or blender. Strain, pressing the solids with the back of a spoon to extract as much juice as possible. Stir liqueur into sauce. *Note:* The sauce will become a jewel-like ruby red if made a day ahead, which allows the air from processing to dissipate. Scrape the foamy residue from the top, if you like.

For the Lemon Cake

1 cup cake flour
1 teaspoon baking powder
½ cup sugar
½ cup skim milk
1 tablespoon vegetable oil
1 teaspoon finely grated lemon rind (zest)
2 egg whites
⅛ teaspoon salt
1 teaspoon vanilla extract

1. Preheat the oven to 375 degrees. Coat a 7 x 11 x 2-inch baking pan with cooking spray. Line with wax paper, spray again, and lightly dust with flour.
2. Sift the cake flour with the baking powder. Mix with sugar. Stir in the milk, oil, and lemon zest. The batter will be quite stiff.
3. Beat the egg whites with the salt until soft peaks form. Beat in vanilla extract. Fold into the batter.
4. Spread in prepared pan. Bake in the lower third of oven 12 to 15 minutes, turning the pan once during cooking. Cake is done when a toothpick inserted slightly off center comes out clean.

To Roll and Assemble

1. Turn cake upside down onto wax paper laid on top of a damp kitchen towel. Peel off and discard the wax paper adhering to the cake. Roll up the cake with the fresh wax paper and towel, starting at a narrow end. Let cool 20 to 30 minutes. Unroll; discard wax paper. Roll up again and rest 15 minutes. (If cake is prepared a day ahead, wrap it in clean wax paper and foil. Refrigerate.) Unroll and spread with chilled lemon mousse. Save any extra mousse to pat onto ends. Roll up again and wrap in plastic wrap. Chill until serving time. The cake is best served within 8 to 10 hours.
2. To serve: Film a dessert plate with raspberry sauce.

Place a thin slice of cake in the center and drizzle a teaspoon of sauce on top.

Yield: 8 servings
✦ Calories per serving: 203
Carbohydrate per serving: 43g
✦ Cholesterol per serving: 34mg

Dietary fiber per serving: 1g
Fat per serving: 8g
Protein per serving: 3g
✦ Sodium per serving: 104mg

❖ Focus: Flour ❖

Ever been confused about the kinds of flour available? This may help:

- **All purpose:** a blend of winter (hard) and spring (soft) wheats, appropriate for general household use.
- **Bread flour:** chiefly hard wheat, this flour has a higher gluten content that makes a better textured bread.
- **Cake flour:** soft wheat with less gluten, this flour is used to produce soft-textured bakery products like cakes.
- **Enriched flour:** may be hard or soft. The nutrients lost during milling are replenished before packaging.
- **Gluten flour:** is made by washing the starch out of wheat flour and drying the residue. This flour has a high protein content.
- **Graham flour:** whole wheat flour with the bran ground coarser than in regular whole wheat.
- **Instant flour:** all-purpose flour that has been wetted, then dried so it won't clump together. Often used in sauces, because it blends easily without lumping.
- **Self-rising flour:** wheat flour with baking powder and salt added.
- **Whole wheat flour:** the bran layer of the wheat berry hasn't been removed.

A PATIO DINNER

Poached Swordfish with Lemon Dill Sauce

Sweet Potato Fries

Zucchini Pancakes with Tomato Relish

**Nectarines and Peaches in Minted
Orange Sauce**

This patio dinner for four supports the theory that a summer dinner should be as relaxed for the hostess as it is for the guests. The tomato relish will actually improve with a day's rest in the refrigerator and the mint sauce for the dessert can also be done ahead, leaving just a few tasks for the last minute.

This menu presents some unorthodox ways to treat common foods. The swordfish—most often grilled, broiled, or baked—is poached here; the zucchini shredded; the sweet potatoes oven "fried"; and the peaches and nectarines, so often eaten out of hand, are bathed in minted orange sauce. Creative—without hours in the creation.

❖Pine nuts, also known as pignolis or Indian nuts, are costly because they must be extracted by hand from the cones of a certain tree. Buy them in small quantity and keep them in the refrigerator, as they go rancid easily.❖

Poached Swordfish with Lemon Dill Sauce

Poaching swordfish results in the same, moist, succulent fish as the more traditionally poached salmon. The cool lemon-dill sauce, which also serves as a marinade, is a pleasure on hot summer nights and simplicity itself for the cook.

> 2 tablespoons mayonnaise
> ¾ cup plain yogurt
> 2 tablespoons minced fresh dill
> 2 tablespoons lemon juice
> 2 drops hot pepper sauce
> 1½ pounds swordfish steaks or other thick-cut
>   firm-fleshed fish such as mako shark
> 2 cups dry white wine
> 1 cup water
> 4 tablespoons white wine vinegar (one flavored
>   with dill would be ideal)
> 2 bay leaves

1. Combine the mayonnaise, yogurt, dill, lemon juice, and hot pepper sauce.
2. Place fish in a plastic bag, add half the lemon-dill marinade, and marinate at least 2 hours or as long as 6 hours. Refrigerate remaining marinade to use as a sauce.
3. Remove fish from marinade. Any marinade that clings to the fish may be scraped off and added to the sauce.
4. Bring the wine, water, vinegar, and bay leaves to a boil in a 12-inch skillet. Reduce heat to a simmer. Add the fish, cover, and simmer over medium-low heat for 12 to 15 minutes, or until the flesh is firm when pressed with a finger. Remove fish from skillet; discard poaching liquid.

5. To serve, top each serving of fish with 2 tablespoons lemon-dill sauce, and pass remaining sauce at the table.

Yield: 4 servings
+ Calories per serving: 292
  Carbohydrate per serving: 4g
  Cholesterol per serving: 107mg

Dietary fiber per serving: 0g
Fat per serving: 14g
Protein per serving: 36g
+ Sodium per serving: 258mg

Sweet Potato "Fries"
❖

Curry powder creates the unexpected in this simple, quick recipe.

1 pound sweet potatoes, peeled
2 tablespoons corn or other vegetable oil
curry powder to taste

1. Preheat oven to 375 degrees. Quarter the potatoes and cut into ¼-inch-thick strips (if too thin, the potatoes will burn). Spread on a baking sheet and toss with oil. Season to taste with curry powder. (I like about ½ teaspoon curry powder to a pound of potatoes, but you'll want to decide for yourself.)
2. Bake in lower third of oven for 30 minutes, stirring occasionally. Season with salt if desired.

Yield: 4 servings
+ Calories per serving: 132
  Carbohydrate per serving: 22g
+ Cholesterol per serving: 0mg

Dietary fiber per serving: 1g
Fat per serving: 7g
Protein per serving: 2g
+ Sodium per serving: 12mg

Zucchini Pancakes
with Tomato Relish

❖

The tomato relish topping, which sets this vegetable dish apart from others, is so good you may want to double the recipe. It is based on one a friend served with slivers of pita bread one hot summer's day as a poolside snack. Best served at room temperature, it will keep two days under refrigeration. Farmstand seconds, even supermarket tomatoes, do just fine here.

If you like, the zucchini pancakes may be made ahead and reheated in a microwave oven on medium-high heat for 4 minutes or warmed in a 300-degree oven for 15 minutes.

For the Tomato Relish

1 tomato, chopped
2 scallions, diced
1 small garlic clove, minced
½ jalapeño pepper, minced, or ½ to 1 teaspoon
*   canned jalapeño pepper, minced*
1 tablespoon extra-virgin olive oil
1½ tablespoons white wine vinegar
3–4 drops lemon juice

For the Zucchini Pancakes

4 small zucchini (about 1 pound)
1 tablespoon salt, kosher or coarse recommended
1 Golden Delicious apple
1 tablespoon cornstarch
1 tablespoon freshly grated Romano cheese
2 egg whites, beaten lightly
1 teaspoon butter
2 tablespoons corn oil

To Prepare the Tomato Relish

1. Combine all the relish ingredients and stir well. Set aside; refrigerate if holding more than 3 hours.

To Prepare the Zucchini Pancakes

1. Trim the stem end of the zucchini. Grate zucchini by hand or in a food processor. Scrape into a colander set in sink, sprinkle with the salt, and rest 20 minutes.
2. Grate the unpeeled apple with a hand-held grater and discard core.
3. Rinse the zucchini thoroughly under running water, squeezing hard to rinse out salt. Squeeze out as much moisture as possible.
4. Combine zucchini with grated apple, cornstarch, cheese, and egg whites. Mix thoroughly.
5. Coat a 12-inch nonstick skillet with cooking spray. Heat butter and 1 tablespoon oil in skillet over high heat. Spoon in the zucchini mixture, forming 4 "cakes." Reduce heat to medium-low after the underside of the cakes is browned. Turn pan often and loosen the pancakes frequently with a spatula as they cook. Adjust the heat to keep them from burning. Turn pancakes over after 10 minutes, adding the remaining tablespoon of oil. Raise heat to brown the cakes, if necessary, and continue cooking until they are nicely browned. Spoon on tomato relish at the table.

Pancakes

Yield: 4 pancakes
+ Calories per pancake: 132
Carbohydrate per pancake: 11g
+ Cholesterol per pancake: 6g

Dietary fiber per pancake: 1g
Fat per pancake: 9g
Protein per pancake: 4g
+ Sodium per pancake: 33mg

Relish

Yield: 12 tablespoons of relish
+ Calories per tablespoon: 17
Carbohydrate per tablespoon: 2g
+ Cholesterol per tablespoon: 0mg

Dietary fiber per tablespoon: 0g
Fat per tablespoon: 1g
Protein per tablespoon: 0g
+ Sodium per tablespoon: 3mg

Nectarines and Peaches in Minted Orange Sauce

❖

Nutritionists tell us nothing beats plain fruit for dessert, but how many taste buds would agree? Here's a quick recipe that makes the most of lackluster, barely ripened, supermarket fruit. You might want to double the recipe. Without the liqueur, it makes a great snack to have on hand.

> 2 tablespoons sugar
> ½ cup water
> 1 tablespoon snipped fresh mint
> 4 fruits, a combination of peaches and nectarines
> 2 navel oranges or 1 cup orange juice
> 2 tablespoons slivered almonds or macadamia
>   nuts
> fresh mint leaves for garnish (optional)
> 1 teaspoon orange liqueur per serving (optional)

1. Dissolve sugar in the ½ cup water in a 1-quart, uncovered saucepan over medium heat. Don't stir, but swirl the pan by the handle.
2. When sugar is dissolved, raise heat to high and boil 2 minutes or until the syrup is reduced to ¼ cup. Add mint, cover, and steep off heat for 30 minutes.
3. The mint sauce may be strained to remove the leaves (be sure to press the solids with the back of a spoon), or used as is. (The recipe may be prepared several days ahead to this point and kept chilled.)
4. Bring 2½ quarts water to a boil in a 4-quart saucepan. Add the fruits. If they are very ripe, boil just 30 seconds to loosen the skin. Unripe fruits will take longer, up to 3 or 4 minutes. Drain, peel, and slice into a glass or ceramic bowl.
5. Squeeze the oranges to extract the juice. Pour juice

over fruit; add nuts. Pour the mint sauce over the fruit; stir gently to combine.

6. To serve, spoon into champagne glasses or small glass bowls. Garnish with mint leaves and a spoonful of orange liqueur, if you wish.

Yield: 4 servings
✦ Calories per serving: 132
Carbohydrate per serving: 5g
✦ Cholesterol per serving: 0mg

Dietary fiber per serving: 1g
Fat per serving: 3g
Protein per serving: 0g
✦ Sodium per serving: 8mg

❖Phyllo (Greek for "leaf") dough (or Fillo) is a tissue-thin pastry made from flour and water much used in Middle Eastern cookery. It is a boon to the waist-conscious, for it is relatively low in calorie. Thaw in the refrigerator and keep the sheets covered with a damp towel when working with a single sheet. Wrap unused phyllo as airtight as possible in plastic and foil before refreezing.❖

CHILL CHASER

"Cream" of Celery Root Soup
Pork Medallions with Cider and Apples
Barley and Mushrooms
Nutted Fall Fruit Tarts

When the scent of apples and the crinkle of leaves fill the air, we welcome hot and hearty fare. This menu makes use of some of the season's best—celery root, apples, fresh cider, and pork, a year-round meat that is particularly welcome this time of year.

Pork's fatty image has been justly deserved in the past, but new breeding and feeding techniques are now producing leaner animals, meaning less fat per serving. Boneless cutlets—be sure to trim off any visible fat—along with tenderloins are among the leaner pork cuts you can buy. There are about 198 calories in a 3-ounce serving along with healthy doses of zinc (a nutrient with an influence on growing tissues and one of the few that the typical American diet may not provide in optimal amounts) and thiamin (used in carbohydrate metabolism). Remember, health experts suggest 3-ounce servings of meat should be the norm, not just a dieting tool. With the other menu items here to satisfy appetites, this is as good as any time to make the resolution—less meat, more grains (like barley) and vegetables rich in fiber (like celery root). If you want yet another vegetable, try the Julienne of Root Vegetables (see page 121).

While this menu has been written for eight diners, you could halve the ingredients for the pork medallions and the barley to serve four or even reduce it to serve two. The soup may be frozen, so there's no need to halve it, and making anything less than eight tarts hardly seems sensible. Do take pan sizes and cooking times into account when reducing or enlarging recipes.

"Cream" of
Celery Root Soup
❖

A thick, hearty soup, just right when the cold winds howl. You may freeze it for up to one month without flavor loss. Reheat it gently in a double boiler.

1 pound celery root, peeled and cubed
1½ pounds leeks, trimmed, sliced, and rinsed
(about 4½ cups)
1 small onion, chopped (about 3 tablespoons)
1 potato, peeled and sliced (about 1½ cups)
3 cups homemade chicken stock or canned broth
3 cups water
1 teaspoon salt
1 teaspoon arrowroot
1 cup plain yogurt
1 tablespoon minced fresh dill
1 teaspoon Dijon mustard
freshly ground black pepper to taste

1. In a 4-quart saucepan combine the celery root, leeks, onion, potato, stock, water, and salt. Cover, bring to a boil, then reduce heat and simmer 25 to 30 minutes or until vegetables are tender.
2. Puree the soup in batches in a food processor or blender.
3. Stir the arrowroot into the yogurt. Stir it into the soup,

then stir in dill and mustard. Add fresh pepper and taste, correcting seasoning if necessary.

Yield: 8 1-cup servings
✦ Calories per serving: 113
Carbohydrate per serving: 21g
✦ Cholesterol per serving: 4mg

✦ Dietary fiber per serving: 2g
Fat per serving: 2g
Protein per serving: 5g
Sodium per serving: 667mg

Pork Medallions with Cider and Apples

❖

Deliciously quick!

1¾ pounds boneless pork cutlets, trimmed of all
    fat
½ teaspoon salt (optional)
freshly ground black pepper to taste
2 tablespoons corn or other vegetable oil
3 Granny Smith apples, peeled, cored, halved,
    and sliced
2 cups apple cider
1 tablespoon applejack or Calvados (optional)
½ teaspoon dried rosemary
1½ tablespoons arrowroot
3 tablespoons plain yogurt
1 tablespoon minced fresh parsley (optional)

1. Pound the meat between pieces of wax paper, flattening to about ¼-inch thickness. Salt and pepper meat if desired.
2. Heat oil in two 12-inch nonstick skillets over high heat. (Or sear meat in one pan in two batches.) Sear meat

one minute, flip, and brown other side, adjusting heat
if necessary to prevent burning.
3. Add sliced apples, cider, applejack, and rosemary.
Cover, reduce heat, and simmer 5 or 6 minutes.
4. Stir arrowroot into yogurt. Whisk yogurt into skillet
without removing the meat. Stir over low heat until the
sauce is thickened, 1 to 2 minutes. Garnish with
minced parsley, if desired.

Yield: 8 servings

Dietary fiber per serving: 1g

✦ Calories per serving: 257

Fat per serving: 14g

Carbohydrate per serving: 14g

Protein per serving: 20g

✦ Cholesterol per serving: 67mg

Sodium per serving: 203mg

Barley and Mushrooms

❖

An all-but-forgotten grain, barley provides a welcome
change from standard starches. And its strong nutritional
profile makes it one well worth serving. A rich source of
carbohydrates with moderate amounts of protein, it is
also a significant source of cholesterol-combatting fiber—
for about the same number of calories per serving as a
baked potato.

The cooking instructions here are for regular barley; if
you can buy quick-cooking barley, follow package directions. Any leftover bones from the Lamb Medallion recipe
(page 22), simmered along with the barley, would add
wonderful flavor. Trim away any fat, and chop the bones
into 4-inch chunks with a mallet before adding them to
the pot. Discard the bones before serving.

1 cup medium pearl barley
2 quarts water
1 teaspoon salt

2 tablespoons unsalted butter
12 ounces mushrooms, sliced
2 tablespoons minced fresh parsley
freshly ground black pepper to taste

1. Bring the barley, water, and salt to a boil in a covered 4-quart saucepan. Reduce heat to a gentle boil and cook, stirring occasionally, until the barley is tender and all water has evaporated. This will take about 2 hours. Stir in butter. (Barley may be made ahead and reheated either conventionally or in a microwave oven on high for 2 minutes before completing recipe.)
2. Coat a 12-inch nonstick skillet with cooking spray. "Saute" the mushrooms over high heat until lightly browned, about 5 to 6 minutes. Stir into the barley with the parsley and pepper.

Yield: 8 ½-cup servings
✦ Calories per serving: 124
Carbohydrate per serving: 21g
✦ Cholesterol per serving: 8mg

✦ Dietary fiber per serving: 2g
Fat per serving: 4g
Protein per serving: 3g
Sodium per serving: 297mg

Nutted Fall Fruit Tarts

❖

You might need a double batch of these to satisfy the peanut-butter-and-jelly crowd as well as company. Comfortable on fine china or a paper plate, they make an after-school snack you'll encourage your children to eat. Minimum mess, maximum taste—who could ask for more?

3 tablespoons unsalted butter
3 pears, peeled, cored, and cubed
2 Granny Smith apples, peeled, cored, and cubed
2 tablespoons maple syrup or dark brown sugar

1 teaspoon cinnamon
a dash ground cloves
a few gratings fresh nutmeg
2 tablespoons slivered almonds
2 tablespoons applejack or Calvados (optional)
2 sheets phyllo dough (about 14 by 18 inches)
1 teaspoon cinnamon and sugar (about ⅞
   teaspoon sugar mixed with ⅛ teaspoon
   cinnamon)

1. Melt butter in a small saucepan over medium heat to clarify. Remove from heat, let rest 5 minutes. Spoon off the foamy top layer (may be used over vegetables); spoon off and set aside the clear, yellow, clarified butter; and discard the bottom, white, liquid layer. (It's easier to clarify a whole stick at a time, and it will keep for weeks in the refrigerator, too.)
2. Heat half the yellow clarified butter (reserving the remaining butter for step 5) in an 8-inch skillet over high heat. When hot add the cubed fruit, maple syrup or sugar, cinnamon, cloves, and nutmeg. Toss to combine, reduce heat to medium, and cover. Cook, stirring occasionally, until fruit is tender (about 3 to 4 minutes for ripe fruit, longer for unripe).
3. Uncover and add almonds and applejack. Boil 30 seconds, then remove from heat to cool.
4. Preheat oven to 375 degrees. Coat an 8-cup muffin tin (each cup a 3-inch diameter) with cooking spray. Cut 32 4-inch squares from the phyllo. (If you don't mind the rest of the phyllo sheets being short, this is most easily done by cutting a 4-inch-wide strip from a one-pound stack of phyllo leaves, and cutting the strip into 4-inch lengths. It is a bit wasteful, but time efficient, and the uncut leaves may be carefully rewrapped and frozen.)
5. Press 2 squares of phyllo into each muffin cup. Divide the fruit among the cups. Press 2 more squares on top of the tarts, tucking in the edges; don't worry that it looks messy now. Brush remaining clarified butter over tart tops, and sprinkle with the cinnamon-sugar.

6. Bake on the top rack of the oven for 15 minutes or until toasty brown. Remove and cool on a rack for 10 minutes before removing the tarts from the tin with a flexible-bladed spatula. The tarts may be made a day ahead or frozen. They may be reheated in the muffin tin (300 degrees for 10 minutes) or on a serving dish in a micro-wave oven (high power for 1 minute).

Yield: 8 tarts
✦ Calories per tart: 118
Carbohydrate per tart: 20g
✦ Cholesterol per tart: 8mg

✦ Dietary fiber per tart: 2g
Fat per tart: 5g
Protein per tart: 1g
✦ Sodium per tart: 31mg

❖ Focus: Cholesterol ❖

Cholesterol is a fatty substance important for a variety of functions. It is a structural component of all cells and is used to make vitamin D (which aids in the absorption of calcium and phosphorus), bile acids (which help in digestion), and some hormones (which regulate many body processes). However, although it is an essential part of body chemistry, our bodies make all we need after the age of six months, so even a cholesterol-free diet poses no problem.

How the Deed Is Done

Atherosclerosis—a thickening of the artery walls caused by the accumulation of cholesterol and connective tissue—begins when cholesterol carrying lipoproteins invade the arterial wall. The damaged wall responds by growing new tissue that traps the cholesterol, resulting in a thickening called plaque. If the plaque becomes pronounced enough it can restrict the blood supply. If a coronary artery is blocked, and part of the heart doesn't get the oxygen it needs and dies, a heart attack results. If blood is restricted to the brain, a stroke results. Sometimes the artery walls respond to the plaque by ballooning. This is called an aneurysm. If a large artery is involved and bursts, it may be fatal. Plaque also can lead to the formation of blood clots.

Two Sides to the Coin

There is as yet no clear-cut proof that elevated cholesterol blood levels are a direct cause of atherosclerosis. Some studies of population groups have found a correlation between high blood cholesterol, triglyceride concentrations, and heart disease, while other studies have not. Based on the enormous amount of evidence now available, many health experts recommend limiting the fats that contribute to high cholesterol levels, while others suggest dietary changes are insignificant in preventing cardiovascular disease.

Who to believe? First of all, remember no one suggests that you absolutely will not die of a heart attack if you eat a low-fat, high-polyunsaturate diet (see *Focus: Heart Disease Risk Factors*, page 314), for, after all, other factors do come into play. But also know that in the last twenty years as Americans have increased their use of polyunsaturate fats while decreasing their intake of saturated fats, fewer deaths have been caused by heart disease, leading some to believe that waiting for incontrovertible proof may prove deadly.

What HDL and LDL Cholesterol Can Mean to You

While levels of cholesterol are of concern, how it is carried in the bloodstream is also important. Like other fats, cholesterol does not dissolve in liquid so it is transported in the blood by lipoproteins—most of it by low-density lipoproteins, known as LDL, the "bad" cholesterol, and to a lesser extent by high-density lipoproteins, HDL, the "good" cholesterol. Generally, high levels of LDL cholesterol appear to increase the risk of heart disease by keeping cholesterol in circulation, while high levels of HDL cholesterol seem protective by clearing the artery walls of cholesterol and transporting it to the liver where un-needed cholesterol is removed.

Some studies have shown moderate to vigorous physical activity may increase the HDL and lower the LDL concentrations in the blood. Genetic factors as well as diet may also influence your lipoprotein profile.

In What Foods?

Cholesterol is only found in animal foods such as meats, fish, dairy products, poultry, and cheese. Highly saturated fats (those which are solid at room temperature) may raise blood cholesterol levels, however, even if they contain no cholesterol themselves. Be wary then of labels proclaiming, "Made with pure vegetable oil," or "No Cholesterol," for the products could be made with coconut or palm oils or hydrogenated vegetable shortening, all of which are high in saturated fats and hence can raise blood cholesterol levels.

Remember too that low-fat foods are not always low-cholesterol foods. Beef liver and veal are both rather low in fat, but liver is very rich in cholesterol and veal is moderately high, too.

If It's Too High, Then What?

A blood test and your doctor will determine if your cholesterol level is dangerously high. Should you decide to control the level there are two steps to take:

First—Restrict your daily cholesterol intake to less than 300 milligrams a day.

Second—Reduce the total fat in your diet to 25 to 30 percent. Ten percent should come from polyunsaturated fats, 10 percent from monounsaturated fats, and no more than 10 percent from saturated fats. (Read *Focus: The Difference in Fats*, page 281.)

FIRST NIGHT

Saffron Consomme with Shrimp

Roast Loin of Lamb Persillade

Green Beans with Pecans

Potato and Fennel Puree

Iced Fruit Mousse

The title for this menu for four is borrowed from Boston's citywide celebration of New Year's Eve, First Night, a clamorous evening of controlled excess. What's in store here is a bit less boisterous, but with all the markings of a festive occasion worth celebrating. There are shrimp, saffron, an elegant loin of lamb, and a special potato puree, all topped off with a light but indulgent fruit dessert.

Happily, many of the cooking chores can be prepared ahead. The consomme will actually improve with a day's rest in the refrigerator. The potato and fennel puree may be made a day before serving and reheated in a double boiler or in a microwave oven. The iced fruit mousse should be made through step 2 at least a day in advance. This will leave only the meat to trim and prepare for roasting, the green beans to trim and steam, and the final whipping of the fruit mousse to be done on the day of the dinner. Like champagne, this menu offers a simple elegance, heady with flavor and long on class.

❖According to a survey conducted by the Department of Health and Human Services, the top five contributors of fat to the typical American's diet are: **Hamburger**—7.0%; **Hot dogs, luncheon meats**—6.4%; **Whole milk**—6.0%; **Doughnuts, cakes, cookies**—6.0%; **Beef steaks, roasts**—5.5%.❖

Saffron Consomme
with Shrimp

❖

Light, with a distinctive splash of Pernod, this soup improves with a day's aging, but add the shrimp just before serving to avoid overcooking them.

    1 leek, white part only
    1 carrot
    1 celery rib
    1 8-ounce bottle clam juice
    1 can (13¾ ounces) chicken broth or 1¾ cup
        homemade chicken stock
    ½ cup dry vermouth or white wine
    2 teaspoons minced fresh parsley
    ¼ teaspoon crumbled saffron threads
    a few shakes paprika
    1 tablespoon Madeira
    1 teaspoon Pernod (optional)
    ⅓ pound medium-size raw shrimp (about 15),
        peeled and deveined

1. Quarter the leek the long way and rinse thoroughly to remove all traces of dirt. Peel the carrot. Julienne the leek, carrot, and celery in a food processor, or shred on the coarse side of a grater.
2. Combine the vegetables with the clam juice, chicken broth, vermouth, parsley, saffron, and paprika in a 2-quart saucepan. Simmer, uncovered, at least 20 minutes or up to 1 hour. (Soup may be prepared to this point and refrigerated 24 hours ahead.)
3. Stir in Madeira, Pernod, and shrimp. Cover and simmer just until shrimp turn pink, about 1 minute. Do not allow to boil. Ladle into consomme cups.

Yield: 4 1-cup servings
✦ Calories per serving: 82
Dietary fiber per serving: 1g
Fat per serving: 1g

Carbohydrate per serving: 6g
Cholesterol per serving: 62mg
Protein per serving: 11g
Sodium per serving: 606mg

Roast Loin of Lamb Persillade

❖

A loin of lamb makes an elegant offering. Succulent, with its own distinctive flavor, it is simple to cook, simple to serve, and subtly suggests this is no ordinary dinner. Such gracious ease must cost, of course; what you don't pay in the kitchen you will at the butcher, but it's money well spent. A loin of lamb—generally, a special order—comes from that unexercised backbone area that tends to be tender. The roast consists of the kidney chops, unsplit, but cracked for easy carving. Order not by the pound but by the number of chops you want; one per diner is certainly sufficient, with perhaps one or two extra for the meat lovers of the group. Don't try to roast fewer than four chops, but you can roast more than specified in the recipe. Be sure to have the butcher crack the bones, and trim the fat yourself as if you were wielding a scalpel.

> a lamb loin of 5 chops, about 1¾ pounds, bone cracked
> ¼ teaspoon salt
> freshly ground black pepper to taste
> 1 tablespoon unsalted butter
> 1 garlic clove, minced
> 3 tablespoons dry bread crumbs
> 2 tablespoons minced fresh parsley
> 1 teaspoon finely grated lemon rind (zest)

1. Preheat the oven to 450 degrees. Trim all fat from the lamb loin. Salt and pepper the meat.
2. Melt the butter in an 8-inch nonstick skillet until foamy. Cook the garlic over medium heat, stirring with a wooden spoon until soft but not browned, about 2 minutes.

3. Add the bread crumbs and saute over medium-high heat until lightly browned, about 4 minutes. Remove from heat and stir in the parsley and lemon zest. (Crumb mixture may be prepared as much as a day in advance, but do not press it onto the meat until just before roasting.)
4. Place the loin on a rack in a roasting pan. Press the crumb mixture evenly onto the meat. Roast in the lower third of the oven for 30 to 35 minutes or until an instant-reading meat thermometer registers 135 degrees for medium-rare (145 degrees for your basic gray with a blush at the center). Rest 10 minutes, loosely covered with foil, before carving.

Yield: 4 servings, one extra chop
✦ Calories per serving: 325
Carbohydrate per serving: 4g
Cholesterol per serving: 131mg

Dietary fiber per serving: 0g
Fat per serving: 14g
Protein per serving: 42g
Sodium per serving: 286mg

Green Beans with Pecans

❖

Green beans are a good source of Vitamin C, which aids in resisting infection, and a B vitamin that promotes good vision and healthy skin. The beans may be done through step 2 and held, covered, at room temperature for up to two hours.

¾ pound fresh green beans
1 tablespoon unsalted butter
1 tablespoon lemon juice

2 tablespoons chopped pecans
½ teaspoon salt
freshly ground black pepper to taste

1. "Tip and tail" the beans by lining up a handful at a time and cutting across both ends.
2. Bring 1½ cups water to a boil in a 2½-quart saucepan fitted with a steamer. Add the beans, cover, and steam 6 to 8 minutes or until beans are tender but still crisp. Drain. (Undercook beans slightly and rinse them under cold water to stop the cooking if you are not immediately continuing.)
3. Melt the butter in a 10-inch skillet until just foamy. Add the beans, lemon juice, and pecans. Season with salt and pepper. Grasp the skillet by the handle and shake the beans once or twice over high heat until beans are coated and heated through.

Yield: 4 servings
✦ Calories per serving: 80
Carbohydrate per serving: 8g
✦ Cholesterol per serving: 8mg

Dietary fiber per serving: 1g
Fat per serving: 6g
Protein per serving: 2g
Sodium per serving: 295mg

Potato and Fennel Puree

❖

If you're cutting back on butterfat, mashed potatoes lose a lot of appeal. Puree them with fennel, though, and a smooth, rich taste is gained, without a lot of saturated fat. The puree may be done several hours in advance and reheated in a double boiler or in a microwave oven on high power for a minute and a half.

2 medium potatoes (12 ounces), peeled and
    halved
1 pound fennel

1 tablespoon plus 1 teaspoon unsalted butter
3 tablespoons low-fat or skim milk
2 tablespoons freshly grated Parmesan cheese
½ teaspoon salt
freshly ground black pepper to taste
a few gratings fresh nutmeg

1. Place the potatoes in a 2½-quart saucepan. Cover them with water, cover the pan, and boil on high heat for 10 minutes.
2. Meanwhile, trim the root end, tough outer shell, and the feathery tops of the fennel bulbs. Mince some of the feathery top and reserve for garnish.
3. Quarter the fennel bulbs and add to the potatoes. Boil, half covered, over medium-high heat for an additional 20 minutes or until tender. Drain.
4. Puree the fennel and potatoes in a food processor or food mill with the butter, milk, cheese, salt, pepper, and nutmeg. Taste to correct seasoning. Garnish just before serving with minced fennel, if desired.

Yield: 4 ½-cup servings
Calories per serving: 228
Carbohydrates per serving: 23g
✦ **Cholesterol per serving: 35mg**

Dietary fiber per serving: 1g
Fat per serving: 13g
Protein per serving: 6g
Sodium per serving: 365mg

Iced Fruit Mousse

❖

A frothy fluff of a dessert. The fruit may be frozen days or even months ahead, then whipped with the egg white and touch of honey the day of serving. Desserts such as this are a great way to take advantage of summer's sweet and fragrant fruits by freezing them for use during cold weather.

1 nectarine
½ cup orange juice, freshly squeezed preferred
1 banana, sliced
1 egg white
1 teaspoon honey
a few drops lemon juice
1 tablespoon Crème de Cassis (optional)

1. Drop the nectarine into boiling water to cover for 30 seconds or until the skin is softened. (This will take longer for unripe fruit.) Cool under running water, peel off skin, and slice fruit.
2. In a food processor or in batches in a blender, puree the orange juice, banana, and nectarine. Freeze until firm, at least 3 hours. (Fruit may be kept frozen up to 5 to 6 months.)
3. Soften the frozen fruit at room temperature for about 1 hour or until it can be roughly broken up with a knife. Combine the fruit with egg white, honey, lemon juice, and liqueur in a food processor (or in a bowl with a hand-held mixer). Beat for 2 to 3 minutes (longer for a hand-held mixer), or until frothy and doubled in volume. Iced mousse is now ready to serve or may be kept chilled (not frozen) for up to 24 hours.

Yield: 4 ½-cup servings
✛ **Calories per serving: 63**
Carbohydrate per serving: 15g
✛ **Cholesterol per serving: 0mg**

Dietary fiber per serving: 1g
Fat per serving: 0g
Protein per serving: 1g
✛ **Sodium per serving: 14mg**

❖Arrowroot is much used in *The Enlightened Gourmet* because it has twice the thickening power of flour, making for a tidy calorie saving. It is made from the root of a tropical plant and is so called because it was once used to treat wounds caused by poison arrows. Arrowroot is flavorless, and for best results, should be cooked neither too long nor at too high a temperature.❖

DINNER BY THE FIRE

Grilled Vegetable Salad
Grilled Ginger-Lime Pork Tenderloin
Potato and Leek Gratin
Red Cabbage with Chestnuts
Meringued Poached Pears

Here is a simple menu for four to enjoy by a fire in the cool of the year. Don't abandon the idea if you don't have a grill; the hot vegetable salad lends itself well to broiling and the pork tenderloin may be roasted. If you've never cooked a pork tenderloin before, you might be surprised by its tenderness and flavor. Best of all it is relatively low in fat and calories, supplying a reasonable 240 calories for a 3½-ounce portion. Pork is high in potassium (important in fluid balance), phosphorus (for bones and teeth), and iron (for building blood).

Serve the pork with a tasty grilled vegetable salad, a low-fat potato gratin, colorful and crunchy red cabbage, and meringued poached pears. These are foods to warm cool nights.

❖The iron from greens is not as readily absorbed as the iron from animal sources. It can be enhanced, though, by eating a good source of vitamin C—oranges, strawberries, or tomatoes for example—at the same meal.❖

Grilled Vegetable Salad

❖

A wonderful change of pace from the ubiquitous tossed salad. If you haven't time to salt the eggplant (which removes the bitterness), omit it, or substitute another vegetable such as summer squash. You will need eight 10-inch-long, thin wooden skewers.

> 1 small eggplant
> 1 tablespoon salt, kosher recommended
> 1 green bell pepper
> 1 red bell pepper
> 1 tomato
> ¼ pound mushrooms

For the Dressing

> 4 tablespoons olive oil
> ¼ cup white wine vinegar
> 2 scallions, minced
> 1 garlic clove, minced
> 1 shallot, minced
> 3–4 leaves fresh basil, snipped
> 1 tablespoon sesame seeds
> ⅛ teaspoon salt
> freshly ground black pepper to taste
> juice of one lemon
> 1 small head Boston or other soft-leafed lettuce,
>   rinsed and spun dry
> oil and vinegar or lemon juice (optional)

1. Soak the skewers in cold water for at least 30 minutes or as much as 2 hours before cooking.
2. Trim the ends from the eggplant. Peel eggplant and cut it into 1-inch-thick slices. Quarter the slices. Place on a double thickness of paper towels, sprinkle both sides with the tablespoon of salt, and rest 20 minutes.

3. Meanwhile, core the peppers and cut them in eighths. Quarter the tomato. Cut mushrooms if necessary or leave whole.
4. Combine the oil, vinegar, scallions, garlic, shallot, basil, sesame seeds, salt, and pepper in a large bowl. Toss with peppers, tomatoes, and mushrooms.
5. When eggplant has rested 20 minutes, rinse it thoroughly to remove all salt. Drain. Combine with marinade and other vegetables. Cover bowl with plastic wrap and refrigerate up to 8 hours or leave on the counter, up to 1 hour while the vegetables marinate. (Or you may complete the recipe to this point a day ahead if desired.)
6. Alternate the vegetables on the skewers. Grill, turning frequently and brushing with any remaining marinade and the lemon juice, until lightly browned, about 20 minutes. To broil, place the skewers on a rack 4 inches from the coils. Turn frequently and brush with any remaining marinade and the lemon juice until lightly browned, about 10 minutes.
7. Meanwhile, line the salad plates with lettuce leaves. Dress them with a sprinkling of oil and vinegar or a few drops of lemon juice, if desired. Slide the vegetables off the skewers onto the lettuce.

Yield: 4 servings
Calories per serving: 219
Carbohydrate per serving: 15g
✦ Cholesterol per serving: 0mg

✦ Dietary fiber per serving: 3g
Fat per serving: 12g
Protein per serving: 4g
✦ Sodium per serving: 99mg

Grilled Ginger-Lime
Pork Tenderloin

❖

Simple and succulent, this pork tenderloin dish may well become one of your standards. For piquant variety, try substituting citrus juices for the lime juice. If you prefer, the meat may be roasted in a 325-degree oven for about an hour.

1 pound pork tenderloin, trimmed of all fat
½ cup reduced-sodium soy sauce
½ cup Chinese cooking wine or dry white wine
juice of one lime
1 tablespoon dark brown sugar
1 scallion, minced
3 tablespoons minced fresh ginger
2 small garlic cloves, minced

1. Place the tenderloin in a leakproof plastic bag or non-metallic baking dish. Combine the remaining ingredients, pour marinade over the meat, and marinate at least 4 hours in the refrigerator or overnight. Turn occasionally.

2. Remove meat from the marinade. Pat it dry so it will sear quickly. Reserve marinade. Grill the meat over a low fire for 40 minutes, turning and basting frequently with reserved marinade. Check the internal temperature after 40 minutes with an instant-reading meat thermometer. Cook until it registers 145 degrees (160 degrees if you prefer the meat without the barest blush of pink). To serve, slice in ½-inch rounds.

Yield: 4 servings
✦ Calories per serving: 186
Carbohydrate per serving: 8g
Cholesterol per serving: 79mg

Dietary fiber per serving: 0g
Fat per serving: 4g
Protein per serving: 27g
Sodium per serving: 1145mg

Potato and Leek Gratin

❖

Potato lovers will feel more than satisfied with this tasty dish and enjoy it all the more knowing it is low in fat. It may be completed several hours in advance and held covered and chilled until baking.

> 3 leeks, white part only, diced and rinsed
> 3 medium baking potatoes, thinly sliced
> ½ cup low-fat cottage cheese
> ⅔ cup homemade chicken stock or canned broth
> 1 rounded teaspoon arrowroot
> ½ teaspoon salt
> freshly ground black pepper to taste
> a few gratings fresh nutmeg
> 2 teaspoons chopped fresh chives
> 3 tablespoons dried bread crumbs
> 1 tablespoon unsalted butter
> 1 tablespoon freshly grated Parmesan cheese

1. Combine the leeks and potatoes in a 2½-quart saucepan. Add cool water to cover the vegetables by 2 inches. Cover the saucepan and place over high heat. As soon as a boil is reached, reduce the heat so the water boils gently. Boil 5 minutes, then drain the vegetables.

2. Coat a quiche pan or a 9-inch baking dish, preferably one which can go to the table, with cooking spray. Layer the potatoes and leeks in the pan. Set aside.

3. Preheat the oven to 350 degrees. In the bowl of a food processor or in a blender, combine the cottage cheese, chicken stock, and arrowroot. Process until smooth.

4. Turn the sauce into an 8-inch skillet. Place the skillet over high heat and whisk until the sauce thickens and is smooth, about 2 minutes. Reduce the heat to medium-high to prevent the sauce from boiling as the pan heats up.

5. When the sauce is thick, pour it over the potatoes and leeks in the baking dish. Season with the salt, pepper, and nutmeg.
6. Sprinkle the dish with the chives, then with the bread crumbs. Dot with the butter. Sprinkle cheese on top. The dish is ready to bake. (If you prefer, the dish may be chilled for several hours, covered with plastic wrap. Drizzle with a few tablespoons of milk if necessary and allow to come to room temperature, or increase baking time by 5 to 10 minutes.)
7. Bake the potatoes in the top third of the preheated 350-degree oven for 15 to 20 minutes. Run under the broiler if necessary to brown the top.

Yield: 4 servings
Calories per serving: 234
Carbohydrate per serving: 41g
✦ **Cholesterol per serving: 11mg**

✦ **Dietary fiber per serving: 2g**
Fat per serving: 4g
Protein per serving: 10g
Sodium per serving: 488mg

Red Cabbage with Chestnuts

❖

Red cabbage is a colorful vegetable, long on spunk yet light on pound-potential. The chestnuts aren't integral, just a nice touch, so don't pass over the recipe if the nuts are nowhere to be found. This dish reheats nicely.

3 ounces chestnuts
12 ounces red cabbage, shredded (5 cups)
¾ cup homemade chicken stock or canned broth
a few drops fruity vinegar, such as raspberry
        vinegar
1 tablespoon brown sugar

¼ teaspoon salt
freshly ground black pepper to taste

1. Cut a cross in the flat side of each nut. Put the nuts in an 8-inch pan and cover them with water. Cover the pan and bring the nuts to a boil. Boil 1 to 2 minutes. Drain, cool under running water, and peel. Roughly chop or leave whole, as you wish.
2. Place the cabbage and the chicken stock in a 12-inch skillet. Add the vinegar, brown sugar, salt, and pepper. Cover and simmer over medium heat until tender, about 15 minutes. (Recipe may be prepared to this point several hours before serving. Refrigerate if holding more than 1 hour. Reheat in a skillet.)
3. A minute or so before serving, add the chestnuts to the cabbage to heat through.

Yield: 4 1-cup servings
✦ Calories per serving: 78
Carbohydrate per serving: 16g
✦ Cholesterol per serving: 0mg
✦ Dietary fiber per serving: 3g
Fat per serving: 1g
Protein per serving: 2g
✦ Sodium per serving: 155mg

Meringued Poached Pears

❖

Here are poached pears in a meringue disguise, stuffed with oats, nuts, raisins, and spices. Save the poaching liquid in your freezer—it will keep indefinitely—for poaching any kind of fruit. If you would like a bit of sauce, either boil a cup of the poaching liquid to reduce it to ¼ cup, or use a few tablespoons of the poaching syrup from Glazed Gingered Oranges (page 89).

The pears may be poached and stuffed up to a day in advance; the meringue may be made an hour ahead and held, covered with a plate. Frost and bake the pears just before serving. If you'd prefer, the pears may be completely baked and reheated on medium power in a microwave oven for 45 seconds.

4 pears, Bosc recommended
2 cups Burgundy wine
2 tablespoons sugar
2 cups water
juice of half a lemon
1 cinnamon stick
1 whole nutmeg
2 tablespoons oats, quick-cooking recommended, not instant
2 tablespoons raisins
1 tablespoon slivered almonds
½ teaspoon ground cinnamon
a dash ground cloves
4 egg whites
2 tablespoons sugar
1 teaspoon vanilla extract
1 tablespoon finely grated unsweetened chocolate

1. Peel the pears. Take a thin slice off the bottom of each pear so it sits upright. Core each pear from the bottom as if it were an apple.
2. In a 3-quart saucepan combine the wine, sugar, water, lemon juice, cinnamon, and nutmeg. Cover and bring to a boil. Add the pears, cover, and adjust heat so pears just simmer (10 minutes for very ripe pears, as long as 45 minutes for unripe pears). Pierce with a fork to check for tenderness. When tender, remove from poaching liquid, drain, and cool. (Poaching liquid may be frozen to use for poaching other fruits.)
3. Meanwhile, coat a baking sheet with cooking spray. Spread the oats on it and toast in a 350-degree oven (no need to preheat). Stir oats once or twice as they cook until lightly browned, about 10 minutes. Leave oven on if you're completing the dessert now.
4. Combine oats with raisins, almonds, and spices. Press 2

teaspoons of this mixture into the cavity of each pear. Place upright on the baking sheet. (Pears may be covered with plastic wrap and held at room temperature up to 2 hours or chilled up to 24 hours before continuing.)

5. Beat the egg whites until stiff, sprinkle in the sugar, and continue to beat until stiff glossy peaks form. Beat in the vanilla. (Meringue may be made an hour before baking pears. Cover bowl with a plate and leave at room temperature.)

6. Frost the pears with the meringue; the meringue need not be smooth. Bake in the lower third of a preheated 350-degree oven just until meringue browns, about 5 or 6 minutes. Divide grated chocolate over pears just before serving.

Yield: 4 servings
Calories per serving: 240
Carbohydrate per serving: 47g
✦ **Cholesterol per serving: 0mg**

✦ **Dietary fiber per serving: 5g**
Fat per serving: 6g
Protein per serving: 6g
✦ **Sodium per serving: 52mg**

❖Chili peppers abound with more than 200 varieties grown for market around the world. Chili peppers, native to the New World, were probably introduced to Europe by explorers who had found them easy to dry and helpful in disguising the less than well preserved food on long ocean voyages. Columbus is said to have named chili peppers by coupling the Indian word "chili" with "pepper" (he mistook them for the Asian peppercorn). The seeds and white membrane are the hottest part of a chili pepper.❖

DINNER AT EIGHT

Gingered Beef Consomme with Crepe Pillows
Grilled Veal Loin Chops
Dilled New Potatoes
Swiss Chard with Bacon and Balsamic Vinegar
Bananas Creole

Here's a meat-and-potatoes meal for traditionalists who like "soup to nuts" but are minding their fats and calories. This chic menu, for eight lucky diners, could easily be organized and carried off in a few hours time if necessary. But it's an ideal do-ahead menu. Advance preparation could include the gingered beef consomme (up to two months in advance, kept frozen), the crepe pillows (one day ahead, kept chilled), the herb butter for the potatoes (may be frozen indefinitely), the potatoes themselves (several hours ahead if you have a microwave oven for reheating), the bacon fried and Swiss chard prepared for cooking (early in the day), the dessert rice (a full day ahead), and the bananas and final dessert assembly (two hours before your guests arrive). If you don't have a grill, instructions are given for oven roasting the veal chops. This menu, simple yet sophisticated, is one meat lovers are sure to enjoy.

Gingered Beef Consomme with Crepe Pillows

❖

Soups make a wonderful first course for they rarely require any last-minute fuss. Do keep the entire menu in mind, though, when planning a first course soup. The soup should be light—an appetite tickler, not satisfier. This jewel-bright, clear consomme with its crepe pillow is a perfect example—a just right start to a wonderfully satisfying meal. If you've neither the time nor the inclination to make and clarify your own beef stock, a canned product will do nicely. The hot oil and sesame oil are available at some supermarkets and at Oriental markets.

For the Consomme

6 cups homemade beef stock or 3 10½-ounce
   cans beef consomme
3 egg whites and the crushed shells (only if using
   homemade stock)

For the Crepe Pillows

½ cup low-fat milk or skim milk
1 egg, lightly beaten
¼ cup flour, instant blending recommended
pinch of salt
1 tablespoon corn oil
2 scallions, green part only, minced
2 teaspoons very finely minced fresh ginger
½ red bell pepper, minced
½ green bell pepper, minced
8 whole chives or strips of scallion green

For the Soup

1 cup Madeira
½ cup reduced-sodium soy sauce
a few drops hot oil
½ teaspoon (or to taste) sesame oil

To Clarify Homemade Stock

1. (Canned consomme does not need clarifying.) Beat 1 cup cold stock with the egg whites and shells in a large bowl. Meanwhile, bring the remaining stock to a boil in a 2½-quart saucepan.
2. Gradually pour the hot stock into the egg white mixture, beating constantly. Pour the whites and stock back into the saucepan and set over medium-high heat. Stir until the stock regains a simmer; stop stirring as soon as it begins to simmer. Reduce heat to low. Move the pan gently half off the burner. Cover and rest 15 to 20 minutes.
3. Set a colander into a large bowl. Line colander with a double layer of cheesecloth that has been wrung out in water. Gently ladle stock-egg mixture into the colander. Discard the shells and whites. The stock should now be clear and may be kept chilled (for 24 hours) or frozen (up to 2 months) until ready to serve.

To Prepare the Crepe Pillows

1. With a beater, food processor, or blender mix together until smooth the milk, egg, flour, salt, and oil. Refrigerate overnight or for 8 hours in a screw-top jar.
2. Coat an 8-inch nonstick skillet with cooking spray and heat over medium-high heat. Ladle 1½ tablespoons of crepe batter into the pan, tipping the pan in a circular motion so the batter spreads over the entire bottom. Cook until lightly browned, about 45 seconds, then flip and cook about 10 seconds more. Remove crepe from pan. Crepes may be stacked between layers of wax paper and held at room temperature up to 5 hours before serving. Continue to cook the remaining crepes,

spraying pan as necessary to prevent sticking. (Makes 8 to 10 crepes.)

3. Mix together the scallion, ginger, and peppers. Set aside 3 tablespoons for the crepe pillows. Reserve the remaining scallion mixture for the soup.

4. Place 1 teaspoon of scallion mixture on the center of each crepe. Gather the edges and tie with a whole chive or scallion strip. Set aside. (Pillows may be held, covered and chilled, for up to 24 hours.)

To Prepare the Soup

1. Combine the clarified stock (or canned consomme diluted according to label instructions) with the wine, soy sauce, hot oil, sesame oil, and remaining scallion mixture in a 2½-quart saucepan. Heat until steaming, then taste and adjust seasoning if necessary. Place a crepe pillow in each consomme cup and ladle soup over it.

Yield: 8 6-ounce servings, each with 1 crepe pillow
✦ Calories per serving: 83
Carbohydrate per serving: 8g
✦ Cholesterol per serving: 35mg

Dietary fiber per serving: 1g
Fat per serving: 3g
Protein per serving: 5g
Sodium per serving: 695mg

Grilled Veal Loin Chops
❖

With no calorie-crutches such as sauces, mustardy bread crumbs, or herb butters, this simple recipe demands the best veal money can buy—creamy textured, with more white than pink. Because a good veal loin chop will run as much as 8 or up to even 12 ounces each, this is the meal for the meat lovers among us. Some of the weight is bone, of course, but this is still quite a hefty serving, so the rest of the meal has been kept light. If the grill is buried beneath a blanket of snow and you don't have an indoor model, instructions are given for oven roasting.

> 8 1½- to 2-inch-thick veal loin chops
> vegetable oil
> ½ teaspoon salt
> freshly ground pepper to taste

1. Trim any visible fat from the chops. Brush oil over the grill rungs or broiler rack. Season meat with salt and pepper. Grill (or broil, but watch timing) 12 minutes on each side or until an instant-reading meat thermometer placed in the center of the chop reads 140 for meat with the barest blush of pink, or 165 for a more well-done chop.
2. For oven cooking: Preheat oven to 400 degrees. Sear the chops in an oven proof skillet, using cooking spray or a bit of safflower oil. Cook 3 to 4 minutes on one side. Flip, reduce heat to medium, and brown the other side another 3 to 4 minutes. Place the skillet in the bottom third of the oven and roast another 7 minutes for medium-rare or 10 minutes for medium.

Yield: 8 generous servings
Calories per serving: 426
Carbohydrate per serving: 0g
Cholesterol per serving: 240mg

Dietary fiber per serving: 0g
Fat per serving: 26g
Protein per serving: 45g
Sodium per serving: 359mg

Dilled New Potatoes

For variety you might like to substitute other herbs, such as mint or a mixture of parsley, rosemary, and thyme, for the dill. The herb butter may be doubled and kept chilled for a week or frozen almost indefinitely. Be sure to bring it to room temperature before using.

> 1 pound red bliss potatoes
> 4 tablespoons unsalted butter, at room
>   temperature
> 4 tablespoons minced fresh dill
> ½ teaspoon salt
> freshly ground black pepper to taste
> sprigs of fresh dill for garnish (optional)

1. Cut a thin slice from the bottom of each potato so it sits upright. Using the larger side of a melon baller, scoop out a ball from the top center of each potato. Discard these trimmings.
2. Bring 3 quarts water to a boil in a 4-quart saucepan. Boil potatoes over medium-high heat, uncovered, for 25 minutes or until tender when pierced with a fork. Drain.
3. Meanwhile, in a food processor or blender, or with a fork, mix the butter, dill, salt, and pepper. Scrape herb butter onto a sheet of wax paper. Roll up herb butter in the paper into a sausage shape and twist the ends tightly in opposite directions.
4. Place the potatoes upright on a serving dish. Place slices of herb butter in the scooped-out center of the potatoes. (If potatoes are to be reheated in a micro-wave oven, cover them with plastic wrap and chill up to 8 hours. Repeat on medium-high heat power for 3 minutes or until steamy.) Garnish with fresh dill.

Yield: 8 servings, about 1 potato each
✦ **Calories per serving: 80**
Carbohydrate per serving: 7g
✦ **Cholesterol per serving: 15mg**

Dietary fiber per serving: 0g
Fat per serving: 6g
Protein per serving: 1g
Sodium per serving: 255mg

Swiss Chard with Bacon and Balsamic Vinegar

❖

Swiss chard is a pleasing change from the more common spinach. Here's a tasty and satisfying way to serve it without butter.

> 6 ounces bacon
> 2½ to 3 pounds Swiss chard, rinsed and stems removed
> 3 tablespoons safflower or corn oil
> 4 tablespoons balsamic vinegar

1. Fry the bacon in a 12-inch skillet until crisp. Remove and drain on paper towels. Drain fat from skillet and wipe clean with paper towels.
2. Stack the Swiss chard leaves, roll up jellyroll fashion, and slice crosswise into thin strips.
3. Heat the oil in the same skillet over high heat. Add the Swiss chard, tossing with two wooden spoons until wilted, about 3 to 4 minutes. Sprinkle with vinegar, crumble bacon over the top, toss again, and serve.

Yield: 8 servings
✦ **Calories per serving: 98**
Carbohydrate per serving: 3g
✦ **Cholesterol per serving: 5g**

Dietary fiber per serving: 0g
Fat per serving: 9g
Protein per serving: 3g
Sodium per serving: 193mg

❖Nutmeg was such an essential ingredient in eighteenth-century European cuisine that women weren't considered well dressed unless adorned with an ornamental nutmeg grater.❖

Bananas Creole

❖

Rice fanciers will take to this showy yet calorie-modest dessert. Prepare the rice the day before serving, and finish assembling the dessert two hours before, leaving broiling and flaming for the last minute.

> 1½ cups low-fat milk
> 1 vanilla bean or 1 teaspoon vanilla extract
> a few gratings fresh nutmeg
> 1 cinnamon stick
> ½ cup converted rice
> 2 tablespoons honey
> 1 teaspoon unsalted butter
> a pinch salt
> 1 egg, lightly beaten
> the zest (grated rind) of 1 lemon
> 4 bananas
> 5 tablespoons rum
> 3 tablespoons brown sugar
> 1 tablespoon oats, quick-cooking recommended, not instant
> 3 tablespoons ground walnuts
> 1 tablespoon unsalted butter, melted
> 1 teaspoon sugar

1. Simmer the milk, vanilla bean (if you are using it), nutmeg, and cinnamon for 10 minutes in a covered 2½-quart saucepan over medium heat. Remove the vanilla bean and cinnamon stick.
2. Add the rice, honey, 2 teaspoons butter, and salt. Simmer, covered, over medium heat until the liquid is absorbed, about 35 to 40 minutes.
3. Remove from heat, beat in the egg, cover, and let rest 15 minutes. Stir in the lemon zest. If you are using vanilla extract, add it now. Set rice aside. (Rice may be

prepared a day in advance and held, covered, in refrigerator.)

4. Cut the unpeeled bananas in half the long way, taking care not to tear the peels. Set the 8 banana skins aside. Slice the fruit in ½-inch-thick slices. Combine 3 tablespoons of the rum with the brown sugar. Add the banana slices and marinate for at least 10 minutes. Cover with plastic wrap if holding more than 30 minutes (they may be held up to 2 hours).

5. Half fill a 2½-quart saucepan with water. Bring to a boil. Drop the banana skins into the water, boil 1 minute, drain, and pat dry.

6. Place the skins in a 10-inch round, ovenproof serving dish as if they were the petals of a flower, tips meeting in the center, yellow side down. Divide the dessert rice among the banana peels. Arrange banana slices on rice.

7. Mix together the oats and walnuts. Sprinkle over bananas and drizzle with melted butter. (Dessert may be held, covered with plastic wrap, for up to 2 hours before finishing.)

8. Broil the dessert until the oats are lightly toasted, about 10 minutes. Rotate dish occasionally for even browning.

9. To flame: Combine the remaining 2 tablespoons rum and the teaspoon of sugar in a long-handled ½-cup pot (a butter warmer with a lip is ideal). Heat just until tiny bubbles appear at the edges, about 1 minute. Ignite and pour over bananas. *Note:* For safety's sake ignite and pour liqueur at the table.

Yield: 8 servings
✦ Calories per serving: 204
Carbohydrate per serving: 35g
✦ Cholesterol per serving: 37mg

Dietary fiber per serving: 1g
Fat per serving: 5g
Protein per serving: 4g
✦ Sodium per serving: 72mg

❖Lemons and limes are juicier if left at room temperature as are tomatoes, plums, grapefruits, and nectarines.❖

A CANDELIGHT CLASSIC

Oyster Basil Pan Roast
Tossed Green Salad with Shredded Radishes
Veal Medallions with Mushrooms and Marsala
Potato and Artichoke Gratin
Baked Apple Slices with Bourbon Sauce

This delightfully satisfying meal for six seems perfect for cold weather and the flickering flames of candelight and a fire. If you'd like to spread out the jobs, let this be your cooking guide: Prepare the salad greens and dressing the day before; leave the apple for the last minute so it does not turn brown. The veal medallions may also be partially prepared the day before, leaving just the sauteing of the meat and finishing the sauce. The bourbon sauce for the dessert may be mixed and frozen a day early as well, though it only takes a few minutes to prepare. The potato and artichoke gratin may be prepared two hours before dinner and held chilled, covered with plastic wrap, or baked and reheated in a microwave oven. The apple slices may be treated the same way. Although the oyster pan roast could be made a day in advance, the oysters will run the chance of getting tough when they are reheated; so if possible, prepare this dish (which is very simple) just before serving.

Oyster Basil Pan Roast

This pan roast, really a soup, takes so very little time to prepare you might want to keep it in mind for a hurried weekday meal with a poppy-seed-dressed salad (pages 82–83) and a loaf of hot French bread. It may be made ahead if necessary, but reheat very gently so as not to overcook the oysters. Serve it in shallow soup bowls.

> 1½ shallots, minced (about 3 tablespoons)
> 3 celery ribs, minced
> 2¼ cups bottled clam broth or homemade fish
>   stock
> 4 tablespoons cottage cheese
> 4 tablespoons plain yogurt
> 2 tablespoons arrowroot
> 12 fresh basil leaves
> 1½ pints shucked oysters, liquor reserved
> 3 tablespoons dry white wine
> a few drops hot pepper sauce
> a dash cayenne pepper (optional)

1. "Saute" the shallots and celery in 1½ cups of the clam broth in a covered 12-inch skillet until limp, about 5 to 6 minutes.
2. Meanwhile, in a food processor or blender combine the cottage cheese, yogurt, and arrowroot. Set aside.
3. Stack the basil leaves, roll up jellyroll fashion, and slice thinly crosswise.
4. Add the remaining broth and oyster liquor to the shallots and celery along with the wine, basil, and oysters. Cover and simmer over medium heat, stirring occasionally, until the edges of the oysters curl, about 5 to 6 minutes.
5. Remove from heat, and cool by stirring constantly for 1 minute. When slightly cooled, stir in the cottage cheese mixture and serve immediately. If soup is pre-

pared in advance, reheat it gently over just simmering water in a double boiler.

Yield: 6 servings
✦ **Calories per serving: 199**
Carbohydrate per serving: 22g
Cholesterol per serving: 93mg

Dietary fiber per serving: 1g
Fat per serving: 5g
Protein per serving: 19g
Sodium per serving: 828mg

Tossed Green Salad with Shredded Radishes

❖

Salads represent a real challenge for the enlightened cook. Although the basic ingredients tip the scale on the low side, the real taste pleasers, such as bacon, croutons, cheese, and oils, deliver unhealthy amounts of saturated fats and calories. A good dressing and a little innovative use of some common crunchables help make the most of salad standards.

The dressing recipe is sufficient for eight servings; save time by doubling it. If it jells in the refrigerator, warm briefly or heat in a microwave oven to liquefy.

For the Dressing:

⅔ cup canned beef consomme or homemade beef stock
½ cup Chunky Homestyle Ketchup (page 352) or store-bought ketchup
⅓ cup extra-virgin olive oil
1 tablespoon grated onion
1 garlic clove, minced
1 tablespoon Worcestershire sauce

For the Salad

5 cups mixed greens, rinsed and torn, such as
   Boston, salad bowl, and red leaf lettuce
1 bunch radishes (6 ounces), roots and stems
   removed
1 apple, any variety
1 cup bean sprouts

To Prepare the Dressing

1. Combine all the dressing ingredients in a screw-top jar. Shake well to combine. Refrigerate any unused portion or if not using immediately.

To Prepare the Salad

1. Toss the greens in a salad bowl. Shred the radishes in a food processor or with a grater. Core the apple and slice thinly. Toss the radishes, apple, and bean sprouts with the greens. Then toss with about 1 cup dressing.

Yield: 6 servings, with some dressing left over
✦ Calories per serving: 126
Carbohydrates per serving: 11g
✦ Cholesterol per serving: 0mg

Dietary fiber per serving: 1g
Fat per serving: 9g
Protein per serving: 2g
✦ Sodium per serving: 110mg

Veal Medallions with Mushrooms and Marsala

❖

This is a light yet rich dish, which you may partially prepare ahead. It may seem odd to start with a rib chop, then remove the bone, but there is method to this madness.

The bones will transform a canned broth (buy the type marked "double strength" but don't add water) into a fairly quick *demi-glace* and the rib chop meat is more tender than a cutlet. However, cutlets will certainly do. *Note:* If you have homemade beef stock, you will not need the carrots, chopped onion, thyme, and water, as it will be flavorful and thick enough to make a good sauce.

> 3 pounds veal rib chops (1 per diner)
> 2 10½-ounce cans beef broth, double strength, or
>   2½ cups homemade beef stock
> 2 carrots, chopped
> 1 onion, chopped
> a sprig fresh thyme or ½ teaspoon dried thyme
> 1 cup water
> ½ pound pearl onions
> 2 teaspoons arrowroot
> 2 tablespoons wine or water
> ¼ cup flour
> 1 tablespoon plus 1 teaspoon safflower oil
> 2 teaspoons unsalted butter
> 8 ounces mushrooms, sliced
> 6 tablespoons Marsala wine

1. Bone the rib chop by following the bone with the tip of a small paring knife to free the meat. Chop the bones into 4-inch lengths with a cleaver.
2. If you are using canned broth, combine it with the bones, carrots, onion, thyme, and water in a 4-quart saucepan. Cover and simmer at least 30 minutes, but preferably 1 hour or more. If you are using homemade beef stock, boil the stock with the bones, uncovered, over high heat until it has reduced to 1½ cups, about 15 to 20 minutes.
3. Meanwhile, butterfly the veal by slicing it sideways, keeping your knife parallel to the work surface, and cutting to within ½ inch of what was the bone side of the meat. Place the meat between 2 sheets of wax paper and pound slightly. Meat may be left unpounded (adjust cooking instructions) if desired.

4. Trim the root end from the onions. Cut a small cross into the bottom of the onions so they won't explode during cooking. Bring a quart of water to a boil, add onions, and boil 3 to 4 minutes. Drain, and when cool enough to handle, slip off the skins.
5. When the broth or stock has simmered the suggested amount of time and reduced to 1½ cups (raise heat to boil to reduce more, or add more broth to adjust level if necessary), strain, pressing the solids with the back of wooden spoon. (Recipe may be completed to this step a day ahead.) Set near stove to have handy for step 8.
6. Dissolve the arrowroot in the wine or water. Set near stove for step 8.
7. Dredge the veal in the flour. Melt the oil and butter in a 12-inch skillet until bubbly. On high heat, saute the veal on one side for 2 minutes. Reduce heat to medium, turn veal over, add the onions and mushrooms, cover, and cook 2 minutes more. Transfer meat to a platter. Return heat to high, cover, and cook vegetables about 1 minute, stirring often, until nicely browned.
8. Add reduced broth or stock and Marsala, and boil, uncovered, for 2 minutes. Over medium-low heat, whisk in the dissolved arrowroot. Add the meat and spoon the sauce over it. Half-cover the pan and simmer 2 minutes more before serving.

Yield: 6 servings
Calories per serving: 568
Carbohydrate per serving: 11g
Cholesterol per serving: 235mg

Dietary fiber per serving: 1g
Fat per serving: 36g
Protein per serving: 44g
✦ Sodium per serving: 295mg

❖For trivia buffs, 75,000 crocuses (I have it on the best authority!) with their three stigmas each must be picked, and the stigmas plucked (by hand), to produce a pound of saffron. Crush the saffron in your fingertips just before adding to the cookpot.❖

Potato and Artichoke Gratin

❖

What we have here is the prince and the pauper—the regal artichoke teamed up with the peasant potato. The butter-thirsty tuber is rendered moist without much fat, thanks mostly to the artichoke bottoms. Although you may use the more convenient frozen artichoke hearts, the fresh will pay off in royal dividends, lending an understated, yet distinctive flavor.

The gratin can be held chilled, covered with plastic wrap, for 2 hours before baking or completely baked and reheated in a microwave oven on medium power for about 8 minutes.

> 3 artichokes
> 6 tablespoons homemade chicken stock or
> canned broth
> 2 teaspoons lemon juice
> 3 large potatoes (1½ pounds), peeled and sliced
> ⅛-inch thick
> 2 tablespoons extra-virgin olive oil
> 1 clove garlic, halved lengthwise
> ½ teaspoon salt
> freshly ground black pepper to taste
> a few gratings fresh nutmeg
> 3 cups whole milk
> 3 tablespoons grated mozzarella cheese

1. Cut off and the stem of one artichoke. With a stainless steel knife, pare the artichoke as if peeling an apple, removing the top 2 or 3 layers of tough, deep green leaves. Cut off the top third of the artichoke. Turn the artichoke upside down and be sure all the tough, dark green leaves are removed from the bottom. (See illustrations on pages 77–78.) Spread the leaves at the top of the artichoke apart. With a spoon, remove the fuzzy center (the choke). Repeat with other artichokes. Turn

PREPARING ARTICHOKES FOR COOKING

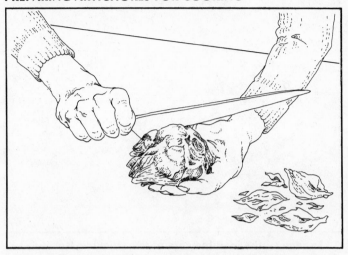

1. To remove the tough outer leaves of an artichoke, pare it as you would an apple.

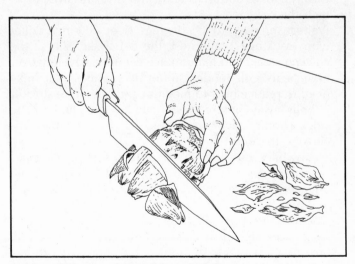

2. Cut off the top third of the artichoke.

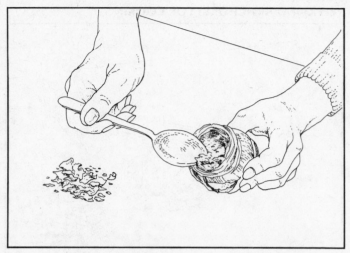

3. To remove the inedible core of the artichoke, spread the leaves apart with your fingers. At the very center will be a cluster of small, sharply pointed leaves and under those a fuzzy core. Remove this with the tip of a teaspoon.

    the artichokes bottom side up and slice crosswise in ¼-inch-thick slices.

2. Preheat the oven to 375 degrees. Coat a 10-inch skillet with cooking spray. Add the artichoke slices, the chicken stock, and lemon juice. Simmer, covered, over high heat until tender, about 10 minutes. You may need to reduce heat to medium and add more stock if it boils away before the artichokes are tender. The stock should have evaporated by the time the artichokes are done.

3. Meanwhile, put the sliced potatoes in a 2½-quart saucepan, cover with cold water, and bring to a boil, uncovered. Once a boil is reached, boil potatoes for 5 minutes, then drain.

4. Uncover the artichokes, add oil to the dry pan, and saute over high heat, stirring frequently, until lightly browned, about 3 to 4 minutes. Toss potatoes with artichokes off heat.

5. Rub a 10-inch quiche dish with the garlic halves, then coat the dish with cooking spray. Put potato and artichoke mixture in dish, smoothing the top. Season with salt, pepper, and nutmeg. Add milk and top with cheese. Bake in the upper third of the preheated 375-degree oven for 45 minutes or until potatoes are tender and most of the milk is absorbed. Broil briefly to brown top if necessary.

Yield: 6 servings
Calories per serving: 210
Carbohydrate per serving: 25g
✦ Cholesterol per serving: 20mg

Dietary fiber per serving: 1g
Fat per serving: 9g
Protein per serving: 8g
Sodium per serving: 290mg

Baked Apple Slices with Bourbon Sauce

❖

Apples and cinnamon, pecans and maple syrup, the buttery crunch of a streusel—you'll do more than just imagine such taste treats with this warm dessert for cold weather. The apples may be prepared for baking up to 3 hours ahead and held covered with plastic wrap, or they may be baked and then reheated in a microwave oven just before serving. The bourbon sauce may be made up to a day ahead and kept frozen.

5 Granny Smith apples, peeled and cored
3 tablespoons cider
1 tablespoon bourbon
2½ tablespoons unsalted butter
4 tablespoons quick-cooking oats, not instant
4 tablespoons chopped pecans
½ teaspoon ground cinnamon

a dash of ground cloves
a dash of ground allspice

For the Bourbon Sauce

1 cup vanilla ice milk
2 teaspoons bourbon
2 teaspoons maple syrup
a few gratings fresh nutmeg

1. Slice the apples into thin slices, crosswise. Coat a 12-inch ovenproof platter or pizza pan with cooking spray. Lay the apple slices on the pan in rings, overlapping as little as possible. Sprinkle with cider and bourbon.
2. Preheat the oven to 375 degrees. Melt the butter in an 8-inch skillet over medium-high heat. When foamy add the oats and pecans, stirring until very lightly browned, 2 to 3 minutes. Stir in spices. Sprinkle this topping over apples. (Set aside, covered, for up to 3 hours if desired.)
3. Bake in the upper third of the oven for 15 minutes. Reduce temperature to 275 degrees and bake 15 more minutes. If the dessert is browning too much, cover it loosely with foil.

To Prepare the Sauce

1. Soften the ice milk in a bowl at room temperature, about 15 minutes, until slightly runny. Stir in the bourbon, maple syrup, and nutmeg. (The sauce may be made a day ahead and frozen. Soften it at room temperature for 15 minutes before serving.)
2. To serve, place a few hot apple slices on a dessert plate. Top with 2 heaping tablespoons sauce.

Yield: 6 servings
✦ Calories per serving: 196
Carbohydrate per serving: 27g
✦ Cholesterol per serving: 16mg

✦ Dietary fiber per serving: 3g
Fat per serving: 9g
Protein per serving: 2g
✦ Sodium per serving: 65mg

LEAN BUT LAVISH

**Watercress, Endive, and Grapefruit Salad
with Poppy Seed Dressing**

Fillet of Beef with Lobster Sauce

Grilled Baby Eggplant Fans

Wheat Pilaf

Glazed Gingered Oranges

Preparing a meal that is long on luxury often ranks pretty high on the calorie and effort scale, too. Here is a very manageable meal in every respect, a lavish dinner for eight that won't demand too much precious time or an extra belt notch. The greens, dressing, and dessert may be prepared a day ahead, leaving the meat, eggplant, and pilaf for the day of the dinner.

A word about beef: As a rule the fattier, the more prized, therefore opt for the less expensive choice grade, rather than prime. If you like you may home-age a choice tenderloin for this recipe. Then you'll combine the best of both worlds, rendering the less fatty meat as fork-tender as the most marbled prime cut. To home-age a tenderloin, purchase a tenderloin weighing at least four pounds. Have the butcher give you the fat that he trims. At home, trim any remaining fat. Retie the meat. Place the meat on a cake rack over a baking sheet. Lay all the fat trimmings on the meat, covering it as much as possible. Crease a piece of aluminum foil large enough to cover the meat down the center. Loosely position the tent of foil over the meat; do not wrap tightly, as air must circulate. Refrigerate for three days, turning the meat and repositioning the fat once a day. During this time, the enzymes that are naturally present in the meat break down the fibers of the muscles, causing them to relax. In the process, the meat softens. You'll notice that any surface not covered by fat will darken and harden. To prepare the meat for cooking, untie the butcher's twine. Carefully pare away all the hardened flesh. Retie the roast; it is now ready for roasting.

Served with the meat is a wheat pilaf. Unlike most starches or grains, bulgur doesn't need lots of butter or other fats to make it moist and tasty. If you enjoy the flavor and texture of this pilaf, you might try it with some added shredded chicken and a few vegetables, as a quick midweek family meal delivering just the combination of foods health experts prompt us to eat more of.

Watercress, Endive, and Grapefruit Salad with Poppy Seed Dressing

❖

Tired of your standard salad, the same ingredients, the same dressing, the boring predictability? Then this salad with its peppery watercress, tart grapefruit, and sassy sauce (terrific with simple green salads, too) might be just the ticket.

For the Dressing

1 egg
1 teaspoon lemon juice
2 tablespoons white wine vinegar
½ teaspoon dry mustard
1 teaspoon sugar
½ cup safflower oil

6 tablespoons canned beef consomme or
  homemade beef stock
2 tablespoons plain yogurt
1 tablespoon mayonnaise
1 tablespoon poppy seeds

For the Salad

1 head red leaf lettuce, rinsed, spun dry, and torn
1 bunch watercress, rinsed, spun dry, and torn
1 small head Belgian endive
1 grapefruit

1. To prepare the dressing: Mix the egg, lemon juice, vinegar, mustard, and sugar in a food processor or blender for 30 seconds. Gradually add the oil in a slow, ultrathin stream with the machine on. Slowly add the consomme, then mix in the yogurt, mayonnaise, and poppy seeds. Keep chilled in a screw-top jar for easy shaking. It will keep for 4 or 5 days.
2. To prepare the salad: Toss the lettuce and watercress in a large bowl. Place 2 leaves endive on each of 8 salad plates, 1 leaf at one o'clock, the other at two o'clock, with the ends at the center of the plate. Place the greens in the center of each plate. Peel the grapefruit as you would an orange. Section the fruit, peeling off as much white membrane as will easily come free. Place about 2 segments in the center of each plate of greens. Shake the dressing and spoon 3 tablespoons over each salad.

Yield: 8 servings, 1½ cups dressing
✦ **Calories per serving: 167**
 Carbohydrate per serving: 4g
✦ **Cholesterol per serving: 32mg**
 Dietary fiber per serving: 1g
 Fat per serving: 16g
 Protein per serving: 2g
✦ **Sodium per serving: 25mg**

Fillet of Beef
with Lobster Sauce

❖

Not your average "surf and turf," but an elegant entree that's easy on the cook. If lobster is unavailable or too dear look for langostino, which is available in the market's frozen fish section. It is a South American product with a flavor very similar to our lobster. The meat may be stuffed and tied for roasting up to four hours before cooking, and kept chilled. Although the recipe calls for stuffing the beef with the lobster, you can save a bit of fuss by using all the lobster in the sauce and omitting the stuffing step.

> 2 tablespoons olive oil, extra-virgin recommended
> 1 shallot, minced (1½ tablespoons)
> 2 garlic cloves, minced
> 2 tablespoons lemon juice
> 12 ounces lobster meat or thawed langostino
> 3 to 3½ pounds beef tenderloin, trimmed of all
>   fat
> 4 tablespoons canned beef consomme or
>   homemade beef stock
> 1 tablespoon plus 1 teaspoon arrowroot
> 1 cup dry white wine
> 2 tablespoons unsalted butter, at room
>   temperature
> 2 tablespoons minced fresh parsley

1. Preheat oven to 450 degrees. Heat the oil over medium-high heat in a 10-inch skillet until tiny bubbles appear. Saute the shallot and garlic, stirring frequently, until soft and transparent, adjusting heat to prevent browning. Add the lemon juice and lobster, and stir over medium heat 1 minute. Remove from heat.
2. Slice meat crosswise to within 1 inch of the bottom. Stuff with half the lobster mixture (refrigerate unused

half), and salt meat if desired. Tie with butcher's or all-cotton twine.

3. Roast in the bottom third of the oven for 40 minutes or until an instant-reading meat thermometer registers 120 for rare. Begin checking temperature after 25 minutes cooking time, because different meat configurations, temperature of meat at time of roasting, and individual ovens will greatly affect the actual cooking time. When roast is done, let it rest 5 to 10 minutes, loosely covered with foil, before slicing.

4. While the meat is resting, complete the sauce: Remove the lobster mixture from the refrigerator and place in an 8-inch skillet. Warm it over medium-high heat for 2 minutes. Stir in the consomme.

5. Dissolve the arrowroot in the wine. Reduce heat to medium. Stir the arrowroot into the lobster mixture, and cook until thickened, about 3 minutes. Whisk in the butter, then the parsley. Spoon sauce over individual servings of beef or pass it at the table.

Yield: 8 servings
Calories per serving: 389
Carbohydrate per serving: 4g
Cholesterol per serving: 189mg

Dietary fiber per serving: 0g
Fat per serving: 30g
Protein per serving: 55g
✦ **Sodium per serving: 181mg**

Grilled Baby Eggplant Fans

❖

Breading the eggplant with just egg whites instead of the whole egg pinches calories and cholesterol—a savings worth far more than the few pennies cost of some discarded yolks. If baby eggplant aren't available, eggplant slices will do as well. Instructions are given for stove-top cooking if grilling isn't viable.

COOKED BABY EGGPLANT FAN

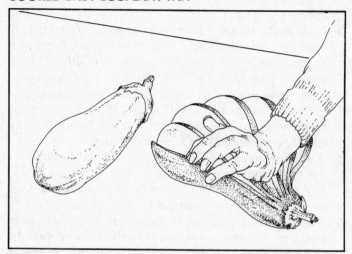

To make an eggplant fan, cut thin slices from the base of the eggplant to within about ½ inch of the tip. Fan the eggplant by pressing it flat with the heel of the hand.

> 8 baby eggplants or 2 1-pound eggplants, stem
>   end trimmed
> 2 tablespoons salt, kosher recommended
> 2 egg whites
> 2 tablespoons water
> 8 tablespoons dry bread crumbs
> 3 tablespoons minced fresh parsley
> 1 scallion, green part only, minced
> a pinch cayenne pepper
> 4 tablespoons olive oil, extra-virgin recommended

1. Fan the baby eggplants by making lengthwise ¼-inch-thick cuts from the base of the vegetable up to within ½ inch of the tip. Press with the heel of your hand to spread the "petals." Refer to the illustration as you do this. (Slice regular eggplant crosswise into ½-inch-thick slices.)
2. Sprinkle one side of the eggplant petals with half the

salt, lay them on paper towels, and rest 10 to 15 minutes. Turn and repeat with remaining salt and let eggplant rest another 10 minutes. Rinse thoroughly and pat dry with paper towels.

3. Beat the egg whites and water together with a fork. Dip eggplants into the egg wash.

4. Mix together the bread crumbs, parsley, scallion, and cayenne on a sheet of wax paper. Dip the eggplants into the crumbs, lifting the petals to crumb all surfaces evenly.

5. Brush half the oil over one side of the eggplants and grill oil side down for 10 minutes. Turn eggplants over and brush with the remaining oil; grill another 10 minutes or until vegetable is tender and golden brown. For stove-top cooking, set a 12-inch skillet with 1 tablespoon of oil over medium heat. Saute the eggplants in the hot oil for 6 to 8 minutes on one side, adjusting heat if necessary. Turn eggplants over, add the remaining oil, and saute until tender and browned, about 4 to 5 minutes.

Yield: 8 servings
Calories per serving: 189
Carbohydrate per serving: 29g
✦ **Cholesterol per serving: 0mg**

✦ **Dietary fiber per serving: 6g**
Fat per serving: 7g
Protein per serving: 6g
Sodium per serving: 365mg

Wheat Pilaf

❖

Nutty and robust, bulgur wheat has been cooked, dried, and cracked when it comes to market in three grinds: fine, medium, and coarse. Generally, coarse is used in salads and for side dishes such as this pilaf, but any will do. It is rich in the B vitamins, which aid in the metabolism of carbohydrates and promote healthy skin, and is a good source of fiber. A handful of golden raisins is a nice addition to this pilaf, stirred in moments before removing from the heat.

> 1 cup bulgur wheat, coarse grind recommended
> 2¾ cup homemade chicken stock or canned broth
> 2 leeks, white part only, sliced (⅔ cup)
> 2 garlic cloves, minced
> 1 tablespoon plus 1 teaspoon olive oil,
>   extra-virgin recommended
> 5 ounces mushrooms, sliced
> 1 tablespoon minced fresh parsley
> freshly ground black pepper to taste

1. Combine the bulgur and 2 cups chicken stock in a covered 2½-quart saucepan. Boil gently for 10 minutes over high heat, stirring occasionally.
2. Meanwhile, combine the leeks and garlic with the oil and ½ cup of the chicken stock, in a covered 8-inch skillet. Cook over high heat, stirring often, until leeks are tender and liquid is evaporated, about 2 to 3 minutes (removing cover or adding liquid if necessary).
3. Uncover, add mushrooms, and cook over high heat until limp and all liquid is evaporated, about 2 to 3 minutes.
4. When bulgur has boiled 10 minutes, remove from heat, and stir in mushroom mixture, parsley, and pepper. Add remaining ¼ cup of chicken stock to the mushroom skillet and deglaze by stirring with a wooden spoon over high heat until about 1 tablespoon of dark brown juices remain. (Note: If the pan is still hot, heat may not be needed.)
5. Stir juices into pilaf and let rest, covered, 15 to 20 minutes before serving. If needed, pilaf may be reheated over low heat or in a microwave oven.

Yield: 8 ½-cup servings

+ Calories per serving: 108
Carbohydrate per serving: 19g
+ Cholesterol per serving: 0mg

Dietary fiber per serving: 1g
Fat per serving: 3g
Protein per serving: 3g
+ Sodium per serving: 5mg

Glazed Gingered Oranges

❖

The nip of the ginger, the succulence of the orange, and the sweet lick of syrup combine to make this easy dessert one you'll want to make often. Besides, it fits your schedule. If time is tight, serve it glazed (step 7) or make it as much as 2 days before and serve it chilled (step 6). Either way, you may dress it up with a ribbon of Raspberry Sauce (see page 26) and a few chopped macadamia nuts if you like.

> 1 quart water
> ½ cup sugar
> 8 navel oranges
> ⅓ cup Triple Sec or other orange-flavored liqueur
> 2 tablespoons minced fresh ginger
> 2 tablespoons Crème de Cassis (optional)
> 8 mint or lemon leaves for garnish, if available

1. Combine the water and sugar in a 4-quart saucepan over medium-high heat until the sugar dissolves and the liquid is clear, about 5 minutes. Do not stir, but swirl the pan by the handle occasionally. Do not allow to boil until all sugar is dissolved.
2. Meanwhile, with a vegetable peeler remove the skin from 4 of the oranges, taking care not to get the bitter white membrane. Stack the skin and cut into very fine strips (julienne).
3. Add the julienned orange zest, orange liqueur, and ginger to the sugar mixture. Boil over high heat until reduced to 1½ cups, about 25 minutes.
4. Meanwhile, remove the white membrane from the 4 oranges and peel the rest of the oranges. Slice all the oranges crosswise in ¼-inch-thick slices.
5. Stir the Crème de Cassis into the reduced syrup off the heat.

6. Oranges may be served chilled or glazed. To serve chilled, marinate the oranges in the syrup in a leak-proof plastic bag or nonmetal bowl at least 2 hours or up to 48 hours before serving. Fan the slices on individual serving plates, drizzle with 2 to 3 tablespoons syrup, and garnish with a mint or lemon leaf.
7. To serve the oranges glazed, marinate them or not, as you prefer. Preheat oven to 375 degrees. Overlap the orange slices in a quiche dish or on individual oven-proof dishes. Spoon 2 to 3 tablespoons of syrup over each serving and bake in the upper third of the oven for 5 minutes. Garnish each serving with a mint or lemon leaf.

Yield: 8 servings
+ Calories per serving: 114
Carbohydrate per serving: 29g
+ Cholesterol per serving: 0mg

+ Dietary fiber per serving: 3g
Fat per serving: 0g
Protein per serving: 1g
+ Sodium per serving: 0mg

❖ Focus: Antibiotics ❖ and Cattle

Some years back, DES (a synthetic hormone) was fed to cattle when it was found the animals would get fatter while eating less (good for the cattle maybe, but not for us!). In 1979, however, the practice was banned for fear humans who ate the meat might develop cancer. Now, the practice of feeding livestock antibiotics has also come under FDA scrutiny. Some animals are given food treated with antibiotics as a preventive measure against disease, on the theory that a healthy animal grows more quickly. Although there is a buffer period between slaughter (or milking) and the last medication dose, some health experts fear that a strain of immunized bacteria could develop. These impervious bacteria could then transfer their antibiotic resistance to other bacteria, which could cause disease in people who ate the meat. Thus, if someone became ill after eating a piece of meat infected with penicillin-resistant salmonella, there would be no cure at the worst, or at best, a cure would take longer to find. The FDA is looking at the issue of adding antibiotics to livestock feed to avoid such problems.

❖Calorie conservationists will want to buy cuts of the leanest beef available. Frequently sold under the store label, this rates the third lowest marking by USDA inspectors, "Good Grade." The sparse marbling and minimal fat makes this meat a good candidate for the braising pot or thinly sliced for quick grilling or stir-frying. Choice is the next best grade for the calorie counter, just remember to trim all fat, and Prime (ironically ranked "best") should be avoided.❖

MENUS FOR INFORMAL ENTERTAINING OR FAMILY DINNERS

❖ Menus for Informal ❖ Entertaining or Family Dinners

Looking for an out-of-the-ordinary do-ahead casserole for a weekend away? Or a quick but special meal to prepare in microwave speed? Maybe a long, leisurely lunch is in order. These, and more, are the subject of this section. Some of the menus are quick, others require a bit more commitment, and all give detailed information on advance preparation when feasible.

As always, the reader is urged to play with the menu items, to mix and match, or combine with your own favorites. If a guilt-free dessert is your hankering, there are several in this section. If you're looking for some interesting ways with vegetables for the family dinner table, you've come to the right place. Love potatoes, but could do without the fat that so improves them? Look no farther than "Back to Basics," on page 132.

These are a collection of meals, for good friends or family, that showcase your good nutritional sense and culinary savvy.

❖Persons attempting to lose weight would do best to restrict their intake of fats and proteins before restricting their carbohydrates. Carbohydrates (4 calories to the gram) are the body's most efficient source of fuel. If these are limited, the body will break down protein (4 calories to the gram), which is best used for tissue building and repair, or fats, which at 9 calories to the gram will take longer to use.❖

REEL GOOD

Crumbed Codfish with Lemon Mustard Sauce
Spaghetti Squash Parmesan
Steamed Broccoli
Cappucino Cream

To ensure "reel-fresh" seafood, check that:

- the fish is kept on ice;
- the store receives daily deliveries;
- the fish is odor-free;
- the flesh is smooth and resilient, not slimy and mushy;
- the fish is weighed as you buy it, not prepackaged.

Once home, keep the fish in a bowl of ice in the refrigerator, just as it is kept at the market, if it won't be cooked within 8 hours. Should it have an off-odor despite all precautions, refresh it by soaking five minutes in a bowl of cool water with two tablespoons added lemon juice. Pat it dry before continuing with the recipe.

Fish in hand, these recipes, each serving four, are uncomplicated. Note that the dessert does require three to four hours overall chilling time, so start it early in the day or even a day ahead. The lemon sauce can be prepared several hours ahead or as the fish cooks. The spaghetti squash can be prepared a day in advance or started before the fish preparation. Use the Steamed Broccoli recipe on page 242, doubled to serve four. If you miss the traditional starch, include a few breadsticks.

❖ Focus: Fish ❖

If you love it you don't need to be convinced, but if the thought of fish brings to mind off-odors and an unpalatable mushiness, there probably isn't much fish in your diet—a food that studies published in the *New England Journal of Medicine* suggest may be instrumental in preventing heart disease.

In one study, Dutch researchers kept track of a large group of men, comparing their health records and diets over a period of 20 years. They found that those who ate as little as an ounce or more of fish a day were two and a half times less likely to die from heart diease than men who ate none at all. Men who ate 7 to 11 ounces of fish per week, that's 2 to 3 servings, had an impressive 64 percent lowered risk.

The researchers investigated other heart disease risk factors such as high blood pressure and high blood cholesterol, but the fact that the fish eaters consumed more cholesterol and fat than the non-fish eaters led them, along with other factors, to conclude that fish consumption all by itself appeared to help protect against heart disease.

Originally, it had been believed that one needed to eat large quantities of fish, particularly cold-water fatty fish—salmon, trout, and mackerel—with their beneficial fatty acids to achieve cardiovascular benefits. But this study suggests that only 2 weekly meals of lean fish may be just what the doctor ordered.

This isn't to suggest that other steps in preventing heart disease—quitting smoking, controlling high blood pressure, or cutting back on total fat—should be ignored; instead fish-eating is considered just one more measure.

How to work fish into a fish-hater's diet? *One:* Be sure the fish is pristinely fresh, absolutely without odor. *Two:* Choose light-tasting fishes such as sole, cod, and haddock rather than strong-flavored ones such as swordfish or bluefish. *Three:* Begin with recipes that use just a little fish in conjunction with other foods, such as the Spicy Shrimp and Cashew Stir-Fry (page 171). *Four:* When ready to serve fish as the entree choose a recipe with a light sauce, such as Crumbed Codfish with Lemon Mustard Sauce, below, or one with a smattering of vegetable flavors, such as Halibut with Nutted Confetti, page 115. Offer them up, hot and tempting with a healthy serving of the facts; it's no fish tale.

Crumbed Codfish with Lemon Mustard Sauce

❖

There's nothing, to my way of thinking, quite so good as fish when it's fresh, or so awful as fish when it's old. If you have access to "reel" fresh seafood, you have one of the healthiest of protein foods and one of the quickest to prepare to boot. This simple recipe's greatest demand is that you stop by a reputable fish market the day you plan to serve it.

Fish does not take well to doing ahead—but this is a quick preparation requiring little more than 15 to 20 minutes. The sauce is easily whipped up while the fish bakes; if you prefer, it may be prepared several hours in advance, kept chilled, and reheated for a minute or two over low heat.

For the Lemon Mustard Sauce

1 teaspoon arrowroot
¾ cup low-fat milk
1 egg yolk
2 tablespoons lemon juice
*1 tablespoon unsalted butter, at room
    temperature*
½ teaspoon dry mustard

¼ teaspoon salt
a few drops hot pepper sauce

For the Fish

1¼ pounds codfish or other thick white-fleshed
    fish
½ cup low-fat milk
2 tablespoons dry bread crumbs
the grated rind (zest) of one lemon
¼ teaspoon salt
a dash cayenne pepper
1 tablespoon lemon juice
2 teaspoons safflower oil

To Prepare the Sauce

1. Dissolve the arrowroot in 2 tablespoons of the milk in a 1-quart saucepan over medium heat. Add the remaining milk, and cook, still over medium heat, stirring, until the mixture thickens, about 2 minutes.
2. With a fork, beat the egg yolk in a measuring cup. Continue beating as you slowly dribble ½ cup of hot milk into the yolk. Return the mixture to the saucepan with the remaining milk and stir over low heat, 1 minute, until thickened.
3. Whisk in lemon juice, butter, and dry mustard. Season with salt and hot pepper sauce to taste. (The sauce may be covered and kept in the refrigerator for several hours.)

To Prepare the Fish

1. Preheat the oven to 450 degrees. Soak the fish in the milk for 10 minutes. Drain and pat dry.
2. With cooking spray, coat a baking dish just big enough to hold the fish. Mix the bread crumbs and lemon zest on a piece of wax paper. Roll the fish in the crumbs, then place it in the baking dish.
3. Season the fish with salt and pepper. Sprinkle with lemon juice and safflower oil.

4. Measure the thickest part of the fish. Calculating 8 to 10 minutes per inch thickness, bake the fish in the upper third of the oven accordingly. The fish may have to be broiled briefly to brown the crumbs.

5. While the fish is baking, reheat the sauce (if it has been chilled) over low heat, stirring frequently, until warmed through—just a few minutes. Pour the sauce over the fish or pass it at the table.

Yield: 4 servings fish, with ⅓ cup sauce each

✦ Calories per serving: 290
Carbohydrate per serving: 10g
Cholesterol per serving: 160mg

Dietary fiber per serving: 0g
Fat per serving: 14g
Protein per serving: 32g
Sodium per serving: 475mg

Spaghetti Squash Parmesan

❖

A relative newcomer to our markets, spaghetti squash has been known in the Orient for many years. Like other hard-skinned squashes it keeps wonderfully well in the refrigerator, assuring a fresh vegetable for the dinner table even if you haven't shopped for several days.

This is a basic way to prepare the crunchy, mild-flavored squash. For variety, top with sesame seeds, mix with minced fresh basil, or combine with chopped tomatoes. A 3-pound squash yields about 6 cooked cups, enough for 6 to 8 servings. The uncooked section may be wrapped in plastic wrap and kept chilled for up to 4 days. Cooked leftovers will keep about 2 to 3 days in the refrigerator, and may be reheated conventionally or in a microwave oven.

½ of a 3½- to 4-pound spaghetti squash
1 tablespoon unsalted butter
1 tablespoon freshly grated Parmesan cheese

¼ teaspoon salt
freshly ground black pepper to taste

1. The squash may be microwaved, baked, or boiled. To microwave: Place the squash cut side down in a pan just large enough to hold it; add ¼ cup water. Microwave on high for 14 to 15 minutes. To bake: Place the squash cut side down in an 8-inch-square baking pan with ¼ cup water. Cook in a 350-degree oven for 45 minutes. To boil: Cut the half into quarters and boil 20 minutes in a covered pot in 4 inches of water.
2. When skin pierces easily with a fork, drain and cool. Scoop out and discard the seeds. With a fork transfer the spaghettilike strands from the shell to a casserole if preparing ahead (may be kept chilled a day in advance), or to a serving dish if serving immediately. Discard the shell.
3. Stir in the remaining ingredients. Taste to correct seasoning. The squash is ready to serve or may be kept covered and chilled for up to a day before serving. Reheat in a 350-degree oven until warmed through or in a microwave oven on medium-high power.

Yield: 4 1-cup servings
✦ **Calories per serving: 80**
 Carbohydrate per serving: 10g
✦ **Cholesterol per serving: 10mg**

✦ **Dietary fiber per serving: 2g**
 Fat per serving: 4g
 Protein per serving: 2g
 Sodium per serving: 200mg

Cappucino Cream

❖

If you love the flavors of coffee and cinnamon with an accent of chocolate, this cloudlike dessert is for you. Start cappucino cream 3 to 4 hours before serving, or up to a day before, as it must chill. Although "Reel Good" is a menu for 4, this dessert makes 7 servings. You may enjoy the extras, confident they are not pound packers.

1 envelope unflavored gelatin
¼ cup plus 2 tablespoons sugar
2 cups skim or low-fat milk
2 eggs, separated
1 teaspoon instant espresso coffee
2 teaspoons Tia Maria or other coffee-flavored
    liqueur
2 tablespoons semisweet chocolate chips,
    pulverized in a food processor
3 tablespoons finely chopped walnuts
7 thin cinnamon sticks for garnish (optional)
grated unsweetened chocolate for garnish
    (optional)

1. Combine the gelatin and sugar in a 2½-quart saucepan. Set aside.
2. Beat together the milk, egg yolks, and coffee in a 1-quart bowl until frothy. Stir into the gelatin saucepan.
3. Cook mixture over low heat for about 7 minutes, stirring constantly. It will thicken very slightly. Remove from heat and transfer back into the 1-quart bowl. Stir in liqueur and chill until the mixture mounds when dropped from a spoon, about 1½ to 2 hours.
4. If the coffee mixture has jelled, beat it to make it smooth. Stir in the pulverized chocolate chips.
5. Beat egg whites until stiff, then fold into the coffee mixture. Divide the cappucino cream among 7 champagne glasses, sprinkle with nuts, and chill for 2 to 3 hours or overnight. To serve, garnish with a cinnamon stick and a dusting of grated chocolate, if you wish.

Yield: 7 servings
✦ Calories per serving: 130
Carbohydrate per serving: 18g
Cholesterol per serving: 80mg

Dietary fiber per serving: 1g
Fat per serving: 5g
Protein per serving: 5g
✦ Sodium per serving: 60mg

VARIATION ON A THEME

Chicken Breasts with Spinach and Feta
Braised Celery with Red Peppers
Rice à la Grecque
Grilled Bermuda Onion Slices

This menu is really just the same old tune—chicken and rice—redone to please the enlightened cook. The chicken skin with its fifty calories and nearly two grams of saturated fat (ironically, the removed fat doesn't lower the cholesterol count!) is gone. The lemon sauce is rich and zesty, but without cholesterol-heavy egg yolks and mounds of butter; the celery is braised rather than raw; and the rice has a golden glow. All the recipes are easy variations on an old familiar theme. These variations make this menu dressy enough for a get-together dinner with friends (although the recipes serve four, they could easily be doubled), or for a family treat.

If you have a willing partner in the kitchen and wish to embellish the theme a bit more, a little knife work can turn the chicken into a dazzler. Cut each cooked breast the long way into about five strips, slanting the knife slightly to create wide slices of spinach-stuffed meat. Film each dinner plate with the lemon sauce. Arrange the chicken like petals of a flower on the plate, filling the spaces with servings of the rice and the celery and red peppers. Cut the onion in half, and set the halves on either side of the plate.

To help plan your work schedule: The chicken may be stuffed and wrapped up to six hours before cooking, and the sauce prepared either as the chicken simmers or a few hours before. The rice is simply put together about one hour before dinner; plan on ten to twelve minutes cooking time for the celery, and about twenty-five minutes for the onions.

Chicken Breasts With Spinach and Feta

❖

A skinless chicken breast offers an excellent source of protein (70 percent of an adult woman's RDA) and niacin, which promotes healthy skin and nerves (95 percent). It's also a good source of phosphorus, a structural component of bones and teeth (27 percent of her RDA) and potassium, important in fluid balance (13 percent), all for a treat-allowing 173 calories (based on average of 3½ ounces per serving). Yet, steamed or broiled without the skin or added fat, pallid poultry can be most unappetizing. Here, stuffed with a tried-and-true spinach-feta combo and drizzled with a complementing lemon sauce, it is a bird of a different feather.

If you have a supply of rich homemade chicken stock, substitute it for the canned broth and eliminate the carrot, onions, celery, and parsley. Omit steps 2 and 8. The lemon sauce could be prepared several hours in advance and kept chilled, but it is quite easily done while the chicken cooks. Parchment paper is available from specialty shops and some supermarkets. Use foil if parchment is unavailable.

*4 chicken breasts, preferably with bones, with or
    without skin*
3 cups homemade chicken stock or canned broth
1 carrot, diced

1 small onion, diced
1 rib celery, diced
a few sprigs parsley
5 ounces raw spinach, backbones removed
2 ounces feta cheese, crumbled
1 tablespoon pine nuts (optional)

For the Lemon Sauce

1 teaspoon arrowroot
½ cup low-fat milk
1 egg, lightly beaten
juice of ½ lemon
2 teaspoons unsalted butter, at room temperature
¼ teaspoon salt
a dash cayenne pepper

To Prepare the Chicken and Cooking Liquid

1. Bone the breasts (reserving the bones if you are using canned broth) and discard the skin. To cut a pocket in the chicken breast, lay one breast on the counter surface with what was the skin side down and with what was the tip of the breast bone pointing away from you. Place one hand on top of the breast meat while slicing from right to left, parallel to the counter, to within 1 inch of the left side. Repeat with each breast. Keep the chicken chilled while preparing the cooking liquid.

2. Break up the bones with a mallet. Combine them with the canned broth in a 2½-quart saucepan. Add the carrot, onion, celery, and parsley. Cover and simmer 30 minutes or up to 1½ hours, adding water if the liquid drops below the original level.

3. Meanwhile, prepare the stuffing: Rinse the spinach leaves and pack them into a 2-quart saucepan. Cover and cook over high heat just until wilted, about 1 minute. Drain any water. Combine the spinach with the feta in a food processor or by hand, mixing well. Turn into a bowl.

4. Toast the pine nuts by tossing them in an ungreased 8-

inch skillet over high heat, about 1 minute, until lightly browned. These burn easily, so watch carefully. Stir the pine nuts into the spinach.

5. Stuff the pockets of the chicken breasts with the spinach stuffing. Press closed with the heel of your hand.
6. Tear off 4 pieces of parchment paper, each about 17 inches by 15 inches. Stack the four sheets together. Fold in half the long way, trimming corners to make a heart shape.
7. Place a chicken breast on one half of each heart. Fold the other half of the heart over it. Starting at the rounded top, fold and pleat the paper, making a tight seal around the chicken. Twist and tuck the pointed end under the packet. (Refer to the illustrations as you do this.) Repeat with remaining chicken and parchment hearts. Set wrapped chicken aside while you complete the cooking liquid.
8. When the broth has simmered at least 30 minutes, set a colander into a medium-size bowl. Pour the chicken broth through it. Press the solids with the back of a wooden spoon, then discard. (Recipe may be prepared to this point early in the day. Refrigerate wrapped chicken and strained broth.)

To Cook the Chicken and Prepare the Sauce

1. Pour the broth into a 12-inch skillet. Add the parchment packets, cover, and simmer over medium-high heat, 8 to 10 minutes. Turn packets over after 4 to 5 minutes of cooking. Adjust the heat to prevent boiling.
2. While the chicken cooks, prepare the sauce. Begin by dissolving the arrowroot in 2 tablespoons of the chicken broth (from the skillet) in a cup.
3. In a 1-quart saucepan set over high heat, heat the milk just until tiny bubbles appear at the edge. Reduce heat to medium-high. Stir in the dissolved arrowroot and continue to stir until the mixture is thickened, about 3 or 4 minutes. Adjust heat to prevent boiling.
4. Remove the pan from the heat. Beat the egg with a fork. Add 3 to 4 tablespoons hot milk to the egg, while

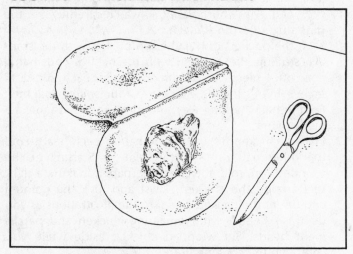

1. Lay the chicken breast, or other food, on half the paper heart, then fold the paper over it.

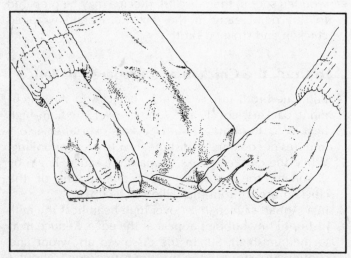

2. Pleat the paper tightly, securing the pleat with your fingertips as you move along the perimeter of the heart. Each pleat is made by making ¼-inch folds at 1½-inch intervals.

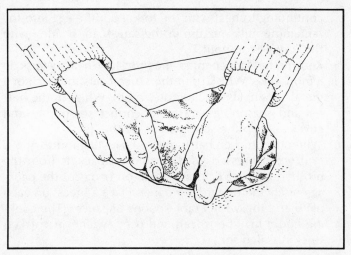

3. Continue making the pleats along the perimeter of the heart.

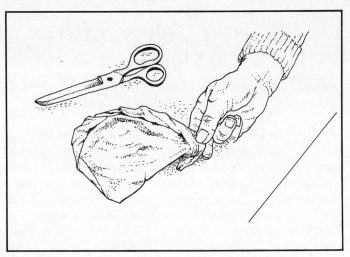

4. Secure the end by tucking the tip of paper under the package.

continuing to beat with the fork. Pour the egg into the remaining milk mixture in the saucepan, beating with the fork as you pour.

5. Return the saucepan to medium-low heat. Whisk in lemon juice. Whisk until the sauce coats the back of a metal spoon, about 2 minutes more. Whisk in the butter and seasonings. Taste to correct seasoning, and cover to keep the sauce warm off the heat.

6. When the chicken has simmered 8 to 10 minutes and is firm when pressed, lift the chicken packets from the broth, draining by tipping them on end. Cut the package open and discard the paper. Place a breast on each plate and top with 3 tablespoons of sauce. (The cooking liquid may be frozen and used whenever chicken stock is called for.)

Yield: 4 servings
✦ Calories per serving: 299
Carbohydrate per serving: 14g
Cholesterol per serving: 162mg

Dietary fiber per serving: 1g
Fat per serving: 12g
Protein per serving: 34g
Sodium per serving: 452g

Braised Celery with Red Peppers

❖

It's a rare vegetable that doesn't require a bit of salt to be tasty, but celery's naturally high sodium content puts that shaker on hold. You won't miss butter here either while you enjoy appreciable amounts of potassium and fiber. Braised celery also provides a tasty alternative to the "Broccoli, again?" glares I sometimes get at my house. For an added spark, it is tossed here with red bell peppers. The recipe may be prepared several hours ahead and reheated, covered, over low heat or in a microwave oven on high power for 1 minute.

2 red bell peppers
4 celery ribs
1½ cups homemade chicken or beef stock or
   canned broth
freshly ground black pepper to taste

1. Cut the peppers in half, lengthwise. Discard the seeds. Flatten the peppers with the heel of your hand. Place on a cookie sheet skin side up, and broil, turning the sheet once to ensure even browning, until the peppers are charred and blackened. Scrape the peppers into a plastic or paper bag, roll tightly closed, and allow to cool. Peel off the skin and slice the flesh into thin strips. Set aside.
2. Trim the celery; remove the strings. Cut each rib lengthwise into 3 to 4 thin strips. Cut the strips across into thirds.
3. Bring the broth and celery to a boil in a 10-inch skillet. Reduce heat to medium-high. Boil gently, uncovered, until the celery is almost tender and the liquid has reduced to about ¼ cup, about 7 to 8 minutes.
4. Add the pepper strips, raise heat to high, and boil until only a few tablespoons of syrupy liquid remain, 2 to 3 minutes. Season with pepper.

Yield: 4 servings
✦ Calories per serving: 26
   Carbohydrate per serving: 4g
✦ Cholesterol per serving: 0mg

Dietary fiber per serving: 1g
Fat per serving: 0g
Protein per serving: 1g
✦ Sodium per serving: 45mg

❖A calorie is a unit of measure. It is the amount of energy needed to raise 1 gram of water (a little less than 1/5 teaspoon) 1 degree Centigrade.❖

Rice à la Grecque

❖

Rice is terrific with chicken, if taste is the sole criteria, but its pale color does little to enhance the poultry. Rice à la Grecque solves the problem nicely with a confetti effect of red pepper and green peas. What's more, this is one rice dish moist enough not to require pat after pat of butter.

> 2 tablespoons minced onion
> 2¾ to 3 cups homemade chicken stock or canned
>   broth
> 1 tablespoon safflower oil
> 1 cup brown rice
> ½ teaspoon salt
> ½ cup fresh shelled or frozen peas
> ¼ cup minced red bell pepper
> freshly ground black pepper to taste

1. "Saute" the onion in 4 tablespoons of the chicken stock in a 10-inch skillet over medium-high heat until the onion is softened but not browned, about 4 to 5 minutes. Add a bit more broth if necessary, or raise the heat to evaporate the liquid when the onion is tender.
2. Add the oil and the rice. Raise heat to high and brown the rice, stirring constantly, about 2 minutes. Add 2½ cups of broth and the salt. Cover and simmer, stirring occasionally, until the rice is tender, about 50 minutes. Add more broth if needed to prevent the rice from sticking.
3. Cook the fresh peas in 2 cups water in a 1-quart covered saucepan for 10 minutes or until they are tender. Drain. If you are using frozen peas, cook them according to package instructions and drain.
4. Stir the peppers and peas into the rice, season with ground pepper, and taste for seasoning adjustment. The rice may be held in a double boiler for up to 1 hour

or reheated in a microwave oven on high for 2 minutes (add a bit more broth).

Yield: 4 servings
Calories per serving: 225
Carbohydrate per serving: 42g
✦ **Cholesterol per serving: 0mg**

✦ **Dietary fiber per serving: 4g**
Fat per serving: 4g
Protein per serving: 5g
Sodium per serving: 315mg

Grilled Bermuda Onion Slices
❖

This simply prepared vegetable does require a grill; unfortunately a broiler won't produce the same results. If you prefer onions on the mild side, soak the slices in warm water 30 minutes before cooking, changing the water once or twice. Vidalia onions would make a delicious substitute for the Bermuda.

> *3 medium Bermuda onions (about 21 ounces),*
> *   peeled and cut into ½-inch thick slices*
> *2 tablespoons olive oil*
> *1 tablespoon homemade chicken or beef stock or*
> *   canned broth*
> *6–8 fresh basil leaves, minced*

1. Brush oil over the rungs of the grill and on one side of the onion slices. Place onions, oiled side down, on the rungs. Grill, twisting the onion slices and loosening them from the rungs with a spatula. Baste occasionally with a little of the oil and stock.
2. After 15 minutes, turn the onions over. Baste again and cook 10 minutes more or until the onions are tender. Be sure the onions don't stick to the rungs. Sprinkle

with basil and drizzle with any remaining oil 5 minutes
before the onions are done.

Yield: 4 servings	Dietary fiber per serving: 1g
✦ Calories per serving: 95	Fat per serving: 4g
Carbohydrate per serving: 8g	Protein per serving: 1g
✦ Cholesterol per serving: 0mg	✦ Sodium per serving: 2mg

❖ Focus: Rice ❖

There are any number of rices available from Italian Ar-
borio to Minnesota wild, but the basic supermarket
choices are brown or white, long-grain or short-grain,
converted or regular. Each type is best suited to a particular use and cooking method. Here are some guidelines:

Brown rice: All rice starts out as the seed of a cereal grass.
The seeds are cleaned and the outer tough husk removed.
This leaves a brown grain with much of the nutritive value
in its now outermost bran layer. Brown rice takes about 50
minutes to cook, has a nutty flavor and texture, and is
moist and compact. It accounts for only 1 percent of the
rice purchased in this country, but is the type most used
where rice is the mainstay of the diet.

White rice: This rice undergoes an additional milling process from brown rice, which removes the outer bran layer,
resulting in a white or polished rice. In America this nutritionally deficient rice is sprayed with a solution of thiamin, niacin, and iron, replacing the nutrients that have
been lost. Such rice is labeled "enriched."

Converted rice: This may be either white or brown. It is
subjected to very high temperatures that force some of
the nutrients of the bran layer back into the grain. This
partial cooking results in less home-cooking time, though
very little less for converted brown rice.

Long-grain, medium-grain, and short-grain: Long-grain
rice cooks a bit more quickly than either medium- or

short-grain rice, and maintains the shape of the individual grains after cooking. This makes a drier, fluffier rice. Medium- and short-grain rice tend to be more tender, moister, and stickier. Generally, long-grain is preferred as a vegetable side dish or for a salad dish, while the medium- and short-grains are used for puddings and molds, or any recipe that has to hold together.

Nutritionally, rice pales in comparison with a potato, as it is somewhat higher in calories and lower in some minerals and vitamin C. But it is an excellent source of carbohydrate, the "fuel" our bodies run on, and is also very easily digested.

A few quick ideas for varying the standard:

1. Cook rice in chicken broth for excellent, full-bodied flavor.
2. Add slivers of dried apricots (3 whole apricots is appropriate for a rice dish serving 4), which have been soaked ½ hour in hot water, and drained.
3. Add currants, white raisins, or other dried fruits, about ½ cup for 4 servings.
4. Add ½ cup tomato juice to the water for Italian- or Spanish-flavored recipes.
5. Add ½ cup orange juice to the cooking liquid when serving with veal.
6. Flavor with sage when serving with pork or poultry, or basil when serving with tomatoes.
7. Color with turmeric or season with saffron for a delicious dish to serve with fish.
8. Mix with other vegetables such as onions, peppers, and peas (see Rice à la Grecque, page 110).

Any of these, singly or in combination, provide a new slant on the predictable.

POUND CHASER

Halibut with Nutted Confetti
Fruited Rice
Honey-Tarragon Dressing for Mixed Greens

Fish, cooked with little fat, is not only excellent for the heart (see *Focus: Fish,* page 96) but also for the waistline. A generous six-ounce serving contributes less than two hundred calories, almost all of an adult woman's daily protein needs, all her niacin and vitamin A, and a healthy dose of some minerals all with a very conservative fifty milligrams of cholesterol (daily intake should not exceed three hundred milligrams). In "Pound Chaser," a menu for four that could be easily adapted to serve as few as two or as many as six, halibut is quickly steamed and topped with a colorful peppering of vegetables and accompanied with an equally speedy rice with apricots and crisp salad. This is a healthy and satisfying meal to prepare, not ahead, but in less than an hour. Diet food? Hardly, just good and good-for-you without superfluous calories and saturated fats. It is indeed a pound chaser.

Halibut with Nutted Confetti

❖

Nutted confetti is very descriptive of this halibut's red and green pepper topping studded with almonds. This is not an etched-in-stone type recipe but a guide for any thick (1 or more inches) white-fleshed fish. Diced tomatoes, carrots, leeks, or celery would be a nice added touch, with or without snipped fresh herbs such as thyme and basil. And while instructions here are for steaming, any number of cooking methods—baking, grilling, or broiling—would do nicely. Do the topping ahead by several hours if it seems easier, but cook the fish just before serving.

> 1 tablespoon olive oil
> 1 small red bell pepper, diced
> 1 small green bell pepper, diced
> 1 shallot, minced (about 2 tablespoons)
> 2 tablespoons slivered almonds
> 1 tablespoon lemon juice
> 2 cups homemade chicken stock or canned broth
>   or homemade fish stock
> 1¼ pounds halibut
> ¼ teaspoon salt
> thin lemon slices for garnish (optional)

To Prepare the Confetti Topping

1. Heat the oil in a 10-inch skillet until hot. Add the peppers and shallot. Cover and saute over medium heat until tender, about 10 to 12 minutes, stirring frequently. Adjust heat as necessary to prevent burning. Add a tablespoon or so of chicken broth or fish stock if the vegetables start to stick.
2. Uncover and raise heat to high. Stir in almonds and cook 1 minute or until heated through. Add lemon

juice. Keep warm on a warming tray or over very low heat until the fish is ready. (Confetti topping may be prepared several hours ahead, kept chilled, and re-heated over medium heat just before serving.)

To Cook the Fish

1. Meanwhile, bring the chicken stock to a boil in a 12-inch skillet. Measure the fish to calculate cooking time (8 to 10 minutes per 1 inch of thickness). Add the fish to the stock, season with salt, and cover. Cook over high heat until the flesh is opaque. Remove the fish from the skillet with a slotted spatula, letting the stock run off.
2. Place the fish on a platter, top with the confetti topping, and garnish with lemon slices.

Yield: 4 servings
✦ Calories per serving: 215
Carbohydrate per serving: 4g
✦ Cholesterol per serving: 70mg

Dietary fiber per serving: 1g
Fat per serving: 8g
Protein per serving: 30g
Sodium per serving: 235mg

Fruited Rice

❖

Apricots provide the simple variation needed to give interest to an otherwise common dish. For other ideas, see *Focus: Rice* on page 112.

3 dried apricots
1 cup long-grain converted white rice
1 cup homemade chicken stock or canned broth
1½ cups water
½ teaspoon turmeric
½ teaspoon salt
1 tablespoon unsalted butter

1. Soak the apricots for 30 minutes in hot water to cover.
2. Place the rice, broth, water, turmeric, and salt in a 2½-quart saucepan. Cover and bring to a boil over high heat. Reduce heat to medium and boil gently, stirring occasionally, until the liquid is absorbed. (Converted rice takes about 15 minutes to cook.)
3. Drain apricots and cut them into thin strips. Add them to the rice 5 minutes before it is done.
4. Toss cooked rice with butter. The rice will keep warm off the heat, covered, for about 10 minutes; it is best made fresh, not reheated.

Yield: 4 servings
Calories per serving: 210
Carbohydrate per serving: 42g
✦ Cholesterol per serving: 10mg

Dietary fiber per serving: 1g
Fat per serving: 3g
Protein per serving: 3g
Sodium per serving: 300mg

Honey-Tarragon Dressing for Mixed Greens

❖

If you've been used to low-cal store-bought dressings, salads are probably something you think you should eat, rather than enjoy eating. This smooth herb dressing might make those thinning greens a favorite again.

When choosing salad greens, remember that the darker green leaves, usually the outer ones, are richest in vitamin A (needed for healthy skin, eyesight, and bones). Select non-garden items for the salad bowl, particularly in winter, to add variety and interest. Apples are delicious, as are pears, sunflower seeds, or pine nuts (use seeds and nuts—high calorie items—sparingly). Canned kidney, shell, or garbanzo beans add important fiber, tastily, while sliced water chestnuts and bean sprouts provide different textures and olives add pizzazz. Canned pimientos add flavorful color, unlike winter's so-called tomatoes, as does a tablespoon or so of canned corn or sliced beets. Grated cheese is great, and so is a shower of grated egg white. Think color and texture contrasts, and salads might just get fun and flavorful again. Particularly nice with this salad dressing is a combination of Boston lettuce, watercress, and sliced apples. Use four cups of salad ingredients, cook's choice.

> 1 egg
> 1 tablespoon tarragon vinegar
> 1 teaspoon Dijon mustard
> 1 teaspoon honey
> 1 teaspoon dried tarragon
> ½ cup safflower oil
> ½ cup canned beef consomme or homemade
>   beef stock

1. In a food processor or blender process the egg, vinegar, mustard, honey, and tarragon for 15 seconds. Add the oil in a very thin, steady stream while the machine runs on high power. Slowly add the consomme. The dressing will keep under refrigeration up to 5 days.
2. Toss the salad with the dressing, estimating 3 tablespoons of dressing per serving.

Yield: 4 servings salad and 1⅓ cups dressing
✦ Calories per serving: 154
Carbohydrate per serving: 1g
✦ Cholesterol per serving: 39mg
Dietary fiber per serving: 0g
Fat per serving: 16g
Protein per serving: 1g
✦ Sodium per serving: 31mg

FLASH IN THE PAN

Pan-seared Lemon Veal
Julienne of Root Vegetables
Poppy Seed Pasta

More often than not, when there just isn't much time for preparing dinner, old standbys get pressed into service. Tried and true as such dishes may be, are they as low in calories as you might wish? Here's a quick (less than one hour) and calorie-conscious menu for two, guaranteed to ease a harried cook's schedule, as well as satisfy that "looking for something good" appetite.

For this meal and anytime when pasta is served, it's a good practice to heat the dinner plates to prevent rapid cooling. A microwave oven is excellent for this, but remember to add a glass of water to absorb energy.

There's not a lot of planning involved in this meal. Because the vegetables hold well without getting too soggy, you might start there, then boil the pasta as you cook the veal.

Pan-seared Lemon Veal

Veal has the deserved reputation of being a fairly lean meat—a good choice for those trying to limit their calories. Oddly, however, it isn't lower in cholesterol than other red meats or even roast chicken. A three-ounce serving of veal contains 84 milligrams of cholesterol (the

American Heart Association recommends eating no more than 250 to 300 milligrams a day), lean beef contains 73 milligrams, roast chicken with or without the skin has 76 milligrams, and flounder has 52 milligrams. Further, a surprising 48 percent of veal's total fat is saturated, the same as beef. Is veal no nutritional bargain then? Yes and no. Overall, it has less total fat than most red meats, but do remember fish is lower in cholesterol and saturated fat.

For those times, though, when red meat and only red meat will do, here is a recipe with tight reins on the fat.

7 ounces veal cutlet
flour for dredging
¼ teaspoon salt
freshly ground black pepper to taste
2 teaspoons safflower oil
1 tablespoon lemon juice
2 tablespoons Marsala wine
thin slices lemon for garnish (optional)

1. Dredge the veal in the flour, then season with salt and pepper. Coat a 10-inch skillet with cooking spray, then heat the oil until it is very hot. Add the veal and sear on one side, about 1 minute. Reduce the heat to medium and continue to cook an additional minute.
2. Flip veal over and turn heat to high, if necessary, to sear. Cook 2 minutes more over medium heat, adjusting heat if necessary to prevent burning.
3. With the meat still in the pan, add the lemon juice. Allow it to boil away (raising heat to high if necessary). Add Marsala and continue to boil. Remove the pan from the heat when just a teaspoon or two of liquid remains. Transfer veal to dinner plates or a serving platter and spoon pan juices over it. Garnish with lemon slices if desired.

Yield: 2 servings
✦ **Calories per serving: 220**
Carbohydrate per serving: 1g
Cholesterol per serving: 100mg

Dietary fiber per serving: 0g
Fat per serving: 16g
Protein per serving: 19g
Sodium per serving: 380mg

Julienne of Root Vegetables

❖

My husband has second helpings of these. Not a bad endorsement from a guy whose idea of vegetables begins with a very well buttered potato and ends with French fries. The combined flavor of root vegetables is much better than any single one and oddly needs no butter or other fat, which most vegetables seem to crave. Of course, you could add a teaspoon or two of safflower oil or a bit of minced garlic or even other vegetables. Don't omit the parsnips, though, even if you think you don't like them. Their slightly sweet flavor and smooth texture are key to the whole concoction.

> 2 small carrots, peeled and julienned
> 2 leeks, white part only, rinsed and julienned
> 2 small purple-top turnips, peeled and julienned
> 2 parsnips, peeled and julienned
> ½ cup canned beef consomme or homemade
>   beef stock
> freshly ground black pepper to taste
> 1 teaspoon minced fresh parsley

1. Coat a 10-inch skillet with cooking spray. Combine the carrots, leeks, turnips, and parsnips with the consomme in the skillet. Cover and bring to a boil over high heat. Stir often and reduce heat to medium after 3 minutes.
2. When vegetables are tender, about 5 to 6 minutes, transfer them to a serving platter. If necessary, uncover the pan, raise heat to high, and boil any remaining broth until only a tablespoonful remains. Pour it over the vegetables. Season with pepper and garnish with parsley.

Yield: 2 generous servings
Calories per serving: 160

Carbohydrates per serving: 38g
✦ Cholesterol per serving: 0g

✦ Dietary fiber per serving: 8g   Protein per serving: 4g
  Fat per serving: 1g   ✦ Sodium per serving: 95mg

Poppy Seed Pasta

❖

Homemade pasta recipes can be found in the PASTA PASSIONS section of this book, but a store-bought product will save considerable time for this "Flash in the Pan" menu recipe. If available, purchased fresh rather than boxed pasta is much nicer.

> *2 ounces fresh fettucine noodles*
> *2 teaspoons unsalted butter*
> *¼ teaspoon salt*
> *freshly ground black pepper to taste*
> *1 tablespoon poppy seeds*
> *zest (grated rind) of 1 lemon*

1. Cook the noodles according to package instructions. Drain, toss with butter, salt, pepper, poppy seeds, and lemon zest. Serve onto warmed dinner plates.

Yield: 2 ½-cup servings
Calories per serving: 170
Carbohydrate per serving: 25g
✦ Cholesterol per serving: 10mg

Dietary fiber per serving: 1g
Fat per serving: 6g
Protein per serving: 5g
Sodium per serving: 295mg

❖ **Focus: Cutting Fat** ❖

Cutting down on fat means more than going easy on the butter. Here are some practical suggestions for limiting this highest calorie nutrient:

1. Trim all visible fat from meats and skin from poultry.
2. Use few processed lunch meats such as hot dogs, bologna, or salami. At the deli counter, choose lean roast beef, ham, or turkey.
3. Use mayonnaise rarely. If a sandwich is your typical lunch, choose one that doesn't need mayonnaise, or at least use it sparingly. Tuna is low in calories only when it isn't mixed with gobs of mayo.
4. Use low-calorie salad dressings at home exclusively. If any are unavailable when eating out, opt for mere droplets of oil and vinegar or lemon juice. An oil and vinegar dressing is generally better than those awful, overprocessed, chemical wonders most salad bars offer, anyway.
5. Use low-fat or skim milk exclusively. And of course no cream. Make "cream" sauces based on cottage cheese. Use plain yogurt instead of sour cream.
6. Avoid hard cheeses. Softer cheeses have a higher water content so they are generally lower in calories, but they are still hardly low-cal. And some soft cheeses, such as Triple Crèmes, are very high in fat, so use caution.
7. Don't be deceived by the ad that says cream cheese has half the calories of butter. Sure it does, but who spreads cream cheese as thinly as butter on a slice of toast?
8. Baked goods are usually high in fat and sugar. Muffins aren't better for you than doughnuts; they may not be fried but they are heavy with sugar and fat.
9. When planning menus emphasize the vegetables, fruits, and starches instead of often fatty meats. Use your energy in preparing a terrific low-fat potato dish instead of the meat course. Over time, these "understudies" will take on heightened significance if you do them justice, and you'll be less tempted by the higher fat foods.
10. Never fry. Steam, boil, braise with minimal fats, bake, grill, microwave, or roast.
11. Use cooking spray and nonstick skillets.

12. Use chicken broth instead of oil when you saute foods such as onions or mushrooms.
13. Snack on unbuttered popcorn, not chips.
14. Buy and use a degreaser whenever you make pan sauces from drippings.
15. Fresh fruit is seldom as appealing to most of us as a thick slab of chocolate cake, but if you buy the best fruits and give them an honest chance you'll be surprised how good fresh, sweet pineapple is or how satisfying a crisp, cool pear can be. Break out of the rut; splurge on exotic fruits and berries. Raspberries may be costly, but you'll pay less where it really counts.

❖Under the all-too-familiar category of possible carcinogens must now fall the common *raw* mushroom. One study has linked cancer in mice with a diet that included raw mushrooms. This discovery has led some researchers to theorize that hydrazines—a natural substance that protects the plant from some predators—may have adverse effects on people too. Mushroom lovers are advised to cook or dry them, which destroys most of the harmful hydrazines. It hasn't yet been determined how many raw mushrooms one would have to eat to be affected.❖

DOUBLE TAKE

Turkey Breast with Port and Mushrooms

Orzo*

Mushroom-stuffed Leek Rolls

Avocado-Pear Salad with Hot Lime Dressing

There's a double take in store for four dinner mates with this menu, for things are not what they may seem. The meat looks like veal, it cooks like veal, it tastes a lot like veal, but it costs less. Yes, it's turkey cutlets. The fluffy white starch looks like rice, it cooks much the same as rice, it has the same texture as rice, but it's somehow different. Yes, it's orzo, a rice-shaped macaroni product. (No recipe needed, just follow package instructions.) You can create interest and variety without hours in the kitchen or lots of fattening additives; all it takes is a little planning.

While the avocado, a high-fat fruit, may seem out of place in a book of thinning foods, let it be a reminder that there are a few forbidden foods in the enlightened cook's repertoire. Used sparingly, almost any food can be enjoyed.

Begin your preparation with the salad dressing and washing the greens. (If greens are washed, spun dry, put loosely in a plastic bag that is left slightly open, and refrigerated, they can successfully be washed a day ahead.) The Mushroom-stuffed Leek Rolls may be prepared early in the day; they reheat nicely. Boil the orzo while doing the turkey. Both are easy to keep hot while you assemble the salad.

Turkey Breast with Port and Mushrooms

❖

Sliced, skinless turkey breast cutlets, now available in many markets, may be used much as you would veal. Supplying about 157 calories and 70 milligrams of cholesterol in a 3½-ounce portion, they are an excellent resource for the health-conscious cook. Further, while 3½-ounce servings of some protein foods, particularly fish, strike many appetites as too meager, it seems quite satisfying here. If you can't buy cutlets, opt for the whole frozen turkey breast and slice and pound your own cutlets. The remainder may be used in a stir-fried recipe, or ground and used as you would ground beef in lasagne or spaghetti sauce. This recipe may be prepared several hours in advance and reheated if a microwave oven is available (3 minutes on medium high). Reheating in the oven or on top of the stove will toughen the turkey. This dish would be very nice garnished with a spoonful of cranberry relish.

> ½ ounce dried Tree Ears, an oriental mushroom available at specialty food shops
> 2 teaspoons arrowroot
> ¾ cup Tawny Port
> 2 tablespoons safflower oil
> 12 ounces skinless turkey cutlets cut from the breast
> ¼ teaspoon salt
> freshly ground black pepper to taste
> 4 ounces mushrooms, sliced
> ½ cup homemade chicken stock or canned broth

1. Soak the Tree Ears in hot water to cover for 20 minutes. Drain. Remove any tough segments, chop, and set aside.

2. Dissolve the arrowroot in 2 tablespoons of the port. Set near stove to have ready for step 6.
3. Coat a 12-inch skillet with cooking spray. Add half the oil, heat over high heat for 1 minute. Sear for 2 minutes as many cutlets as will fit in the pan without overlapping. Season with salt and pepper, adjusting heat to prevent burning. Turn cutlets over and brown. Reduce heat to medium and cook 2 minutes more. Transfer cutlets to a serving platter. Cover them with a kitchen towel and foil to keep them warm while you complete the sauce. Repeat with the remaining turkey and oil.
4. Add the Tree Ears and mushrooms to the skillet. Stir over high heat until the mushrooms are lightly browned, about 2 to 3 minutes.
5. Add the remaining port and broth to the skillet. Boil until they are reduced to a little more than a half cup, about 2 minutes.
6. Reduce heat to medium. Stir in the dissolved arrowroot. When the sauce has thickened, about 1 to 2 minutes, return the turkey to the skillet. Cover and heat through, about 2 to 3 minutes, stirring from time to time.

Yield: 4 servings
✦ Calories per serving: 180
Carbohydrate per serving: 7g
Cholesterol per serving: 50mg

Dietary fiber per serving: 0g
Fat per serving: 8g
Protein per serving: 22g
Sodium per serving: 215g

❖Potatoes are natural partners with other vegetables, too: potato and turnip puree, flavored with garlic; potato and leek puree, flavored with garlic and Parmesan cheese; potato and celery root, flavored with mustard; potato and beet puree, flavored with a hint of orange and orange zest; sweet potato and squash or pumpkin, flavored with curry.❖

PREPARING LEEK ROLLS

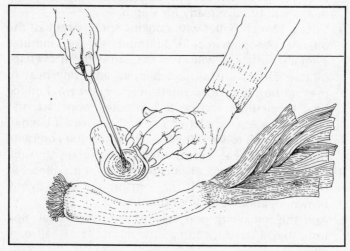

1. Cut three-quarters of the way through the leek, leaving the outer two or three layers intact.

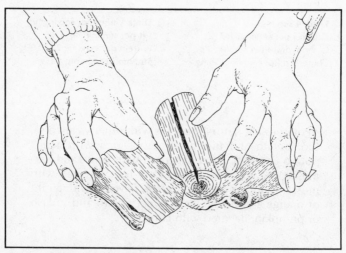

2. You will now have two or three uncut outer leaves for the leek rolls.

Mushroom-stuffed Leek Rolls

❖

These slender rolls are easily prepared early in the day and heated conventionally or in a microwave oven. Buy the largest leeks available or the rolls will be pitifully tiny, and be sure to trim off the outer leaves that are stringy and tough.

 4 very large leeks
 2 carrots, scrubbed
 8 ounces mushrooms
 2 tablespoons olive oil
 1 garlic clove, minced
 ½ cup plus 1 tablespoon homemade chicken
      stock or canned broth
 ¼ teaspoon salt
 freshly ground black pepper to taste
 a few gratings fresh nutmeg

1. Cut through each leek where the color turns from white to green. Discard the green stalk. Trim the root end. Peel away and discard the 2 or 3 tough outer layers surrounding the white, bulb end. Make a cut running from the bulb to the tip, three-quarters of the way through the leek. Do not cut all the way through. Peel off the intact, uncut, outer leaves; there will be 2 or 3 such leaves per leek. (Refer to the illustrations as you do this.) Set these aside in a colander. Chop the remaining leek and put in the colander. When all the leeks have been prepared, rinse them thoroughly. Leave them to drain while continuing.
2. Half-fill a 2-quart saucepan with water and bring it to a boil. Blanch the whole leek leaves 1 to 2 minutes or until tender. Rinse under cool water and drain. Set aside.

3. Julienne the carrots in a food processor or shred with a grater. Set aside.
4. Mince the mushrooms in a food processor or very finely by hand. Scrape into an absorbent towel and twist the ends to form a ball. Wring out over a sink to remove excess moisture from the mushrooms. Set aside.
5. Coat a 10-inch skillet with cooking spray, then place it over high heat. Add the oil, heat it for 1 minute, then add the garlic. Cook the garlic over medium heat until tender but not browned, about 1 minute.
6. Add the chopped leeks, carrots, and ½ cup chicken stock. Cover and cook over medium-high heat until the vegetables are tender, about 3 to 4 minutes.
7. Add mushrooms and cook, stirring, over medium heat 4 to 5 minutes, or until the vegetables are tender and dry. Season with salt, pepper, and nutmeg. Remove from heat.
8. Preheat the oven to 300 degrees. To assemble the rolls, lay the leek leaves on the work surface with the whitest end facing you. Put a rounded teaspoon of the mushroom stuffing on the end closest to you and roll up loosely. Coat an oven- or microwave-proof serving dish with cooking spray. Arrange the leek rolls, seam side down, in a column in the center of the dish. Spoon the remaining filling over the center of the rolls. Sprinkle with the remaining broth. (The rolls may be completed to this point early in the day and held in the refrigerator until baked.)
9. Bake the rolls in the lower third of a preheated 300-degree oven for 10 to 15 minutes (30 minutes if chilled) or in a microwave oven on medium-high for 3 minutes.

Yield: about 8 rolls; 4 servings
✦ Calories per serving: 105
Carbohydrate per serving: 10g
✦ Cholesterol per serving: 0mg

Dietary fiber per serving: 1g
Fat per serving: 7g
Protein per serving: 2g
✦ Sodium per serving: 165mg

Avocado-Pear Salad with Hot Lime Dressing

❖

A spicy-hot, citrus-cooled dressing on avocado and pear wedges creates a clean, refreshing salad. The dressing may be made a day or so ahead, but slice the avocado and pear at the last minute to keep them from turning brown.

For the Dressing

juice of 1 lime (about 1½ tablespoons)
¼ to ½ fresh jalapeño chili pepper, minced, or 2
*   teaspoons minced canned jalapeño chilis*
1½ tablespoons lemon juice
1 tablespoon plain yogurt
1 tablespoon mayonnaise
⅛ teaspoon salt

For the Salad

2 cups torn soft-leafed salad greens, Bibb
*   recommended*
1 small, ripe avocado, peeled and pitted
1 pear, cored
½ small red bell pepper, minced

1. Combine all dressing ingredients in a screw-top jar. Shake vigorously and refrigerate until serving time.
2. Divide the greens among 4 salad plates. Slice the avocado and pear; divide the slices among the plates, alternating a pear slice with an avocado slice. Spoon 1 to 2 tablespoons dressing over each serving. Garnish with the pepper.

Yield: 4 servings, ½ cup dressing
✦ Calories per serving: 140
Carbohydrate per serving: 13g
✦ Cholesterol per serving: 0mg
✦ Dietary fiber per serving: 3g
Fat per serving: 11g
Protein per serving: 2g
✦ Sodium per serving: 110mg

BACK TO BASICS

Grilled Stuffed Flank Steak
Cheese-stuffed Potatoes
Hot Beet and Parsnip Salad on Beet Greens

Here's a back-to-basics meal featuring steak and potatoes, but prepared under a sharp nutritional eye. The beef cut is among the leanest and lowest in cholesterol, the potatoes are deliciously smooth and rich with very little added butter, and the hot vegetable salad serves six, but with a mere two tablespoons of highly polyunsaturated safflower oil. Yet, there is absolutely no hint of restriction or denial, for this is a menu full of flavor and satisfaction.

This seems the perfect meal for a cool summer evening, leaving you plenty of time for the beach; but it would be just as welcome any time of year when you want to entertain six casually or treat the family to a special meal. Marinate the meat the day before, and bake and stuff the potatoes the morning of the dinner. The stuffing could be done then, too, as well as the initial cooking of the beets and parsnips. At dinnertime, stuff, tie, and grill the meat, bake the potatoes, and finish the hot beet salad. Voila! there's a meal to enjoy as much for what's missing (fats and calories) as for what it delivers (taste, followed in short order by compliments).

Grilled Stuffed Flank Steak

❖

Let the meat soak in its marinade while you soak up the sunshine; stuffing and tying the steak are quickly accomplished while someone else washes out the lunch cooler. If the lazy days of summer are just a hazy memory, perhaps a sniff of grilling beef—despite the nip of the air—will bring them closer.

For the Marinade

1 12-ounce can beer
4 tablespoons reduced-sodium soy sauce
3 scallions, minced
2 tablespoons dark brown sugar
1 tablespoon minced fresh ginger
2 garlic cloves, minced
¼ teaspoon Oriental hot oil, available at some markets and specialty food shops

For the Meat and Stuffing

1½ pounds flank steak
¼ ounce dried Tree Ears (oriental mushrooms) or dried Porcini mushrooms, available at specialty food shops
2 tablespoons safflower oil
1 garlic clove, minced
1 large shallot, minced (about 2 tablespoons)
4 ounces mushrooms, chopped
½ cup dry bread crumbs
1 tablespoon minced fresh parsley

1. Combine all the marinade ingredients in a glass or ceramic bowl. Add the meat. Cover and refrigerate at

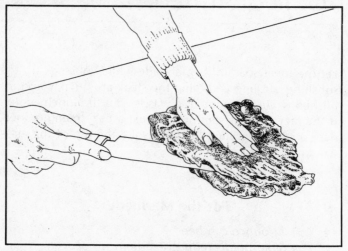

1. To cut a pocket in a flank steak, place one hand on top of the meat. Insert the knife about 2 inches from the top and slice through the middle of the meat to within 2 or 3 inches of the left side and the bottom end.

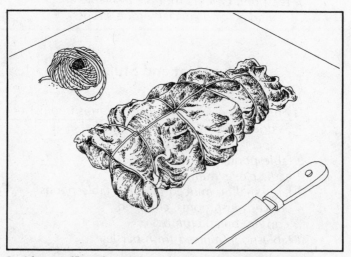

2. After stuffing the pocket, skewer the opening closed. Tie the meat with butcher's twine at 2-inch intervals, compressing the meat into a cylinder.

least 8 hours or up to 24 hours, turning meat occasionally.

2. To prepare the stuffing: Soak the dried mushrooms in
hot water to cover for 30 minutes. Drain. Slice if using
Porcini; Tree Ears do not need slicing. Remove any
tough segments. Set aside.

3. Coat an 8-inch skillet with cooking spray. Add 1 tablespoon of the oil and heat over high heat for 15 seconds.
Add the garlic and shallot, and stir until tender, but not
browned, about 1 minute. Lower heat to medium to
prevent browning as the garlic cooks.

4. Add the regular mushrooms, and stir-fry until
browned, about 4 to 5 minutes over medium-high
heat. Stir in the bread crumbs, and stir-fry until lightly
browned, about 2 to 3 minutes. Stir in the Tree Ears or
Porcini and parsley. Stir-fry until heated through, about
30 seconds. Remove stuffing from stove. (The stuffing
may be completed to this point early in the day and refrigerated.)

5. Remove the meat from the marinade; pat dry. Reserve
the marinade. To cut a pocket in the meat: Place the
meat on the counter so the length of it stretches north
and south. Place one hand on top of the meat. Insert
the knife into the meat 2 inches from the tip and slice
through the meat, holding the knife parallel to the
counter, to within 2 or 3 inches of the left side and 2 or
3 inches from the bottom (south) end.

6. Stuff the pocket with the bread crumb and mushroom
stuffing. Skewer the opening closed by threading skewers through the bottom and top flaps of meat at 2-inch
intervals down the length of the flank steak. Wrap the
flank steak tightly with butcher's or all-cotton twine at
2-inch intervals. This will compress the meat into a
compact cylinder. See illustrations opposite. (The recipe may be prepared to this point up to 4 hours before
grilling. Keep refrigerated.)

7. Grill the flank steak, turning and basting with the
marinade and the remaining tablespoon of oil, 35 to 40
minutes or until an instant-reading meat thermometer
registers 120 degrees for rare meat or 130 degrees for

medium-rare. Rest 10 minutes, loosely covered with foil. Remove the strings and skewers, and carve meat into thin slices on an angle.

Yield: 6 servings	**Dietary fiber per serving: 0g**
✦ **Calories per serving: 232**	**Fat per serving: 27g**
Carbohydrate per serving: 13g	**Protein per serving: 24g**
Cholesterol per serving: 75mg	**Sodium per serving: 500mg**

Cheese-stuffed Potatoes

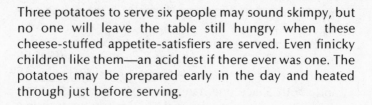

Three potatoes to serve six people may sound skimpy, but no one will leave the table still hungry when these cheese-stuffed appetite-satisfiers are served. Even finicky children like them—an acid test if there ever was one. The potatoes may be prepared early in the day and heated through just before serving.

> *3 large baking potatoes, scrubbed*
> *⅔ cup low-fat cottage cheese*
> *1 ounce Parmesan cheese, grated (about 2*
> *tablespoons)*
> *½ cup low-fat or skim milk*
> *1 tablespoon unsalted butter*
> *¼ teaspoon salt*
> *freshly ground black pepper to taste*
> *freshly grated nutmeg*
> *1 tablespoon minced fresh parsley*

1. Pierce the potatoes with a fork in a few places and bake in a 400-degree oven (no need to preheat) for 1 hour or until tender. Potatoes may also be microwaved on high power for 15 minutes or until tender. Let cool.
2. With a paring knife, cut an oval-shaped lid from the

top of each potato. Scrape the potato from the lid into a bowl or food processor; discard the skin. Scrape out the inside of the potato into the same bowl with a teaspoon leaving a ½-inch-thick shell. Repeat with remaining potatoes. Reserve the potato shells.

3. Combine the cheeses, milk, butter, salt, pepper, and nutmeg with the potato in the food processor or bowl. Pulse the machine just to combine, being careful not to overprocess, or mash potatoes in the bowl.

4. Divide this mixture among the potato shells, smoothing the mounded potato with a knife. (Potatoes may be held for several hours, refrigerated, before heating.)

5. Preheat oven to 325 degrees. Place the potatoes on a baking sheet and bake in the lower third of the oven for 20 minutes if the potatoes are room temperature, or for 30 to 35 minutes if they are still cold. Broil briefly to brown tops if necessary. Garnish with parsley. To serve, cut potatoes in half.

Yield: 6 servings
Calories per serving: 125
Carbohydrate per serving: 14g
✦ **Cholesterol per serving: 15mg**

Dietary fiber per serving: 0g
Fat per serving: 4g
Protein per serving: 8g
Sodium per serving: 300mg

Hot Beet and Parsnip Salad on Beet Greens

❖

What a waste when the beet greens are tossed out in favor of the beet! One-half cup of cooked greens have 300 times the vitamin A found in a half cup of cooked beets; and considerably more of some minerals such as iron for a mere 18—yes, count them, 18!—calories. Coupled with the parsnips, another pretty good source of calcium, what we've got here is a nutritional bargain. And it tastes as good as it is good for you.

> 2 bunches beets with greens (5 to 6 beets)
> 3 parsnips
> ¾ cup homemade chicken stock or canned broth
> 2 tablespoons balsamic vinegar or to taste
> 2 tablespoons safflower oil

1. Break the beets from the greens leaving 2 inches of stem on the beets. Half cover the beets with water in a 2½-quart saucepan. Cover and bring to a boil over high heat. Reduce heat to medium-high and boil gently until beets are tender, about 30 to 40 minutes, or longer if the beets are old. Drain and cool under running water.
2. While the beets are cooking, peel the parsnips. Cut them in half the long way, then cut into thin strips and halve the strips. Place the parsnips in a 1-quart saucepan with ½ cup chicken stock. Cover, bring to a boil over high heat, then reduce heat to medium-high. Boil until tender, about 10 minutes, adding a little more stock if needed. Drain and set aside in the pan.
3. When the beets are cooled, peel off the skin. Trim off the root and stem end. Slice the beets in ¼-inch-thick slices, then cut the slices into sticks. Add the beets to the parsnips. Set aside.
4. Remove the red stems from the greens. Wash the greens. Stack them and slice into thin strips. (The recipe can be completed to this step several hours in advance. Refrigerate cooked vegetables if holding them more than 1 hour.)
5. Bring ¼ cup water to a boil in a 10-inch skillet. Add the greens and stir over high heat until they are wilted and the water has evaporated, about 1 minute. Season with 1 tablespoon of vinegar. Remove from heat, cover to keep warm, and set aside.
6. Combine the oil, the remaining ¼ cup broth, and the remaining tablespoon of vinegar in the 1-quart saucepan with the beets and parsnips. Over high heat, toss

the beets and parsnips in the pan until heated through, about 2 to 3 minutes. Remove from heat.

7. To serve, divide the greens among 6 salad plates or spread in the center of a serving platter. Surround with a ring of beets and parsnips.

Yield: 6 servings
✦ Calories per serving: 135
Carbohydrate per serving: 21g
✦ Cholesterol per serving: 0mg

✦ Dietary fiber per serving: 4g
Fat per serving: 5g
Protein per serving: 3g
✦ Sodium per serving: 70mg

❖Aerobic exercise, such as running, swimming, biking, cross-country skiing, rowing, brisk walking, or aerobic dancing, improves your heart-lung condition, promotes weight loss or maintenance, can raise HDL ("good") cholesterol levels, and reduce stress. The American College of Sports Medicine recommends aerobic exercise three to five times weekly, for 15 to 60 minutes at a time. This raises the heart rate to within 60 to 90 percent of the maximum. (To compute your maximum heart rate, subtract your age from 220.) Exercising less than three times a week will produce only minimal results, while exercising more than five times a week will not improve cardiovascular condition, but will help use up calories.❖

VEGETARIAN DELIGHT

Eggplant and Spinach Cheese Strata
Tossed Salad with Creamy Herbed Dressing
Hot Bakery Italian Bread*

The focus of this do-ahead dinner for six is a meatless mélange very like a lasagne, except there is no pasta or meat. Eggplant takes the place of the starch, while five cheeses, including feta, deliver the protein quotient. Because it takes very nicely to freezing, it makes the perfect take-away weekend meal, particularly if assembled in a disposable baking pan. Supplement with a bakery Italian bread and a salad, and dinner's done.

If something seems missing without a sweet, make it fruity. Should you be in the mood for cooking, Glazed Gingered Oranges (page 89) or Pineapple Sorbet (page 173) would be right. If convenience is key, however, an icy store-bought lemon sherbert would be most welcome.

❖When nutritional information is given in grams, milligrams, and the like, it's hard to translate in your mind's eye unless you have scientific training. As a starting point, remember 1 tablespoon (there are 16 in a cup) equals 14 grams or 14,000 milligrams. As an example, the recommended daily amounts of thiamin (1 milligram) and riboflavin (1.2 milligram) are each equal to the weight of a grain or two of sugar.❖

Eggplant and Spinach Cheese Strata

❖

This slimmed down and somewhat simplified recipe was inspired by one I once read. While it will require a fair amount of time to put together (a good hour), once done it may be frozen or just refrigerated, requiring nothing more than a twist of the oven or microwave dial (use medium-high power) at dinner time. We love it after a frosty day of skiing.

For the Sauce

2 carrots, scrubbed and chopped
1 leek, white part only, chopped
1 large onion, chopped
2 garlic cloves, minced
1¼ cups homemade chicken stock or canned
    broth
1 28-ounce can tomatoes
1 bouillon cube
1 bay leaf
4–5 leaves fresh basil, snipped
1 teaspoon sugar
freshly ground black pepper to taste

For the Strata

2 1-pound eggplants
2 tablespoons salt, kosher recommended
1½ tablespoons olive oil
1 10-ounce package raw spinach
3 ounces feta cheese, crumbled
½ cup part-skim ricotta cheese

½ cup low-fat cottage cheese
1 egg
2 tablespoons minced fresh parsley
1 tablespoon lemon juice
3 ounces mozzarella cheese, grated
1 ounce Parmesan cheese, grated

To Make the Sauce

1. In a cast-iron 12-quart Dutch oven or other large, heavy pot, "saute" the carrots, leek, onion, and garlic in ½ cup of the chicken broth, covered, over medium-high heat until the vegetables are tender, about 5 to 6 minutes.
2. Add the tomatoes with their juice, breaking them up with a spoon. Add the bouillon cube, bay leaf, basil, sugar, pepper, and remaining chicken broth. Bring to a boil, reduce to a simmer, and cover. Cook 1½ hours, stirring occasionally.
3. Remove the bay leaf. Puree the sauce in a food processor, food mill, or in batches in a blender. Set sauce aside.

For the Strata

1. While the sauce cooks, trim the ends from the eggplant. Slice unpeeled eggplant lengthwise into ¼- to ½-inch-thick slices. Lay the slices on a double thickness of paper towel and sprinkle their tops liberally with salt to draw out excess moisture and bitterness. Let rest 15 minutes, turn and sprinkle the other side with salt. Let rest 15 more minutes. Rinse very thoroughly and pat dry.
2. Coat a large baking sheet with cooking spray. Arrange eggplant slices in a single layer on the sheet. Brush the top surface of the eggplant with a bit of the oil. Broil about 4 inches from the heat, about 4 to 5 minutes on each side, turning pan once to ensure even browning. Away from the heat, spray pan with cooking spray

when slices are flipped. Repeat with remaining egg-plant. Set aside.

3. Rinse the spinach and pack it into the wiped out Dutch oven or other large saucepan. Cover and cook over high heat until wilted, about 1 minute. Transfer spinach to a strainer. Press with the back of a wooden spoon to remove excess moisture.

4. To make the filling: Combine the spinach, feta, ricotta, cottage cheese, egg, parsley, and lemon juice in a food processor. Process just until feta is broken up but mixture is still chunky. If you are doing it by hand, finely chop the spinach, beat the egg and cheeses with a mixer, and combine with parsley and lemon juice.

To Assemble and Bake

1. Preheat the oven to 325 degrees if you are cooking the strata immediately. To assemble: Coat the bottom of a 7- by 11-inch ovenproof or microwave-proof serving dish with some tomato sauce. Arrange a third of the eggplant slices in a single layer, cutting slices if necessary to fit pan. Spread half of the spinach-cheese mixture over the eggplant. Arrange second third of eggplant slices, and cover with the remaining spinach-cheese mixture. Arrange the final third of the eggplant slices and cover with a thick coating of tomato sauce. (There will be some sauce left over; it may be frozen and used whenever tomato sauce is called for.) Sprinkle mozzarella and Parmesan cheeses over the top.

2. The strata may be frozen for up to 2 months, refrigerated for up to 4 to 6 hours before baking, or baked immediately in the upper third of the oven for 25 minutes or until heated through. Broil briefly to brown cheese, if necessary. Let strata rest 10 minutes before cutting it into rectangles to serve.

Yield: 6 servings
✦ Calories per serving: 330
Carbohydrate per serving: 33g
✦ Cholesterol per serving: 80mg

✦ Dietary fiber per serving: 5g
Fat per serving: 14g
Protein per serving: 18g
Sodium per serving: 615mg

Tossed Salad with Creamy Herbed Dressing

❖

If you keep it, that is nice,
Eat it and it's paradise:
The radicchio of Treviso.

So goes a very freely translated Italian jingle praising the lettucelike, rose-colored specialty of the Italian district of Treviso. Once found only there, it is now available in nearly every New York corner produce store and maybe even your supermarket as well. It looks much like a miniature red cabbage, but its price tag boasts another pedigree. You might like to try mixing a few leaves in with other greens, or if you are in an extravagant mood, make a salad of radicchio all by itself.

The dressing is a spritely one, heavy with garlic and oregano as befits an Italian dressing. Because the bread crumbs serve as a thickener, the dressing is best made at least an hour before it is served, to allow the crumbs time to swell. The dressing will keep several days in the refrigerator.

For the Dressing

1 egg
¼ cup olive oil, extra-virgin recommended
1 garlic clove, minced
2 tablespoons white wine vinegar
4 tablespoons canned beef consomme or
homemade beef stock
2 anchovy fillets (optional), mashed
2 tablespoons dry bread crumbs
½ teaspoon dried oregano

For the Salad

2 slices white bread
½ head curly-leaved lettuce
*½ head radicchio (optional) or a few chopped red
    cabbage leaves*
1 small head Bibb or Boston lettuce
½ bunch watercress

To Prepare the Dressing

1. Beat the egg in a food processor or blender on high for
   10 seconds. Gradually add the oil while the machine
   runs. Add the remaining dressing ingredients and combine well. Store, chilled, in a screw-top jar.

To Prepare the Salad

1. Cube the bread by stacking the slices and cutting them
   into 5 equal strips. Turn the bread 90 degrees and cut
   into fifths again. Spread the cubes on a cookie sheet.
   Coat lightly with cooking spray and toast in the upper
   third of a 350-degree oven (no need to preheat) for 10
   to 12 minutes or until the croutons are lightly browned.
   Stir occasionally. Set aside. (May be prepared a few
   hours ahead and held on the counter.)
2. Rinse and spin dry the greens. Tear into a salad bowl.
   At serving time, toss with the dressing and garnish with
   the croutons.

Yield: 6 servings
✦ Calories per serving: 130
Carbohydrate per serving: 8g
✦ Cholesterol per serving: 45mg

Dietary fiber per serving: 1g
Fat per serving: 10g
Protein per serving: 3g
✦ Sodium per serving: 105mg

❖ Focus: Fats and Oils ❖

Deciding on a cooking oil or purchasing a food processed
with a fat means making some choices. To consider are 1)
taste, 2) the effect the fat will have on your health, and 3)

cooking characteristics such as the temperature at which the oil smokes, and its stability in the presence of heat. (Heating an oil to the smoking point releases an off odor, and may open the way for many of the unsaturated fatty acid molecules to become saturated.) Here is a capsule guide to fats and oils. And remember, a label may boast "No Cholesterol" (no vegetable oils contain cholesterol) but still be high in the saturated fats that raise blood cholesterol levels. (For an explanation of the terms saturated, monounsaturated, and polyunsaturated, see page 281).

Butter: Made from cream, superior flavor. "Sweet" butter isn't sweet, it simply isn't salted. Because of its very low smoking point (temperature at which fat starts to burn), it is best to mix butter with a bit of oil (which has a higher smoking point) if it is used for sauteing. One teaspoon butter contains 11 milligrams of cholesterol (300 milligrams is the daily recommended norm). It is a saturated (46 percent) fat.

Coconut oil: Used by food manufacturers in non-dairy creamers, cookies, cakes, mixes, and the like. Unlike most vegetable oils, very high (87 percent) in saturated fats.

Corn oil: An all-purpose oil with virtually no taste and a high smoking point, so it is excellent for sauteing of foods but poor for taste enhancement. High in polyunsaturates.

Grapeseed oil: Found in specialty markets, grapeseed oil has a very high smoking point so it is excellent for sauteing. Excellent odor and flavor make it good in salad dressing, too. High in polyunsaturates.

Hot or chili oil: Used very sparingly for seasoning. Made from soy (a polyunsaturate) or other vegetable oils and an extract of hot red peppers or chilis.

Lard: Rendered pork fat. Used (but not in *The Enlightened Gourmet*) to produce flaky pie crusts. High (about 40 percent) in saturated fats.

Margarine: A blend of vegetable oils, water, flavorings, and preservatives. Cholesterol watchers should be discerning label-readers. Select brands that list liquid safflower or corn oil first. The process of hydrogenating (chemically hardening) oils reverses the initial health benefit, saturating previously unsaturated molecules.

Olive oils: Olive oils have come into their own in the '80s, gaining respect not only in culinary circles but medical circles as well. Once thought to play a neutral role in blood cholesterol levels, a new study suggests olive oil may actually help decrease such levels. Olive oil comes in different qualities from the ironically titled "pure" (after all, the oil has been chemically refined and mixed with virgin oil to improve flavor) to the much vaunted extra-virgin (the first cold pressing of high quality olives, with a legal maximum of 1 percent acidity and no chemical refinement). A low smoking point makes olive oil best as a seasoning oil rather than as a cooking oil. It is high in monounsaturated fats.

Peanut oil: Used in Oriental and some French cooking. Has a high smoking point. Generally tasteless. Monounsaturated.

Safflower oil: Popularized by a diet book that falsely attributed magical fat burning powers to this light, virtually tasteless oil. Safflower oil is very high in polyunsaturates (74 percent) but lacks vitamin E, so it should not be the sole fat in a dietary plan.

Sesame oil: Used sparingly after cooking to season Oriental dishes and for some salad dressings. Moderately high (42 percent) in polyunsaturates.

Soybean oil: Used mostly by food manufacturers and in Oriental cooking. A high smoking point and high in polyunsaturates (if not hydrogenated).

Vegetable shortenings: A solid, highly saturated fat. Moderate smoking point.

Walnut oil: A light, "clean" oil perfect for salad dressings. Like olive oil, high in monounsaturated fats.

Oils are pure fat and run about 120 calories a tablespoon, butter and margarine have about 100 calories for the same amount, and solid vegetable shortenings vary from 106 to 115 calories. Buy oils in amounts that will be used within 3 months. Refrigerate walnut oil after opening; refrigerate olive oil if desired. A few seconds in a microwave oven or a warm pan of water will liquefy a chilled, hardened oil.

❖Celery root or celeriac is not the root of celery as we know it, but the root of a celerylike plant. Available in the winter months, it will keep for several days in the refrigerator. Choose small knobs with as few roots as possible. It is also delicious raw, dressed with mustard, mayonnaise, and lemon juice, or pureed and served as one would a potato.❖

LANAI LUNCH

Grilled Shrimp and Lobster Patties

**Corn and Tomato Salad with
Blue Cheese Dressing**

Sesame Breadsticks*

Tropical Fruits with Apricot Cream

Things seem to move at a slower pace in Hawaii, land of the lanai (porch), so it seemed only appropriate to conjure up that wonderfully relaxed spirit in the title for this porch luncheon or light dinner for four. It's a very undemanding menu, for what little there is to be done can be prepared an hour or so ahead, leaving only the grilling of the seafood patties to be done about 20 to 25 minutes before serving time.

A few explanatory notes about the ingredients: The seafood patties may be made with langostino, a frozen lobsterlike shellfish available in most stores' freezer section. Of course, you may use either crab or lobster or certainly all shrimp would do just as well. I've also found supermarket frozen shrimp to be quite good in this recipe; what they lack in flavor is made up for by the other ingredients.

If you are grilling outside, prepare the fire far enough ahead so the flames are gone; if using a gas grill, use the lowest temperature setting. The seafood patties also can be broiled.

Consider the Tropical Fruit with Apricot Cream recipe a guide only. Any number of fruit and "cream" combinations can be tried, such as strawberries with orange cream, peaches and nectarines with blueberry cream, or bananas and papayas with pineapple cream.

The breadsticks are purchased, allowing the hostess longer on the lanai to work on that tan.

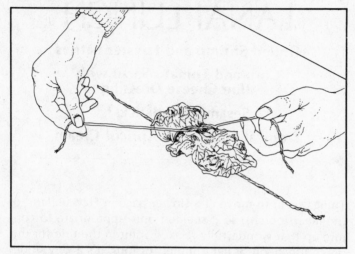

1. To form the patties, cross two 12-inch-long cotton strings on a counter. Center a lettuce leaf on the strings, and place the shrimp mixture in the center of the lettuce. Tie the top and bottom strings together, wrapping the lettuce around the shrimp filling.

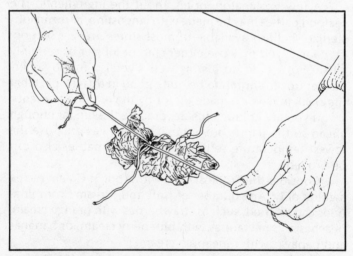

2. Now tie the two remaining strings, as shown. Tie another length of string around the corners if necessary. Snip excess string.

Grilled Shrimp and Lobster Patties

❖

This is a sort of seafood sausage with a lettuce casing. It may be grilled (or broiled) until the greens have charred but still retain a bit of green and the seafood has steamed. Call it an Oriental barbecue if you will.

> 1 pound raw shrimp (35 to the pound), peeled and deveined
> 6 ounces langostino, lobster meat, or crabmeat
> 3 scallions, minced
> 1 teaspoon grated fresh ginger
> 2 tablespoons plus 1 teaspoon peanut oil
> 3 tablespoons cornstarch
> hot pepper sauce to taste
> 8–10 outer Romaine lettuce leaves, stiff stems removed
> 2 tablespoons Chinese cooking wine or sherry
> ¼ cup reduced-sodium soy sauce
> a few drops hot oil, available at Oriental and specialty food shops
> 2 carrots, grated

1. In a food processor combine the shrimp, langostino, ⅓ of the scallion, ginger, 1 teaspoon oil, cornstarch, and hot pepper sauce. Pulse just to chop; do not puree. (Seafood may be prepared to this point early in the day and kept chilled.)
2. Refer to the illustrations as you prepare the patties. Lay two foot-long pieces of all-cotton twine or butcher's twine in a cross on the work surface. Center a lettuce leaf on the twine. Spoon a generous ⅓ cup of seafood mixture on the center of the leaf. Pull the lettuce over the seafood, and tie the north-south strings, snugly but not too tight. Then tie the east-west strings. Tie the cor-

ners if any lettuce pokes out with any remaining string or use another length of string. Repeat with remaining seafood and lettuce leaves. (The patties may be prepared and refrigerated up to two hours before grilling.)

3. Combine the 2 tablespoons oil with another ⅓ of the minced scallion and all the cooking wine. Brush a bit of this mixture on the bottom of the seafood patties and the grill rungs or broiler rack. Grill the patties over low coals for 20 to 25 minutes. Turn them over once and baste with the remaining oil–wine mixture. (Grilling will require less time if the grill can be covered.) To broil, arrange patties on a broiler pan rack or in a shallow baking pan. Broil 10 to 12 minutes, basting, and turning once to char lettuce nicely. To test for doneness, snip the string, lift the lettuce, and flake the seafood with a fork. If shellfish appears gray, not pink, return the patties to heat for a few more minutes (no need to retie). Note: Grill and broiler temperatures differ widely, so check seafood often.

To Prepare the Dipping Sauce

1. Mix together soy sauce, remaining scallion, and a few drops hot oil. To serve, arrange packets on a serving platter, then snip and remove strings. Garnish tops with grated carrot (or ginger if you prefer). Pass the dipping sauce at the table.

Yield: 4 servings

✦ Calories per serving: 270
Carbohydrate per serving: 18g
Cholesterol per serving: 165mg

Dietary fiber per serving: 1g
Fat per serving: 9g
Protein per serving: 27g
Sodium per serving: 755mg

❖Despite its name, buttermilk is usually made from skim or low-fat milk with a fat content of less than 1 percent, compared to a butterfat content of 3.5 percent for whole milk.❖

Corn and Tomato Salad with Blue Cheese Dressing

❖

It is best to serve this when naturally ripened, full-fla-vored tomatoes are at hand—about the same time corn on the cob is plentiful. This is a good way to use a leftover cooked ear of corn. Because the dressing also makes a de-licious dip for raw vegetables and will keep in the refriger-ator about 5 or 6 days, you might consider doubling the recipe.

For the Dressing

3 tablespoons plain yogurt
1 tablespoon low-fat milk
1 teaspoon mayonnaise
½ teaspoon Dijon mustard
2 tablespoons crumbled blue cheese

For the Salad

1 cooked ear of corn
2 very ripe tomatoes
5–6 leaves fresh basil, minced
2 strips bacon, cooked, drained, and crumbled
freshly ground black pepper to taste

1. Whisk together the yogurt, milk, mayonnaise, and mustard. Stir in the blue cheese. Set aside or refrigerate.
2. Scrape the corn from the cob onto a piece of wax paper. Slice the tomatoes and halve the slices. Arrange the tomato slices in a crescent shape on the upper half of 4 luncheon plates. Garnish with the corn kernels. Pour a ribbon of dressing down the middle of the to-

matoes. Sprinkle with the basil and bacon. Season with pepper.

Salad

Yield: 4 servings	**Dietary fiber per serving:** 1g
Calories per serving: 160	**Fat per serving:** 10g
Carbohydrate per serving: 12g	**Protein per serving:** 7g
✦ **Cholesterol per serving:** 15mg	**Sodium per serving:** 375mg

Dressing

Yield: 4 servings	**Dietary fiber per serving:** 0g
Calories per serving: 170	**Fat per serving:** 14g
Carbohydrate per serving: 4g	**Protein per serving:** 8g
✦ **Cholesterol per serving:** 30mg	**Sodium per serving:** 525mg

Tropical Fruits with Apricot Cream

❖

A quickly fixed, refreshing dessert that serves up a little extra calcium so very tastily. When making the apricot cream, look for all-fruit, no-sugar jellies and jams, available at most specialty food shops and some markets. Fructose, the type of sugar found in fruits, has the same sweetening effect as sugar, but with half the calories, making all-fruit jellies just as sweet but with a few less calories.

For the Apricot Cream

4 tablespoons plain yogurt
4 tablespoons cottage cheese
2 tablespoons all-fruit apricot (or flavor of your choice) jam

For the Fruits

1 ripe mango
1 ripe kiwi
½ teaspoon cinnamon mixed with ½ teaspoon
*   sugar*
4 ripe strawberries, with stems if possible

1. To prepare the cream: Process the yogurt, cottage cheese, and jam in a food processor or blender until smooth, about 1 minute. Keep chilled. (This will keep in the refrigerator for about 2 days.)
2. Peel and slice the mango. Fan the slices on four dessert plates. Peel and slice the kiwi very thinly. Cut rounds in half. Make circles with kiwis at the base of the mango fans. Mound cream in the circles, sprinkle the cream with cinnamon sugar, and top with a strawberry.

✦ **Yield: 4 servings**
Calories per serving: 100
Carbohydrate per serving: 20g
✦ **Cholesterol per serving: 5mg**

Dietary fiber per serving: 1g
Fat per serving: 1g
Protein per serving: 2g
✦ **Sodium per serving: 80mg**

❖Proteins require more energy to digest than either fats or carbohydrates and thus are often touted as the food of choice for reducing regimens. However, the reason high-protein diets don't work (other than restricting calories) better than any other sort of diet is this: When protein is mixed with fat and carbohydrate, which is inevitable, less energy is used to metabolize the food. The body does not need extra energy to digest it. Further, high-protein diets are often high-fat diets (meat and dairy foods) and don't retrain poor eating habits.❖

PLAYIN' CAJUN

Pan-blackened Swordfish

Hoppin' John

Okra and Tomatoes

Pan-blackened fish, okra, and black-eyed peas; say it with a drawl and smell the magnolias. It also starts one thinking; for a nation of adventuresome eaters who have been drawn to foreign cuisines like moths to a flame, we've been amazingly slow to experience the culinary diversity within our own borders. Until now that is. Red, white, and blue are the current colors of choice in many a leading restaurant. Only a few years back, a translator was needed for a menu that now proudly boasts of "American specialties."

Paul Prudhomme, Cajun cooking guru, has been largely responsible for today's interest in New Orleans-style cooking and "pan-blackening." Be forewarned: It's a technique to be used only in well-ventilated kitchens or outdoors; if your kitchen is so equipped, do give it a try. It is a very quick cooking method and wonderful for thick fish steaks. My recipe is not a strictly authentic rendition; Prudhomme mixes chilies, herbs, and spices for a delightfully hot dish, and here lemon and soy create a piquant glaze. Because of the smoke, I think it's best to prepare the fish for no more than four, cooked all at one time either in a twelve-inch cast-iron skillet or simultaneously in two eight-inch skillets.

The serving size of fish in this menu for four is small, a modest quarter pound, for the black-eyed peas and rice are an excellent source of protein (see *Focus: Complete Vegetable Protein*, page 274) all by themselves. As well as contributing healthy amounts of carbohydrate, some vitamins, and minerals including iron, legumes (the catch-all term for dried beans) are an excellent source of Type II fiber, a suspected anticholesterol agent.

Another Southern "import" one rarely used to find north of the Mason-Dixon line is okra. Quick-cooking and low in calories, it adds another possibility when you're green-beaned out. It has a natural affinity for tomatoes and corn, which provides a colorful concoction.

Start the meal by soaking and cooking the black-eyed peas and rice recipe; the okra takes about fifteen minutes, the fish the same.

Pan-blackened Swordfish

❖

Due to the immense popularity of Cajun cooking, many cookbooks, scads of restaurants, and nearly every food magazine offer their version of a pan-blackened something. It's a technique particularly well suited to health-conscious cooks—just overlook the usual final butter drenching. You'll need an inexpensive, well-seasoned cast-iron skillet, which is best reserved for pan blackening only, and a very efficient kitchen fan. Disconnect any nearby smoke alarms. Choose thick (at least ¾-inch), firm-fleshed fish for this, such as halibut, swordfish, or tuna.

1 pound swordfish steaks
4 tablespoons lemon juice
3 tablespoons reduced-sodium soy sauce

1. Heat a 12-inch cast-iron skillet over high heat until the bottom turns a grayish color, about 8 to 10 minutes. Add the fish and sear it on one side for 1½ minutes. Flip

it over and sear the other side another 1½ to 2 minutes. Poke with a finger or flake with a fork to determine doneness; different fishes will cook at varying rates.

2. While fish cooks, mix the lemon juice and soy sauce. When the fish is done, remove the pan from the burner (leaving fish in skillet), but keep it close to the fan.

3. Pan cover in hand, add the lemon-soy to the skillet, and cover immediately. Rest until smoke subsides, about 1 minute. Uncover. If more than 2 tablespoons of sauce remain, return the skillet to high heat to boil briefly.

4. Transfer fish to plates or a serving platter. Spoon a bit of sauce over fish and serve.

Note: If you must do fish in two batches or in two skillets, add another tablespoon lemon juice and another tablespoon soy sauce.

Yield: 4 servings	Dietary fiber per serving: 0g
✦ Calories per serving: 150	Fat per serving: 5g
Carbohydrate per serving: 2g	Protein per serving: 23g
✦ Cholesterol per serving: 60mg	Sodium per serving: 500mg

Hoppin' John
❖

Hoppin' John, or black-eyed peas and rice, is a well-known Southern dish that everyone, regardless of region, would do well to give a try. Not only tasty and easily prepared, it ranks high on the nutritional scale as well. That's because rice and beans (or in this case black-eyed peas) together make a complete protein—as nutritionally complete a protein, in fact, as that found in meat, poultry, or fish, but without the cholesterol or saturated fats of animal foods. Unlike most bean recipes, the cook needn't start 24 hours ahead preparing this simple one, for the peas will boil up tender in just 15 minutes after a mere hour's soak. If your family isn't yet accustomed to meatless meals, but you'd like to offer up more fat-lowered menus, begin by serving big dishes of vegetable protein foods, such as this Hoppin' John, with small servings of meat, poultry, and fish. Gradually reduce the animal protein until an occasional meatless meal (see "Farm Fresh," page 256 or "Vegetarian Delight," page 140) is as accepted as spaghetti.

¾ cup dried black-eyed peas
2 cups boiling water
½ small onion, minced (about 2 tablespoons)
¼ cup chopped celery (use mostly leaves)
2¾ cup homemade chicken stock or canned broth
½ cup long-grain white converted rice
½ teaspoon salt
1 teaspoon cumin or to taste
hot pepper sauce to taste
1 tablespoon minced fresh parsley
1 tablespoon unsalted butter

1. Cover the peas with the boiling water and let rest 1 hour. Pour off water, rinse, and drain. (Peas also can soak overnight, if you wish.)
2. Combine the onion and celery with ½ cup of the chicken stock in a 2½-quart saucepan. Cover and cook over medium-high heat until they are tender, about 3 to 4 minutes.
3. Add the peas and remaining chicken broth, cover, and bring to a boil over medium-high heat. Reduce heat to a simmer and cook until peas are tender, about 15 to 20 minutes.
4. Stir in the rice, salt, cumin, and hot pepper sauce. Cover and simmer until rice is tender, about 15 minutes.
5. Toss with parsley and butter, and serve. (Although it is better served freshly cooked, Hoppin' John can be prepared ahead and kept warm in a double boiler or re-

heated 2 minutes on medium-high power in a microwave oven.)

Yield: 4 servings

+ **Calories per serving: 160**

Carbohydrate per serving: 28g

+ **Cholesterol per serving: 5mg**

Dietary fiber per serving: 1g

Fat per serving: 3g

Protein per serving: 5g

Sodium per serving: 320mg

Okra and Tomatoes

❖

Okra is relatively low in calories—46 in a cooked cup—
and a fair source of both vitamin A and calcium. Another
plus, preparing it is quite simple, requiring nothing more
than snipping off the stem end and slicing the pod into
rounds. Don't overcook okra, though, or the mucilaginous
quality that makes it so crucial to gumbo will leave this
simple recipe a gummy mess. For that reason, it is best
cooked just before serving. While fresh tomatoes and
corn would definitely be tastier, canned products can be
used.

> 8 ounces fresh okra, trimmed and sliced into
>   rounds (about 2 cups)
> 3 tomatoes (about 1½ pounds), cored, peeled (see
>   page 177), and diced
> 1 ear corn, uncooked but scraped from the cob
> 2 tablespoons minced onion
> 1 tablespoon safflower oil
> 1 bay leaf
> ½ teaspoon salt
> hot pepper sauce to taste

1. Place all ingredients in a 2½-quart saucepan. Cover.
   Place on high heat. When a boil is reached, uncover,

and simmer for 12 minutes, stirring occasionally. Remove bay leaf before serving.

Yield: 4 servings
✦ Calories per serving: 90
Carbohydrate per serving: 14g
✦ Cholesterol per serving: 0mg

✦ Dietary fiber per serving: 2g
Fat per serving: 4g
Protein per serving: 3g
Sodium per serving: 310mg

❖ Focus: Hidden Fat ❖

Most of us consume about 35 to 40 percent of our total calories in fat, but health experts warn fat should account for no more than 35 percent, and ideally no more than 20 percent, of our calorie intake. Short of having a dietary analysis done, it's hard to pinpoint the amount of saturated and other fats we eat. Learning to spot hidden fat, however, will save calories, and avoiding saturated fats could save your heart. Remember, a gram of fat contributes more than twice the calories of protein or carbohydrate.

It's far from being just the butter spread on toast or the oil in the frying pan—nearly everything we eat has some fat. A banana has some fat, as does a shrimp; even a carrot has some, though in tiny amounts. But these aren't the sorts of hidden fats we need to be wary of. The single largest contributor of saturated hidden fat is the very food we baby boomers were brought up to eat more of—meat. In fact, many high-protein foods are also high-fat foods. Take cheese, a delicious protein substitute for meat. With a few exceptions, cheese is a high fat item.

Below is a chart of some common fatty foods with a few lower fat items thrown in for comparison. Note, SFA stands for saturated fatty acids (given in grams); this is only a portion of the fat found in a food. In addition there are polyunsaturates and monounsaturates, but other than being contributors of calories, these fats are not a health threat. Tips on how to cut the fat in your diet are given on page 122 in *Focus: Cutting Fat.*

FOOD	CALORIES	SFA
BEEF		
3½ ounces		
chuck, lean and fat	409	13.89
chuck, lean only	299	7.65
bottom, lean and fat	274	6.78
bottom, lean only	224	4.01
sirloin steak, lean and fat	297	8.37
sirloin steak, lean only	219	4.11
POULTRY		
chicken, light meat, with skin	222	3.1
chicken, light meat without skin	173	1.3
egg, 1 poached	79	1.7
CHEESE		
cheddar, 1 ounce	114	0.6
cottage cheese, regular, 4 ounces	117	3.2
cottage cheese, low-fat, 4 ounces	82	0.7
cream cheese, 1 ounce	99	6.2
feta, 1 ounce	75	4.2
muenster, 1 ounce	104	5.4
ricotta, part skim, ½ cup	171	6.1
MILK		
whole, 1 cup	150	4.9
low-fat, 2 percent, 1 cup	121	2.9
skim, 1 cup	86	0.3
vanilla ice cream, 10 percent fat, 1 cup	269	8.9
SALAD DRESSINGS		
farm style, from mix, 1 tablespoon	53	0.9
French, from mix, 1 tablespoon	97	1.4
Italian, from mix, 1 tablespoon	69	1.4
Russian, 1 tablespoon	76	1.1
mayonnaise, 1 tablespoon	100	1.6

MICRO-EASE

Salmon Steaks with Green Sauce
Mapled Buttercup Squash
Brown Rice with Walnuts

A microwave oven isn't required to cook this menu for four, but it does streamline one or two of the cooking tasks. Microwave ovens are particularly well-suited for cooking winter squashes. Not only are they quick, but because they require only a tiny amount of water, the squash is kept from being soggy. A microwave oven is also used here to poach the fish, but either job can be done conventionally.

At the heart of this "Micro-ease" dinner is salmon, a cold-water fish with unique kinds of fats that are more polyunsaturated than vegetable oils, meaning they may actually help to unclog the arteries. Because of its high fat content, salmon takes well to poaching. The cooking liquid in turn is quickly whirred into a green sauce, rich in taste but not in calories.

Accompanying the fish recipe are jiffy ways to enliven the flavor of butternut squash and simple brown rice.

PREPARING BONELESS AND
SKINLESS SALMON STEAKS

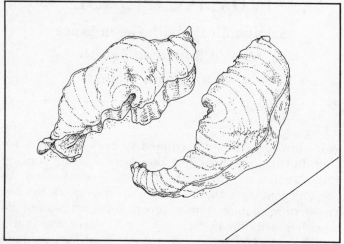

1. Remove the skin and bones from a salmon steak with the tip of a small knife, leaving two strips of meat. Each will be a little thicker at one end than the other.

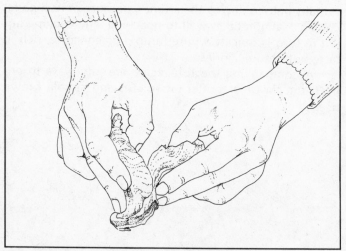

2. To re-shape the salmon steak, hold the thick end of one salmon strip against the thin end of the other salmon strip.

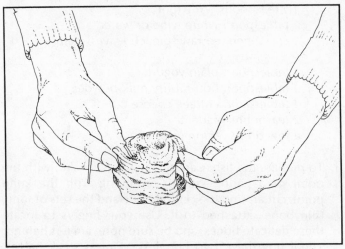

3. Curl the remaining thin end around the other thick end, forming a boneless, skinless steak.

Salmon Steaks
with Green Sauce

❖

This recipe makes a lovely presentation with the coral of the salmon accented by the soft green of the sauce. It may be prepared on the stove top, as well as in a microwave oven.

> 1 pound salmon steaks, each about ¾- to 1-inch
>   thick
> 1 bottle (8 ounces) clam broth
> ⅓ cup dry white wine
> 1 bay leaf
> 1 tablespoon minced chives

1½ teaspoons arrowroot
1 tablespoon white wine or water
1 cup julienned raw spinach leaves, stems
    removed
1 tablespoon plain yogurt
1 tablespoon non-fat dry milk powder
1 tablespoon cottage cheese
2 teaspoons Madeira
a few drops lemon juice

1. To prepare the fish: Carefully remove the skin with the point of a paring knife. Continuing with the knife point, cut around the central bone and the sets of long, thin bones attached to it. Use your fingers to locate these delicate bones, and be sure none are left behind. You'll now have two boneless, skinless steak halves, each a little thicker at one end and tapering to a thinner tail. Place them on the counter so one thick end abuts the other half's thin end. Secure with a toothpick. Press the other thicker end snug against the now secured thicker end and press the free thin tail to the outside of both thicker ends. This will form a solid, circular salmon steak. Secure with another toothpick. Repeat with each salmon steak. (See illustrations on pages 164–65.)
2. Place a serving platter in the oven and heat it to 150 degrees.
3. To poach the salmon in a microwave oven: Combine the clam broth, wine, bay leaf, and chives in a microwave-proof dish just large enough to hold the fish. Add the salmon. Cover or use plastic wrap to hold in steam. Microwave at medium-high for 8 minutes or until the flesh is resistant when pressed. Flip once during cooking. (To cook on a stove burner: Combine ingredients in a 12-inch skillet, cover, and simmer 15 minutes, turning fish over once.)
4. Transfer the fish to the warmed platter, remove the toothpicks, and keep the fish warm in oven.

To Prepare the Sauce

1. Dissolve the arrowroot in the tablespoon of wine or water. Set near stove to have handy for step 3.
2. Remove bay leaf from the poaching liquid. Transfer liquid to a food processor. Add the spinach, yogurt, dry milk powder, cottage cheese, and Madeira. Pulse just to combine; don't puree spinach.
3. Pour sauce into a 10-inch skillet. Over medium-high heat, whisk in the arrowroot until the sauce is lightly thickened, about 2 minutes. Season to taste with lemon juice. Pour over salmon steaks and serve.

Yield: 4 servings	**Dietary fiber per serving:** 1g
✦ **Calories per serving:** 270	**Fat per serving:** 16g
Carbohydrate per serving: 4g	**Protein per serving:** 28g
✦ **Cholesterol per serving:** 75mg	**Sodium per serving:** 340mg

Mapled Buttercup Squash

❖

This vegetable, ultrarich in vitamin A and potassium, is a snap to prepare with the help of a microwave oven. If you prefer, try it with acorn squash, although the relative dryness of the buttercup lends itself ideally to this method.

1 2-pound buttercup squash
1 tablespoon unsalted butter
2 tablespoons maple syrup
2 teaspoons rum
½ teaspoon salt

1. Cut the squash in half at its "equator." Remove the seeds with a spoon. Place the halves, cavity side up, in a microwave-safe baking dish with ½-inch water. Divide the butter, maple syrup, rum, and salt between the

halves. Cover with plastic wrap. (The squash may be held up to one hour on the counter before cooking.)
2. Microwave at high power for 10 to 12 minutes, or until tender when pierced with a fork. To serve, cut the halves in half. (To bake, prepare as for microwave cooking, but don't cover with plastic wrap. Bake in a 350-degree oven for 45 to 50 minutes, or until tender when pierced with a fork.)

Yield: 4 servings
Calories per serving: 175
Carbohydrate per serving: 38g
✦ Cholesterol per serving: 10mg

✦ Dietary fiber per serving: 3g
Fat per serving: 3g
Protein per serving: 3g
Sodium per serving: 300mg

Brown Rice with Walnuts

❖

Brown rice is the whole grain before the outer bran layer has been removed (for more on rice see *Focus: Rice*, page 112). It has nearly three times the cholesterol-binding type of fiber of white rice. Here, its nutty flavor and texture are perfectly complemented by the small addition of chopped walnuts. Because it only cooks 10 minutes faster in a microwave oven, save that appliance for the fish and squash in the menu, and cook the rice on a stove burner.

¾ cup long-grain brown rice
2¼ cups homemade chicken stock or canned broth
½ teaspoon salt
2 tablespoons chopped walnuts
1 tablespoon unsalted butter, at room temperature
freshly ground black pepper to taste

1. Place the rice, broth, and salt in a 2½-quart saucepan. Cover and bring to a boil over high heat. When a boil is reached, reduce heat so the liquid simmers. Simmer 45 to 50 minutes or until the liquid is absorbed. Stir occasionally with a fork and adjust heat as needed to prevent sticking.
2. Remove rice from heat, stir in walnuts and butter, and season with pepper.

Yield: 4 servings
Calories per serving: 180
Carbohydrate per serving: 30g
✦ **Cholesterol per serving: 10mg**

✦ **Dietary fiber per serving: 3g**
Fat per serving: 6g
Protein per serving: 4g
Sodium per serving: 305mg

❖It's been estimated that 200 to 600 milligrams of sodium a day is adequate for a healthy diet. A daily intake (for healthy persons) of 1100 to 3300 milligrams is considered safe. Most Americans consume 2300 to 6900 milligrams of sodium daily. To help you gauge added salt (though sodium is also found in foods and water) remember 1 teaspoon of table salt equals 2300 milligrams of sodium.❖

ORIENT EXPRESS

Spicy Shrimp and Cashew Stir-Fry
Boiled Rice*
Pineapple Sorbet

Here's a stir-fry for four who like theirs hot and spicy, although it could be tamed by modifying some of the ingredients. The Oriental ingredients called for—hot oil, sesame oil, chili paste with garlic, and Chinese cooking wine—are increasingly available at supermarkets and specialty food shops. Fish market shrimp, as opposed to those sold frozen in plastic bags at supermarkets, are much more flavorful and worth the extra cost for this recipe.

Although a wok makes for a more authentic dish because vegetables don't become overcooked, a nonstick skillet would be just fine. Be sure to heat the wok before adding the oil, and add the next ingredients immediately or they will have a tendency to stick. Most importantly, to borrow a phrase, "be prepared." Once the heat is on, there'll be no time for measuring four tablespoons of this and two of that, so have everything premeasured in little bowls and lined up. While a stir-fry can be reheated in a microwave oven on medium-high power for about a minute, the vegetables will be crisper and the shrimp more moist if it is prepared just before serving. Prepare the rice, according to package directions, while chopping and assembling the stir-fry ingredients. Keep it warm while preparing the entree.

In the way of a finale, why not pineapple? But for this meal, pineapple pureed and frozen into a melt-in-the-mouth sorbet. Prepare the sorbet early in the day or even up to two days ahead. The bit of added gelatin helps to prevent ice crystals from forming. Remember to remove the sorbet from the freezer and place it in the refrigerator about 30 minutes before serving.

Spicy Shrimp and Cashew Stir-fry

❖

Spicy, succulent shrimp (not frozen supermarket shrimp, but fresh fish-market shrimp) and lots of crisp vegetables make this meal-in-a-wok one you'll want to enjoy again and again. If you want to make it less hot, reduce the chili paste with garlic by half and omit the hot oil. Once cooking begins there's no time to gather, measure, or prepare ingredients so be sure to have everything close at hand before you heat the wok. This makes four generous servings, but ingredients may be cut in half across the board to serve two.

> 1 pound raw, large shrimp (25–30 to the pound),
>   unpeeled
> 6 tablespoons reduced-sodium soy sauce
> 1 egg white, lightly beaten
> 1½ tablespoons Chinese cooking wine or sherry
> ¾ teaspoon chili paste with garlic
> 6 ounces pea pods, stringed
> 1½ tablespoons cornstarch
> 3 tablespoons sherry
> ¾ cup homemade chicken stock or canned broth
> 2 tablespoons peanut oil
> 2 scallions, minced
> 1 garlic clove, minced
> 2 teaspoons grated fresh ginger
> 1½ carrots, julienned
> 1½ red bell peppers, julienned
> ½ teaspoon sugar

6 ounces mushrooms, sliced
2 cups loosely packed, julienned raw spinach,
    stems removed
3 tablespoons cashews
3 drops hot oil (optional)
a few drops sesame oil

1. Peel and devein the shrimp. Combine 2 tablespoons of the soy sauce with egg white, cooking wine, and chili paste. Mix well with a fork. Marinate the shrimp in this mixture for 1 hour, covered, in the refrigerator.
2. Meanwhile, bring 1 quart water to a boil in a 2½-quart saucepan. Blanch the pea pods 1 minute, rinse under running water to cool, and drain. Set aside.
3. Mix together the cornstarch, sherry, 4 tablespoons of the chicken stock, and remaining 4 tablespoons soy sauce in a small bowl. Set near the stove to have handy for step 8.
4. Heat the wok over high heat until a drop of water skitters on contact. Add the peanut oil, immediately add the scallions, garlic, and ginger, and stir-fry for 10 seconds.
5. Add the carrots, peppers, sugar, and 4 tablespoons of the chicken stock. Stir-fry until carrots are tender, about 2 to 3 minutes.
6. Add the shrimp and marinade. Stir-fry until the shrimp turn pink, about 2 minutes. Add the mushrooms, and stir-fry until tender, about 1 minute.
7. Add the pea pods, spinach, and 4 remaining tablespoons chicken stock. Stir-fry until the spinach is just wilted, about 1 to 2 minutes.
8. Stir the cornstarch mixture from step 3, then add it to the wok. Stir-fry until the sauce is thickened, about 1 minute.
9. Add the cashews, hot oil, and sesame oil. Stir-fry just to combine. Serve.

Yield: 4 servings
✦ **Calories per serving: 300**
Carbohydrate per serving: 21g
Cholesterol per serving: 170mg
✦ **Dietary fiber per serving: 3g**
Fat per serving: 12g
Protein per serving: 27g
Sodium per serving: 1090mg

Pineapple Sorbet

❖

Enjoy a dish of frozen fruit! More interesting than the ubiquitous pineapple-on-a-toothpick served by the standard Chinese restaurant, this packs a clean, bright flavor, the perfect "palate cleanser."

A very ripe pineapple is essential. Look for one that is more yellow than green (a sign of under-maturity), heavy for its size, soft but not squishy to the touch, and rich with a pineapple-y scent. Canned pineapple is certainly adequate, but use only half the juice.

The sorbet may be eaten as soon as it firms up in the ice cream maker (instructions for pan-freezing are also given); or it may be stored in an airtight container in the freezer for up to 1 week. Remove it from the freezer and place it in the refrigerator 30 minutes before serving to soften slightly. Serve the sorbet in the hollowed-out pineapple shell, garnished with fresh strawberries, if desired.

> 1 ripe, fresh pineapple
> ⅓ cup sugar
> ⅓ cup water
> 1 package unflavored gelatin

1. Lay the pineapple sideways on a work surface; slice off the top third, taking care not to cut into the green leaves.
2. Remove and discard the core. Remove fruit by cutting around the pineapple, leaving a ½-inch-thick shell. Make crosswise cuts through the pineapple flesh at 1-inch intervals, taking care not to cut through the shell. Run the knife under the flesh, again leaving a ½-inch-thick shell on the bottom. Scrape the fruit free with a spoon and put it and the juice into a food processor. Remove fruit in a similar fashion from the pineapple lid as well. Add it to the food processor.

3. Add sugar to the fruit and puree, but leave slightly chunky.
4. Combine the water and gelatin in a 1-quart saucepan. Stir to soften, then stir over low heat until gelatin is completely dissolved. Combine thoroughly with fruit.
5. Freeze in an ice cream maker according to manufacturer's directions. If you do not have an ice cream maker: Pour mixture into a 9-inch-square metal pan and place in freezer until ice forms around the edge. This will take between 1 and 3 hours, depending on the freezer. Meanwhile, chill a bowl in the refrigerator. Transfer the sorbet to the bowl and beat with an electric mixer until smooth. Cover the bowl with plastic wrap and return to the freezer. Repeat twice.

Yield: 5 1-cup servings
✦ Calories per serving: 90
Carbohydrate per serving: 23g
✦ Cholesterol per serving: 0mg

Dietary fiber per serving: 1g
Fat per serving: 0g
Protein per serving: 0g
✦ Sodium per serving: 0mg

❖Over half the calories of a popular fast-food chain's fish sandwich come from fat. The same for its chicken pieces and super burgers. The single hamburger, at 35 percent fat, is the better choice, if the choice must be made.❖

SUNDAY SUPPER

Eggs Imposter

Asparagus*

Garden Goodness Cheese Rolls

Homework's in order for this elegant luncheon or light supper for two, but it's time well spent if you savor food that is light, lovely, and satisfying. Although Eggs Imposter would be welcome anytime, asparagus season, which seems to lengthen with each year, seems perfect. Gladden the table with daffodils, and enjoy!

Do-it-ahead cooks will want to start with the yeast rolls as much as a week early while the-better-under-pressure types should begin no later than four hours before serving. Simpler than most, this roll recipe requires only one rising; the rolls are shaped right after kneading. You'll have lots left over for the freezer. These rolls reheat wonderfully in a microwave oven if they are wrapped in a dampened kitchen towel (the time will depend on how many you heat at once).

Components of the Eggs Imposter may also be done far in advance (a day or two) or started about one hour before serving. Despite the great length of the recipe, the eggs and the asparagus require no more than an hour to whip up. Peel the asparagus (no recipe included here, just steam or boil and top with a little of the Lemon Cream Sauce from the egg recipe) before beginning the Eggs Imposter, and cook the spears just before poaching the eggs.

Eggs Imposter

❖

Eggs are not inherently elegant, but here they are, posing convincingly, as the focal point of a chic luncheon or supper dish. Picture the plate; a puddle of tomato coulis speckled with parsley, a centered artichoke bottom topped by a poached egg, which is in turn dappled with lemon sauce, and the whole artfully garnished with several chive strips. Overwhelming? Not when you take it step by step. Organization is the only skill needed to carry off this recipe and menu. Start with the tomato coulis as much as 2 days or as little as an hour before. Next, whip up the lemon sauce (could be done up to 24 hours ahead), then trim and cook the artichoke bottoms either early in the day or just before serving. (Sorry, frozen artichoke hearts or bottoms won't do.) Just before serving, warm the plates (an important step in keeping this easily cooled-off food hot) while poaching the eggs. Steam or boil asparagus to serve with the remaining lemon sauce.

For the Tomato Coulis

3 medium tomatoes (about 1 pound, 3 ounces)
1 small onion, minced
1 garlic clove, minced
4 tablespoons homemade chicken stock or
    canned chicken broth
5–6 fresh basil leaves, snipped
½ teaspoon sugar
½ teaspoon salt
freshly ground black pepper to taste
2 tablespoons minced fresh parsley

For the Lemon Cream Sauce

1 teaspoon arrowroot
6½ tablespoons low-fat milk
1 tablespoon cottage cheese
2 tablespoons lemon juice
1 egg, lightly beaten
1 teaspoon butter
a shake salt
a dash paprika
a dash cayenne pepper

For the Artichokes

2 large artichokes
half a lemon
1 teaspoon vegetable oil

For the Eggs

1 to 2 eggs per diner
1 tablespoon cider or white vinegar
10–12 5-inch-long chives or strips of scallion

To Prepare the Tomato Coulis

1. Fill a 2½-quart saucepan three-quarters full with water
   and bring it to a boil. Remove the core from each of the
   tomatoes and cut a cross into each bottom. Add the
   tomatoes to the boiling water. Boil 15 seconds for ripe
   tomatoes, and as long as 1 minute for firm ones.
2. Drain the tomatoes and cool under running water.
   Starting at the cross, peel off and discard the skin. Place
   a sieve over a bowl. Quarter the tomatoes and pop the
   seeds into the sieve with your thumb. Remove juice
   from seeds by pressing with the back of a wooden
   spoon. Roughly chop the pulp. Combine the tomato
   pulp and juice. Set aside.
3. Combine the onion and garlic in the chicken stock in a
   10-inch skillet. Cook over medium-high heat, covered,
   until tender, about 3 to 4 minutes.

4. Add the tomato pulp and juice to the skillet, stirring to combine. Season with basil, sugar, salt, and pepper. Cover and simmer for 20 minutes or until the tomatoes are thick and somewhat reduced. (If tomatoes are very juicy, it will take longer.) Remove the skillet from heat, stir in parsley, and taste for seasoning adjustment. Set aside.

To Prepare the Sauce

1. Mix together with an electric beater, food processor, or blender, the arrowroot, milk, and cottage cheese until smooth. Pour into a 1-quart saucepan and stir over medium-high heat until slightly thickened, about 2 to 3 minutes.
2. Whisk in the lemon juice and egg, and cook 2 to 3 minutes more, whisking constantly.
3. Remove from heat and whisk in the butter and seasonings. Cover and set aside. (If sauce is to be held more than 30 minutes, refrigerate. Reheat over low heat, stirring constantly, adding a drop or so of milk or chicken stock, if necessary, to thin.)

To Prepare the Artichokes

1. Cut off the stem of the artichokes. With a stainless steel knife, pare each artichoke as if peeling an apple, removing the top 2 or 3 layers of tough, deep green leaves. It is very important to remove any stringy leaves; it is better to overpare than underpare. Cut off the top half of the artichokes. (See illustrations on pages 77–78.)
2. Half fill a 2½-quart saucepan with water and bring it to a boil. Add the lemon and artichokes. Boil, covered, until the artichokes are tender when pierced with a fork. Begin testing at 15 minutes, but they could take as long as 25 minutes. Drain and cool under running water.
3. Gently pull open the artichokes from the top so you can see the fuzzy center (choke). Remove all the choke

with a spoon. Inspect again for any stringy leaves. (If preparing artichokes more than 30 minutes ahead, wrap in wax paper and chill.) Heat the artichokes in a nonstick skillet coated with cooking spray and 1 teaspoon vegetable oil for 2 minutes or until heated through. Cover the pan and hold over very low heat while cooking the eggs.

To Prepare the Eggs

1. Heat the plates in a preheated 150-degree oven or in a microwave oven with an added glass of water to absorb the energy. If necessary, reheat tomato coulis over medium heat on a stove burner or in a microwave oven. Reheat the lemon sauce on the stove or in the microwave on medium power for 1½ minutes.
2. Fill a 10-inch skillet seven-eighths full with water and the vinegar. Bring to a gentle boil. Reduce heat so the water just simmers.
3. Break each egg, one at a time, into a cup. Slip, one at a time, into the simmering water. Spoon hot water over eggs from time to time, and check that they aren't sticking. Cook until the desired degree of doneness (about 3 to 4 minutes for a runny yolk and set white).
4. While the eggs cook, divide the tomato coulis between the heated plates. Center an artichoke bottom on the coulis. Remove the eggs from the water with a slotted spoon and slip into the artichokes. Dollop three-fourths of the lemon sauce over the eggs. (Save remaining sauce to serve on steamed or boiled asparagus.) Garnish with crisscrossed chives. Serve with asparagus on the plate.

Yield: 2 servings
✦ Calories per serving: 320
Carbohydrate per serving: 40g
Cholesterol per serving: 420mg

✦ Dietary fiber per serving: 5g
Fat per serving: 13g
Protein per serving: 20g
Sodium per serving: 1160mg

Garden Goodness
Cheese Rolls

❖

Yeast breads bring to mind long, laborious hours in the kitchen, but here's a yeast roll recipe that only needs one rising. If you use the new "rapid-rise" dry yeast available at some markets, the process is all the quicker. The actual mixing, kneading, and shaping of the rolls can be easily accomplished in 30 minutes.

> ½ cup water at 105–115 degrees
> 2 teaspoons sugar
> 2 packages dry yeast
> 1 teaspoon salt
> 2 eggs, lightly beaten
> ½ cup low-fat cottage cheese
> 1 teaspoon minced stalk of a scallion
> 1 teaspoon grated carrot
> 2 teaspoons minced fresh parsley
> 4–5 fresh basil leaves, minced
> 3½ cups flour

1. Combine the water, sugar, and yeast in a 2-cup measure. Set aside until doubled in volume, about 10 to 15 minutes.
2. Meanwhile, beat together in a large bowl the salt, eggs, cottage cheese, scallion, carrot, and herbs.
3. When the yeast has doubled in volume, stir it into the egg mixture with 1 cup of the flour. Mix well. Gradually beat in more flour to make a firm dough. Toss dough onto a lightly floured board and knead, adding more flour as needed, for 8 to 10 minutes or until it is smooth and elastic.
4. Divide the dough into quarters. Divide each quarter into six equal parts. Roll the pieces between the palms of your hands to form balls. Place the rolls 2 to 3 inches apart on baking sheets that have been coated with cooking spray. Cover with a kitchen towel and let rise

in a warm, draft-free spot until doubled or even tripled in volume.

5. Preheat oven to 375 degrees. Bake the rolls in the middle of the oven for 15 minutes. Serve at once. If you prefer soft-crusted rolls, brush them with some melted butter when you remove them from the oven. (Rolls may be reheated in a microwave oven if they are wrapped in a dampened kitchen towel.)

Yield: 26 rolls
Calories per roll: 70
Carbohydrate per roll: 13g
✝ Cholesterol per roll: 20mg

Dietary fiber per roll: 1g
Fat per roll: 1g
Protein per roll: 3g
Sodium per roll: 115mg

❖ Focus: Factor out Fat ❖

On reading that most nutritionists recommend limiting fat in the diet to no more than 35 percent of the total (but that 20 percent is better), do you think, "I don't eat much fat, so I don't have to worry about it"? If the following foods make up a significant part of your diet, you might just think about making some changes:

- luncheon meats
- mayonnaise
- butter, margarine, saturated oils, including those used in cooking
- whole milk and ice cream
- ham, pork, hamburger, steak, lamb
- eggs, scrambled or fried
- hard cheeses and some soft cheeses such as Triple Crèmes
- bacon and sausage
- cookies, cakes, doughnuts, croissants
- foods processed with lots of fat such as commercial salad dressings, potato chips, granola bars, candy bars, some crackers
- nuts, such as peanuts, for snacking
- peanut butter
- skin on poultry

PASTA PASSIONS

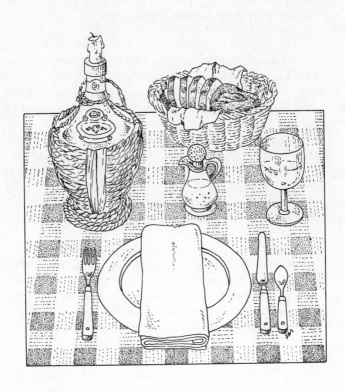

❖ Pasta Passions ❖

When I was growing up, we called them noodles and spa-ghetti—welcome food, homey food, comfortable stuff to sink your teeth into. Now the word is pasta, covering an entire array of noodles in countless shapes and fascinating flavors, with innumerable sauces, and presented in all kinds of combinations. It's still great stuff to sink your teeth into, but it needn't be predictable anymore.

If you've never made noodles, the length of these recipes may seem intimidating and the thought of buying special equipment yet another deterrent, but I urge you to reconsider with these simple arguments:

1. A hand-cranked, chrome pasta maker, which kneads, rolls, and cuts the dough into two basic shapes, is rela-tively inexpensive and easy to store and clean.
2. After one batch you'll be a pro at any shape pasta, from angel hair (vermicelli, very thin) to lasagne noodles (flat and broad).
3. The instructions for making noodles may seem compli-cated or long, but they are detailed to help you suc-ceed. Unless you live within a block of a store that carries fresh pasta, you can probably make it faster than if you go out to pick up a package.
4. Fresh pasta is much tastier and offers more possiblities than packaged products.

Not convinced? You'd still settle for a P.B. & J. rather than make your own noodles? Get out the grated cheese, because fresh noodles are increasingly available in spe-cialty stores and supermarkets everywhere. And every pasta recipe here, with the exception of the Seafood Ravi-olis with Tomato Cream Sauce, can be made with store-bought noodles.

To me, pasta dishes are among the most creative and fun to cook. Combinations and variations are seemingly endless, proportions rarely need to be exact, and many dishes are as good at room temperature as they are hot, making them perfect for casual entertaining or take-along meals. Even finicky children like noodles served up with just a little butter and without that "icky" sauce (more for the grown-ups, thank you!). And joy of all joys, nutritionists urge us to eat more complex carbohydrates and fewer fats. A plate of noodles interestingly sauced with vegetables and perhaps a smattering of shellfish, gets a clean bill of health.

A few cautionary words: Do watch the butter or oil drizzled on those noodles. Olive oil, rich in monounsaturates and recently suspected of actually helping to lower blood cholesterol levels, is a healthier choice than butter, when feasible. But for calories' sake, do be stingy with either. Always heat the plates or soup dishes that a hot pasta dish will be served in, for noodles cool off quickly. And never attack the aftermath of a noodle-making session with a sponge, or you'll have glue for your efforts. Scrape the work surface with a pastry blade or knife, then scrub with a dry brush, and finally wipe up with a damp sponge. A chrome pasta machine never needs washing. To prevent rust, simply dust off with a dry cloth.

It is always difficult to say how many people a recipe will feed, and even more difficult with noodles. So much depends on the individual's appetite and what else is offered. If you use any of these recipes out of context, for example as a side dish when it was intended as a main course, keep proportions in mind. The recipes may feed more people or fewer, depending on the rest of the meal.

Noodles are healthful, delicious, and fun. After a glance through this chapter, and maybe a sample, I hope you'll agree.

❖ Focus: Pasta ❖

The most basic of ingredients (flour, salt, and water) combine to form an enormous variety of noodle shapes to be eaten at a range of temperatures and at nearly any course. Pasta, literally "dough," was supposed to have originated in the Orient, but records show that as early as a century before the citizens of Pompeii were feasting on noodles.

Thomas Jefferson returned from Italy with a spaghetti machine, and Americans, along with many of the world's people, have been noodle fans ever since. Macaroni and cheese, and spaghetti and meatballs rank right up there with apple pie and the Statue of Liberty as all-American symbols.

Fresh pasta, though, is a bit of an unknown to many of us without Italian grandparents or big city stores. Contributing to the mystery can be the confusion over names. Even in Italy a pasta by one name in one district may go by another name in a neighboring one. But finding or making a recipe's specified pasta shape is often unnecessary, since pasta by any other name is still pasta.

Fresh pasta is best cooked within an hour of being made, though it may be dried for later use or wrapped in a plastic bag and refrigerated for up to 12 hours. Uncooked pasta may be frozen, but will be brittle and break easily. Fresh pasta doesn't expand when it is cooked as much as dried pasta, which may double.

Salt is sometimes added to the cooking water 1) on the theory it is absorbed by the pasta and 2) it ever so slightly raises the temperature of the boiling water, and the hotter the water the better the pasta. (I don't bother with salting the water.) Oil is added to prevent sticking (more important with fresh noodles) and boil-overs. Stir pasta several times when it is cooking to also help prevent it from clumping together. Use 3 quarts of water for every 8 ounces of pasta; too little water makes for sticky pasta, as does overcooking. Some have been known to test spaghetti by throwing a strand on the wall, but a more hygenic method is to pinch a noodle in half. If any white starchiness is visible at the core, boil the pasta a bit longer, but test it often.

❖Sodium-conscious consumers should keep in mind that a product with little or no salt added is not necessarily sodium free. There are 70 different sodium compounds used in processed foods, to say nothing of the sodium naturally occurring in foods.❖

UP SCALE

Dry-fried Salmon Fillets

Red Pepper Pasta with Vegetables and Herb Vinaigrette

Three-Green Salad with Champagne-Orange Vinaigrette and Melted Goat Cheese

Strawberry-Buttermilk Sherbet

Here's a decidedly "up scale" meal with salmon, goat cheese, and red pepper pasta that will not up your weight scale. An easy-on-the-cook, informal gathering of spring's best, this dinner for eight may be started early on the day of serving and completed in just a few hours, leaving only the salmon to dry-fry and the cheese to briefly heat at dinner time. This menu epitomizes *The Enlightened Gourmet*, for it is delicious as well as healthy. Salmon, for example, has been found to contain a particular kind of fat that can actually help reduce the amount of cholesterol in the bloodstream; pasta mixed with lots of fresh vegetables gives a strong serving of important complex carbohydrates; olive oil has recently been shown, in one study where the subjects were fed a diet with forty percent-fat content (two-thirds of it being monounsaturated like olive oil), to be *more* effective in lowering blood cholesterol than only a twenty percent-fat diet; buttermilk and goat cheese offer up a bit of bone-strengthening calcium. All in all, not a bad way to eat well and eat right.

Dry-fried Salmon Fillets

❖

One of spring's many gifts is salmon, and one of the best ways to cook it is as little as possible. This "dry-fry" (there's no butter or oil) requires a good nonstick skillet and a decent fan, but there is nowhere near the smoke of the Pan-blackened Swordfish on page 157. Be sure to buy the freshest possible salmon and keep it on ice in the refrigerator if it isn't to be cooked within a few hours.

> 2 lemons
> 1 tablespoon minced fresh parsley
> 2½ pounds salmon fillets

1. With a zester (a small tool that cuts a ridge in the lemon; its use is optional) remove strips about ½-inch apart around one lemon working from the blossom end to the tip. Reserve the strips of zest for another use or discard.
2. Slice this lemon crosswise into 8 thin slices. Poke out the seeds. Hold a lemon slice so the center is pushed out and the edges are up. Dip the center of the lemon slice in the parsley. Repeat with remaining lemon slices. Set slices aside for garnish.
3. Coat two 12-inch nonstick skillets lightly with cooking spray. (Or dry-fry the fish in two batches.) Heat the pans over high heat until a drop of water skitters on contact. Put the fish, skin side down, in the hot pans. Dry-fry the fish, frequently loosening it from the skillets with a spatula and turning the pans to ensure even heat, about 2 minutes on the skin side. Reduce the heat only if the fish starts to stick. Flip the fish over and cook at high heat for 2 minutes more on the other side. Season with the juice of the remaining lemon when the fish has about a minute left to cook.
4. Transfer the fish from the pans to a serving platter. Garnish each fillet with a parslied lemon slice. If fish is

done in 2 batches, keep the first batch warm in a pre-heated, then turned off, 150-degree oven, or on a warming tray.

Yield: 8 servings
✦ Calories per serving: 171
Carbohydrate per serving: 1g
✦ Cholesterol per serving: 50mg

Dietary fiber per serving: 0g
Fat per serving: 5g
Protein per serving: 28g
✦ Sodium per serving: 91mg

Red Pepper Pasta with Vegetables and Herb Vinaigrette

❖

Ribbons of homemade red pepper pasta generously tossed with crisp vegetables and a garden fragrant herb sauce—what could be better? Moreover, because the dish is served at room temperature or slightly chilled, it is completely prepared ahead. As a take-along or eat-at-home recipe, this is sure to be the star of any meal. It will serve 8 as a side dish, or 5 to 6 as the main dish.

Of course, store-bought fresh or boxed fettucine egg noodles will do fine in place of the homemade. And view the vegetable list (types and proportions) with an eye toward availability.

For the Red Pepper Pasta

2 cups all-purpose flour
1 teaspoon salt
½ teaspoon dried red pepper flakes
1 tablespoon olive oil
2 eggs

a few drops water
1 tablespoon vegetable oil for the cooking water

For the Vinaigrette

½ cup snipped fresh basil
½ cup minced fresh parsley
2 tablespoons minced fresh tarragon
2 tablespoons balsamic vinegar
¼ cup olive oil, extra-virgin recommended
⅓ cup homemade beef stock or canned beef
    consomme
3 tablespoons freshly grated Parmesan cheese
freshly ground black pepper to taste

For the Vegetables

6 ounces fresh asparagus
2 ounces fresh pea pods from snow peas or sugar
    snap peas
2 ounces fresh green beans
½ package frozen artichoke hearts (thawed and
    sliced) or 2 fresh artichokes
4 ounces mushrooms, sliced
juice of ½ lemon (about 2 tablespoons)
1 red bell pepper, diced

To Prepare the Pasta

1. To make the pasta in a food processor: Pour the flour into the bowl of a food processor. Add the salt, red pepper flakes, olive oil, and eggs. Process, adding drops of water, until the dough can be formed into a ball. To make the pasta by hand: Pour the flour, salt, and red pepper flakes into a mixing bowl. Make a well in the center and put the oil and eggs in it. Mix together with a fork or your fingertips, adding drops of water, until the dough can be formed into a rough ball.
2. Pinch off half the dough and work with one half at a

time. To knead the dough, set the smooth rollers of the pasta machine as far apart as possible (generally, the lowest setting on most pasta machines). Dust the dough with flour and feed it through the rollers. Reroll this strip 4 or 5 more times, folding under the ragged edges. Dust the dough with flour to prevent sticking, when necessary.

3. To roll out the dough: Set the machine to the second notch and feed the strip through the rollers. Repeat, advancing the notch a setting higher after each rolling so the rollers progressively come closer together and the dough gets thinner. Roll until dough has gone through the second to last setting (6). Leave the dough on the counter as you repeat steps 2 and 3 with the remaining half of dough.

4. To cut the pasta, feed the rolled strips through the wide blades of the pasta machine. Hang to dry slightly (10 to 20 minutes) on a pasta rack or over the back of a chair in a single layer.

5. To cook the pasta: Bring 6 to 8 quarts water with the tablespoon of vegetable oil to a boil. Gently stir in the noodles, stirring from time to time to prevent them from sticking together. Place a strainer or colander in the sink. When noodles are tender and cooked through—this will take about 2 minutes for fresh ones, 4 to 5 minutes for dried (to test for doneness, pinch a noodle in half; if traces of pure white remain at the center, boil for a few seconds more)—pour the noodles into the strainer.

6. Rinse the noodles with cool water and drain them. Set aside in a large bowl while you prepare the vinaigrette and vegetables. (If you are holding noodles more than half an hour, toss them with a bit of olive oil to prevent clumping.)

To Prepare the Vinaigrette and Vegetables

1. Combine all ingredients listed under vinaigrette in the bowl of a food processor or a blender. Process until well blended. Toss with the noodles.

2. Snap off and discard the tough white end of each asparagus stalk. Peel the stalks with a vegetable peeler if they are thick. Cut the stalks into bite-size pieces. Set the asparagus aside.

3. Remove the strings from the pea pods. Add to the asparagus.

4. Line up a handful of green beans and cut off the "tips and tails." Repeat with remaining beans.

5. Fit a 2½-quart saucepan with a removable steaming basket. Add an inch of water, cover, and bring the water to a boil. Add the green beans. Cover. Re-cover, and time 1 minute. Add the asparagus and pea pods. Add the frozen artichoke hearts if you are using them. Time 4 to 5 minutes, stirring vegetables once or twice, until vegetables are tender but still crisp.

6. Lift the steaming basket from the pan, and immediately run the vegetables under cold water to stop the cooking. Allow the vegetables to drain.

7. To prepare the fresh artichoke hearts: Cut off the stem of one artichoke. With a stainless steel knife, pare the artichoke as if peeling an apple, removing the top 2 or 3 layers of tough, deep green leaves. Cut off the top third of the artichoke. Turn the artichoke upside down and be sure all the tough, dark green leaves are trimmed from the bottom. (See illustrations on pages 77–78.) Spread the leaves at the top of the artichoke apart. With a spoon, remove the fuzzy center (the choke). Slice the heart into ⅛-inch-thick slices. Repeat with the remaining artichoke.

8. Coat an 8-inch skillet with cooking spray. Heat the pan over high heat, uncovered, until a drop of water skitters on contact. Add the mushrooms, sliced fresh artichoke hearts, and lemon juice. Saute at high heat until the liquid is evaporated, about 4 minutes. Add mushrooms and artichokes to other cooked vegetables.

9. Toss the cooked vegetables and the diced red pepper with the noodles. The pasta is ready to serve or may be held, covered with plastic wrap, at room temperature up to 3 hours or refrigerated up to 24 hours before

serving. If you do chill it, allow it to come to room temperature before serving. Pass extra grated Parmesan at the table if desired.

Yield: 8 side dish servings
+ **Calories per serving: 256**
  Carbohydrate per serving: 33g
+ **Cholesterol per serving: 62mg**

+ **Dietary fiber per serving: 2g**
  Fat per serving: 11g
  Protein per serving: 9g
+ **Sodium per serving: 378mg**

Three-Green Salad with Champagne-Orange Vinaigrette and Melted Goat Cheese

❖

This special salad with its delightfully light vinaigrette is a tangle of arugula, red leaf, and salad bowl lettuces served with a dollop of warmed, runny goat cheese.

Arugula is a perfumy, tangy green better known in southern European countries than in the United States. In peak season from May to October, it's a treat not to be missed, particularly if you enjoy the flavor of watercress. It is very high in calcium, vitamin A, and vitamin C.

One needn't buy a fine champagne for the dressing; any drinkable bottle will do. On the outside chance you'd rather cook with the remaining champagne, there is a recipe for Mimosa Sherbet in *Gourmet Light*. The walnut oil is available at specialty food stores; keep it refrigerated after opening.

Prepare the dressing and wash and dry the lettuces up to 24 hours in advance. The cheese may be crumb-coated several hours ahead, but slide it into the oven (a microwave oven won't do) just 10 to 15 minutes before serving. The cheese should still be warmed when served with the crisply cool greens.

For the Dressing

4 tablespoons walnut oil
3 tablespoons dry champagne
2 teaspoons lemon juice
1 teaspoon sugar
grated rind (zest) of an orange

For the Salad

3 ounces goat cheese, such as Montrachet or
    Bucheron
2 tablespoons dried bread crumbs
1 teaspoon walnut oil
1 bunch arugula, rinsed and spun dry
½ head red leaf lettuce, rinsed and spun dry
½ head salad bowl lettuce, rinsed and spun dry

To Prepare the Dressing

1. Combine all the dressing ingredients in a screw-top jar. Shake well to combine. The dressing may be used immediately or held up to 48 hours before using.

To Prepare the Salad

1. Preheat oven to 400 degrees. Coat the cheese in the bread crumbs. Place the cheese in a small baking dish. Drizzle with the teaspoon of walnut oil.
2. Bake the cheese until it is runny, about 10 minutes. Slide it under the broiler briefly, if needed, to brown the crumbs.
3. Meanwhile, tear the greens into a salad bowl and toss with the vinaigrette. Serve the salad onto 8 chilled

salad plates, making a little well in the center of each plate.

4. Place a spoonful of cheese in the well and serve.

Yield: 8 servings
✦ Calories per serving: 113
Carbohydrate per serving: 3g
✦ Cholesterol per serving: 8mg

Dietary fiber per serving: 0g
Fat per serving: 10g
Protein per serving: 3g
✦ Sodium per serving: 92mg

Strawberry-Buttermilk Sherbet
❖

Who would believe buttermilk could be the base of a most delicious, waist-conscious dessert? Yet here it is, smooth and tangy-sweet, and you need nothing more complicated than your refrigerator. Start the sherbet the day before serving to allow for adequate chilling; it will keep in the freezer about 2 to 3 days before becoming grainy. Don't worry about wasting the leftover quart of buttermilk; there are several recipes using buttermilk in this book (Whole Wheat Oatmeal Muffins, Buttermilk Salad Dressing, and more). The leftover strawberries are excellent spooned over Honeyed Lemon Frost, page 203, or spooned on this sherbet.

1¼ cups frozen strawberries with sugar
2 cups skimmed buttermilk
4 tablespoons sugar
2 egg whites
1 teaspoon vanilla extract

1. Thaw the strawberries on the counter or in a microwave oven.

2. Combine the berries with the buttermilk and sugar in a food processor or blender. Blend.
3. Pour the strawberry mixture into an 8-inch-square baking pan or other shallow container and freeze until it has the consistency of mush, about 1 to 2 hours. Chill a mixing bowl at the same time the strawberry mixture goes into the freezer.
4. Scrape the strawberry mixture into the chilled bowl. Add the egg whites and vanilla. Beat with a hand-held mixer until the sherbet is well blended and smooth.
5. Return the mixture to the shallow pan and freeze until firm, about 3 hours, stirring every so often. Sherbet is now ready to serve or may be beaten and refrozen for greater smoothness. Soften the sherbet at room temperature about 20 minutes before serving.

Note: An ice cream freezer will give a smoother product with fewer ice crystals, of course. Follow steps 1, 2, and 4, omitting the freezing and chilled bowl step. Follow manufacturer's directions for freezing in the ice cream maker.

Yield: 1 quart; 8 ½-cup servings
✦ Calories per serving: 93
Carbohydrate per serving: 20g
✦ Cholesterol per serving: 3g

Dietary fiber per serving: 0g
Fat per serving: 1g
Protein per serving: 3g
✦ Sodium per serving: 78mg

❖A study to determine the single largest contributor of salt to a teen-ager's diet found a rather surprising culprit. It wasn't the salt shaker on the table or at the stove, nor the chips or other salty snack foods kids seem to crave, but bakery products—cookies, cakes, muffins, breads, and the like—that accounted for the largest dose of sodium.❖

ICY HEAT

**Angel Hair Pasta with Ham
and Peas in "Cream" Sauce**

Mediterranean Salad

Honeyed Lemon Frost

Making a cream sauce without any cream or a sherbet with very little sweetener *and* having them both taste terrific is the focus of "Icy Heat." This menu for four to six shows there are no secrets, no need for tedious kitchen workouts, just knowledge of some basic low-calorie cooking techniques to turn out some terrific nonfattening foods.

The pasta dish is as healthful as it is delicious. Long on complex carbohydrates and low-fat calcium sources, it keeps often-high-fat proteins and other saturated fats, like butter, cheeses, and oils, in check. Used here as the focal point, a small serving of the angel hair pasta would also make a nice beginning for a more formal dinner, perhaps followed by a simple grilled, broiled, or steamed fish.

Should you cook the menu in its entirety, begin the day before by completing the Mediterranean Salad and preparing the Honeyed Lemon Frost through the first or second freezing. You'll only have to make the noodles (or buy them), whip up the sauce, and complete the final steps of the lemon dessert on the day of the dinner.

Angel Hair Pasta with Ham and Peas in "Cream" Sauce

❖

It's hard to believe this creamy pasta dish studded with peas, mushrooms, and ham never sees a cream carton. The secret lies in lowered-fat dairy products, such as cottage cheese and milk, which easily blend into a velvety smooth sauce with fewer calories—but all of the flavor— of a traditional cream sauce. If you've neither the time nor inclination to make your own angel hair (very thin) pasta, purchase fresh angel hair noodles or even boxed thin spaghetti. The sauce takes little more than 15 minutes to prepare, but may be made several hours early and held, covered and chilled, until serving time. But if you're cooking just before serving, start with mixing the noodle dough, kneading it, and rolling the strips. Next, make the sauce while the pasta dries (unlike other pastas, angel hair needs to rest at least 15 minutes and as long as 30 minutes before cutting or the strands "glue" together). Finally, cut and boil the pasta, and voila!

For the Sauce

½ cup homemade chicken stock or canned
    chicken broth
2 tablespoons olive oil, extra-virgin recommended
12 ounces mushrooms, sliced
2 garlic cloves, minced
6 ounces ready-to-cook ham, diced
1⅓ cups fresh or frozen peas
2 blanched, peeled, and seeded (see page 177)
    tomatoes (optional)
1 cup low-fat milk

8 tablespoons low-fat cottage cheese
2 tablespoons freshly grated Parmesan cheese
1 tablespoon plus 1 teaspoon arrowroot
freshly ground black pepper to taste

For the Angel Hair Noodles

1½ cups all-purpose flour
1 teaspoon salt
2 eggs
a few drops water

To Complete the Dish

1 tablespoon vegetable oil for the cooking water
1 tablespoon unsalted butter, at room
    temperature
freshly grated Parmesan cheese to pass at the
    table

To Prepare the Sauce

1. Heat the stock and olive oil in a 10-inch skillet over high heat until bubbly.
2. Add the mushrooms and garlic. Saute over medium-high heat until the mushrooms are lightly browned and the garlic is softened, about 2 minutes.
3. Add the ham. Cook over medium-high heat about 1 minute. Stir the peas into the skillet. Cook about 30 seconds over medium-high heat. Turn the mixture into a bowl.
4. Chop the tomato pulp and stir it into the ham-mushroom mixture. Set aside.
5. In a food processor or blender combine the milk, cottage cheese, Parmesan cheese, arrowroot, and ground pepper. Blend until smooth. Pour into the empty skillet. Cook the mixture over medium-high heat, whisking

constantly, until the sauce thickens, about 4 minutes.

6. Stir mushroom-ham mixture into sauce. Taste and adjust seasoning. (The sauce may be made several hours ahead. Cover and chill, or keep warm up to half an hour on the stove, covered, over very low heat.)

To Prepare the Noodles

1. To make the dough in a food processor: Pour the flour into the bowl of a food processor. Add the salt and eggs. Process, adding tiny drops of water, until the dough can be formed into a ball. To make the dough by hand: Pour the flour and salt into a mixing bowl. Make a well in the center and put the egg in it. Mix together with a fork or your fingertips, adding tiny drops of water, until the dough can be formed into a ball.

2. Pinch off half the dough and work with one half at a time. To knead the dough, set the smooth rollers of the pasta machine as far apart as possible (generally, the lowest setting on most machines). Dust the dough with flour and feed it through the rollers. Reroll this strip 4 or 5 more times, folding the dough in half and the ragged edges under. Dust the dough with flour, as necessary, to prevent sticking.

3. To roll out the dough: Set the machine to the second notch and feed the strip through the rollers. Repeat, advancing the notch a setting higher after each rolling so the rollers progressively come closer together and the dough gets thinner. Roll the dough through the second-to-last setting (6) or the last setting (7) if the dough doesn't tear. (Should the dough tear, fold it in half and start rolling from the second setting again.) Dust the strip thoroughly with flour and dry it at least 15 minutes or up to 30 minutes before cutting. Repeat steps 2 and 3 with the remaining dough.

4. To cut the dough into angel hair noodles, feed a single pasta strip through the narrow cutting blades of the pasta machine. Drape the noodles in one layer over a chair or pasta rack to dry slightly. They may be cooked

after 10 minutes of drying time or may be dried as long as 2 hours, but they will be brittle and may break easily if held longer.

To Cook and Assemble

1. Heat the sauce, if necessary, over low heat, stirring often. Heat 6 dinner plates. Set a strainer or colander in the sink.
2. Bring 6 to 8 quarts of water with the tablespoon of vegetable oil to a boil. Gently drop the noodles into the water. Stir to prevent sticking. Freshly made noodles will be done (no bright white center when the noodle is pinched) in 2 to 3 minutes, and dried ones in 5 to 6 minutes. Drain the noodles.
3. Toss the noodles immediately with the tablespoon of butter. Combine with the sauce in the skillet. Toss gently to combine. Divide among heated plates. Pass grated Parmesan cheese at the table.

Yield: 6 servings
✦ Calories per serving: 299
Carbohydrate per serving: 33g
Cholesterol per serving: 112mg

Dietary fiber per serving: 1g
Fat per serving: 11g
Protein per serving: 20g
Sodium per serving: 564mg

Mediterranean Salad

—————————————— ❖ ——————————————

Unlike most salads, this one actually improves with age. It may be served two, even three days after being made, and is a great snack to have on hand in the refrigerator. Let these ingredients and their proportions be nothing more than a guide; most vegetables are a welcome addition. This is pretty and particularly appealing served on glass plates.

For the Vegetables

½ head cauliflower, about 8 ounces
1 stalk broccoli, about 5 ounces
1 small summer squash
8 asparagus spears
3 tablespoons homemade chicken stock or
    canned chicken broth
4 ounces mushrooms, sliced
1 red bell pepper, thinly sliced

For the Dressing

3 tablespoons olive oil, extra-virgin recommended
2 tablespoons canned beef consomme or
    homemade beef stock
2 tablespoons lemon juice
1 small garlic clove, minced
1 teaspoon sugar
6–7 leaves fresh basil, snipped
1 scallion, minced
1 tablespoon minced fresh parsley
½ teaspoon salt
freshly ground black pepper to taste

1. Fill a 2½-quart saucepan three-quarters full with water. Bring it to a boil. Meanwhile, core the cauliflower and separate the flowerets. Cut the broccoli flowerets from the stems. Cut the broccoli and cauliflower flowerets into thin strips. Peel and julienne the stems.
2. When the water is boiling, add the cauliflower and broccoli. Boil, uncovered, 4 minutes or until vegetables are just tender when pierced with a fork. Drain and cool the vegetables under running water. Drain.
3. Half-fill the same saucepan with water and bring it to a boil again. Meanwhile, cut the summer squash in half across. Cut the halves in half the long way. Cut each quarter into thin sticks. Set aside.
4. Peel the asparagus spears with a vegetable peeler.

Grasp the spear at the tip; pull the peeler down the length of the stalk, rotating the spear as each length is finished. Cut the spears crosswise into 2- or 3-inch lengths. When the water is boiling, add the summer squash and asparagus. Boil, uncovered, for 4 to 5 minutes. Drain and cool under running water. Drain.

5. Add the chicken stock to the empty saucepan and place over high heat. When small bubbles appear, add the mushrooms and "saute" until the mushrooms are limp and the stock has evaporated, about 3 to 4 minutes. Turn into a large bowl.

6. Add the pepper, broccoli, cauliflower, summer squash, and asparagus to the mushrooms in the bowl. Toss gently to combine.

7. Combine all the dressing ingredients in a screw-top jar and shake to combine.

8. Pour the dressing over the vegetables and toss gently. Cover with plastic wrap. The salad can sit at room temperature up to 3 hours or be refrigerated. But if it is refrigerated, it should be brought to room temperature before serving. The salad will keep up to 3 days, chilled.

Yield: 6 servings
✦ Calories per serving: 103
Carbohydrate per serving: 9g
✦ Cholesterol per serving: 0mg
✦ Dietary fiber per serving: 2g
Fat per serving: 7g
Protein per serving: 3g
✦ Sodium per serving: 213mg

Honeyed Lemon Frost

❖

Here is a cool, lemony sherbet to prepare ahead without the aid of an ice cream maker. Serve it in lemon cups, frosty from the freezer, for a sweet finish to a meal. A dollop of raspberry or strawberry puree (see page 26) is perfect with it. Start the recipe (and finish it if you like) a day or two before serving or at least 7 to 8 hours before.

> 8 lemons (6 should be large and nicely shaped)
> 1½ cups low-fat or skim milk
> ½ cup non-fat dry milk powder
> ⅓ cup honey
> mint or fresh lemon leaves and 6 strawberries for garnish (optional)

1. Sort the lemons, choosing the 6 largest as serving cups. Set aside. Rub the remaining 2 lemons over the fine side of a hand-held grater to remove the zest. Reserve the zest. Squeeze the two lemons and reserve the juice. Discard the seeds.
2. In a bowl or a large measuring cup combine the milk, dry milk powder, honey, lemon zest, and lemon juice. Whisk or mix with a hand-held mixer to combine.
3. Pour the mixture into a shallow 8-inch-square pan. Cover with plastic wrap and freeze until the edges are frozen and the middle remains somewhat soft, about 3 hours.
4. Scrape the mixture into a food processor and process until the mixture is smooth. Return it to the pan, cover, and freeze again until firm, about 3 hours or overnight.
5. Soften lemon frost at room temperature until it is easily removed from the pan, about 20 minutes. Meanwhile, prepare the lemon cups.
6. Take a thin slice off the bottom (pointed end) of the lemon so it sits upright. Slice off the top inch of the lemon. With a paring knife, free the lemon flesh from the shell by reaming the knife around the flesh from both the top and bottom ends of the lemon. Be careful not to pierce the shell. The lemon flesh will easily push out. With a spoon, scrape the inside of the lemon shell to extract the juice. Repeat with the remaining lemons. Reserve the juice and flesh for another use.
7. Scrape the lemon frost into a food processor and process until smooth. Set lemon cups upright on a serving platter that can go into the freezer. Spoon the lemon

frost into the lemon cups. Cover with plastic wrap, then with foil. Refreeze for at least 1 hour or for as long as 24. Allow the lemon frost to soften at room temperature (this will take about 20 to 25 minutes if it is frozen hard) before garnishing with mint or lemon leaves and strawberries and serving.

Yield: 6 servings

✦ Calories per serving: 126

Carbohydrate per serving: 26g

✦ Cholesterol per serving: 4mg

Dietary fiber per serving: 0g

Fat per serving: 1g

Protein per serving: 6g

✦ Sodium per serving: 85mg

❖Foods grown organically (that is without "chemical" fertilizers) do not have more vitamins than those grown with the aid of fertilizers. Such is the mutual conclusion of three different studies, one ongoing for 34 years. The tests agreed bettered soil can improve the yield and size of the crop but not the major nutritional characteristics, which are determined instead by the genes of the plant. Fertilizers can influence the mineral makeup of plants, however. Trace elements such as zinc, cobalt, iodine, and selenium will vary with the amount of these minerals found in the soil.❖

PERFECT PARTNERS

Basil Fettucine with Mussels in Red Wine Sauce

Crusty French Bread*

Shredded Cucumber Salad

Basil and tomatoes, mussels and red wine make perfect partners when paired with fresh egg noodles in this informal pasta supper for six.

Until recently mussels weren't much enjoyed here in America, although they've long been highly prized in Europe. Perhaps due to the rising costs of other shellfish, however, the demand for these nutritious, low-fat bivalves has quadrupled in recent years; Americans now eat about four million pounds a year. Many of these are cultivated—grown in undersea farms—with all the flavor of "wild" mussels but considerably cleaner. With the low cost and low calories (3½ ounces of mussel meat have only 95 calories) come a good source of protein, calcium, and iron. They are mild in flavor with a pleasant texture. They are never eaten raw, unlike clams or oysters. What's keeping even more people from cooking with them then? Probably not knowing what to do with them.

Cleaning is the hardest part. Instructions are included in the Basil Fettucine recipe. Scrub any shells that seem particularly dirty, and remove barnacles with a dull knife. (Cultivated mussels are nearly barnacle-free.) Be thorough, as one shell filled with mud or grit can ruin an entire dish. When purchasing, buy only from a store with a high turnover rate. Mussels are dead (and should be discarded) if they refuse to close when tapped or float to the surface when soaked. Use the mussels within a day or two of purchase, keeping them on ice in the refrigerator if you are keeping them more than four or five hours.

The mussel sauce for this pasta dish may be prepared

several hours ahead. Serve a loaf of crusty French or Italian bread for hungry supper-mates and set the meal off with the cool do-ahead cucumber salad.

Basil Fettucine with Mussels in Red Wine Sauce

❖

Red wine, garlic, shallot, and tomatoes are the basics that make this do-ahead sauce for basil fettucine an appetite pleaser with a heady aroma. It is a dish for those who like hearty fare that is also fair to the heart.

Three ingredient notes: If the thought of making your own pasta elicits nothing so much as tiresome sighs, pick up a package of fresh fettucine noodles or dried egg noodles from the grocery store. Second, for the ½ cup of tomato sauce, any leftover or canned tomato or spaghetti sauce would do nicely, or you might like to make up a batch of Tomato Sauce (see page 351) to have on hand in the freezer. Third, be very sure the mussels are perfectly clean. One shell full of mud or grit can ruin all your effort.

Both the shellfish sauce and pasta may be made several hours ahead, if you wish. And don't forget to warm those plates!

For the Sauce

4 pounds mussels
2 shallots, minced
2 leeks, white part only, diced and rinsed
1 large garlic clove, minced
3 cups dry red wine
½ cup minced fresh parsley
12 ounces mushrooms, sliced

½ cup tomato sauce (store-bought or
     homemade—see page 351) or 2 ripe
     tomatoes
5-6 fresh basil leaves, snipped
1 teaspoon orange zest
freshly ground black pepper to taste

For the Fettucine

2 cups all-purpose flour
2 eggs
8-10 fresh basil leaves, snipped, or ½ teaspoon
     dried basil
1 tablespoon olive oil
1 teaspoon salt
a few drops water

To Complete the Dish

1 tablespoon vegetable oil for the cooking water
1 tablespoon unsalted butter, at room
     temperature
freshly grated Parmesan cheese to pass at the
     table

To Prepare the Sauce

1. Soak the mussels in a big bowl, covered with water.
   Add a handful of cornmeal (theory has it the mussels
   ingest the cornmeal, forcing them to expel grit and
   sand) and let the mussels soak for 20 minutes.
2. Meanwhile, combine the shallots, leeks, garlic, wine,
   and parsley (reserve 2 tablespoons of parsley for garnishing the finished dish) in a 12-inch skillet. Bring to a
   boil over high heat, cover, and simmer 15 to 20 minutes
   while you clean the mussels.
3. To clean the mussels, lift them from the bowl to a colander (don't pour, or all the sand will be washed back
   into the mussels). Rinse the shellfish thoroughly in the

colander. Then pull off the beards—the black thread-like strings—with a small knife. Try to slide the top and bottom shells in opposite directions between your thumb and index finger. Disregard any shells that move easily, are open, or full of mud. Rinse the mussels again under lots of running water. Drain.

4. Add the mussels to the simmering wine mixture. Stir, cover, and bring to a boil over high heat. Mussels are done when all shells have opened, about 3 to 5 minutes. (Discard any mussels whose shells remain closed.) Pour the wine mixture and mussels into a sieve set over a bowl. Lift the sieve from the bowl and set it on a double thickness of paper towel to let the mussels cool and allow the broth to rest undisturbed so the inevitable bits of grit and sand settle to the bottom.

5. Coat a nonstick 12-inch skillet with cooking spray. Saute the mushrooms until lightly browned, about 5 minutes, stirring often. Remove from the heat and set aside.

6. Remove the empty half of each mussel shell. Add mussels in the remaining half-shell to the mushrooms.

7. Line a sieve or colander with a wrung-out cheesecloth or a thin kitchen towel. Place the sieve over a bowl. Pour the cooking broth (but not the grit that has settled to the bottom) through, pressing the solids with the back of a spoon. Add the broth to the mushrooms-mussels. Discard the solids and grit on the bottom of the bowl.

8. Stir the tomato sauce, basil, orange zest, and pepper into the mussels and broth. Stir well to combine ingredients. (Sauce may be made to this point several hours ahead and chilled, or made 1 hour ahead and kept, covered, over very low heat.)

To Prepare the Fettucine

1. To make the pasta in a food processor: Pour the flour into the bowl of a food processor. Add the eggs, basil, olive oil, and salt. Process, adding drops of water, until

the dough can be formed into a ball. To make the pasta by hand: Pour the flour and salt into a mixing bowl. Make a well in the center and put the eggs, basil, oil, and salt in it. Mix together with a fork or your fingertips, adding drops of water, until the dough can be formed into a rough ball.

2. Pinch off a third of the dough and work one third at a time. To knead the dough, set the smooth rollers of the pasta machine as far apart as possible (generally, the lowest setting on most pasta machines). Dust the dough with flour and feed it through the rollers. Reroll this strip 4 or 5 more times, folding under the ragged edges and dusting the dough with flour, when necessary, to prevent sticking.

3. To roll out the dough: Set the machine to the second notch and feed the strip through the rollers. Repeat, advancing the notch after each rolling so the rollers progressively come closer together and the dough gets thinner. Finally roll the dough through the last (7) notch setting to make the dough as thin as possible.

4. To cut the pasta, feed the rolled strips through the wide blades of the pasta machine. Hang to dry slightly in a single layer on a pasta rack or over the back of a chair. (Pasta may be made a few hours in advance and allowed to dry before cooking. Increase cooking time by 3 to 4 minutes for dried pasta.) Repeat steps 2, 3, and 4 with remaining two thirds of dough.

To Assemble and Serve

1. Heat the sauce if necessary over medium-low heat until steamy. Keep warm while cooking the noodles. Heat the plates.

2. Bring 6 to 8 quarts of water with the tablespoon of vegetable oil to a boil. Gently stir in the fettucine noodles, stirring from time to time to prevent them from sticking together. Place a strainer or colander in the sink. When noodles are tender and cooked through, about 2 minutes for fresh noodles (pinch a noodle in half; if traces

of pure white remain at center, boil for a few seconds more), pour them into the strainer.

3. Drain. Toss the noodles with the butter. Slip the noodles into the steaming sauce and toss with two spoons to combine. Divide the pasta and sauce among the heated plates. Garnish with the reserved 2 tablespoons of parsley. Pass grated Parmesan cheese at the table.

Yield: 6 servings
Calories per serving: 468
Carbohydrate per serving: 53g
✦ **Cholesterol per serving: 86mg**

✦ **Dietary fiber per serving: 3g**
Fat per serving: 9g
Protein per serving: 24g
Sodium per serving: 749mg

Shredded Cucumber Salad

Cucumbers and carrots pair up here to make a deliciously different salad that will hold, chilled, for 3 or 4 hours before being served. Besides being delicious with the Basil Fettucine, this salad also makes an ideal dish for picnics or other movable feasts when a salad is called for but impractical to transport. Try to buy the long, English, nearly seedless cucumbers for this salad; they seem a bit less watery. They are available at most supermarkets.

1 large seedless English cucumber, unpeeled
2 small carrots
1 green pepper, diced
3 scallions, minced
3 tablespoons safflower oil
1½ tablespoons raspberry or white wine vinegar
½ teaspoon salt
dash of cayenne pepper to taste
8–10 leaves lettuce to line plates

1. Shred the cucumber and carrot on the coarse side of a hand-held grater into a bowl. Stir in the green pepper and scallions.
2. Season with oil, vinegar, salt, and cayenne. Stir well to combine. Cover and chill for 3 to 4 hours or serve immediately. To serve, line 6 salad plates with lettuce. Scoop cucumber salad onto lettuce.

Yield: 6 servings
✦ Calories per serving: 85
Carbohydrate per serving: 6g
✦ Cholesterol per serving: 0mg

Dietary fiber per serving: 1g
Fat per serving: 7g
Protein per serving: 1g
✦ Sodium per serving: 302mg

❖An improved, healthier American diet is paid lots of lip service but, with few exceptions, we are eating pretty much as we did 20 years ago. We may be eating a little less red meat in the 1980s than we did in 1970, but still more than we did in 1960. We do eat more poultry and fish and fewer eggs now, but fat consumption, considered the single largest dietary problem by many health experts, is actually up. And we eat fewer grains and cereal products, those complex carbohydrates we should be getting more of while the quantity of fruits and vegetables remains the same. As a nation, we've come a long, long way in many aspects, but in terms of a healthy diet, we did better at the turn of the century.❖

EAST MEETS WEST

**Buckwheat Pasta Salad with
Spinach and Scallops**

**Tomato Slices with Basil and
Extra-virgin Olive Oil**

Buckwheat, soy, mirin, and ginger—trademarks of Oriental cuisine—ally here with tomatoes, basil, and olive oil to form a most compatible union. This is casual stuff, great for a foursome as a picnic or a light patio supper on a hot summer night. Prepare the buckwheat pasta salad early in the day, and dinner's a breeze with nothing more taxing than tomatoes to slice. Easily varied, the salad is good with sliced radishes, shrimp instead of scallops or as a complement for them, and slices of water chestnuts. A spoonful of tahini paste (available at specialty food shops and some grocery stores) would be delicious stirred in with the soy sauce and cooking wine. Serve the salad dish warm, at room temperature, or slightly chilled, but not too cold (low temperatures dull the flavors).

If you prefer not to make your own noodles, buckwheat noodles may be purchased at most Oriental and some health food stores.

❖Cigarettes, alcohol, and medication can interfere with the body's normal vitamin requirements. Cigarette smokers may need extra vitamin C. Drinkers or those who eat lots of sugar may need more of the B vitamins, as may persons on antibiotics for long periods of time. A vitamin supplement is not necessarily in order, though; extra helpings of fruits and vegetables will do the trick.❖

Buckwheat Pasta Salad with Spinach and Scallops

❖

When you've tired of the increasingly predictable pasta salad, give this one a try. Very Japanese in spirit with its buckwheat noodles, ginger, and soy, this dish is as good the second day as the first. It's eminently portable too—a natural candidate for the picnic basket if you choose. Pack chopsticks rather than forks, for after all, with this dish, East meets West.

Buckwheat flour—prepared from the seeds of an herb plant, not a grasslike wheat—is available at health food or specialty food shops, and some supermarkets. If there's none to be found in your area, buckwheat pancake mix, which is carried at most stores, will do just fine. (Or buy buckwheat noodles at Oriental markets or health food stores.) Because the buckwheat pasta strips need to dry at least 15 minutes but no more than 30 minutes, begin by making the noodles. While the strips dry, put together the sauce, then cut the noodles and cook them. Toss the two together and serve the salad warm, room temperature, or slightly chilled.

The Chinese cooking wine or mirin, hot oil, and sesame oil are available at Oriental food shops and specialty food shops.

For the Buckwheat Noodles

½ cup buckwheat flour or buckwheat pancake
   mix
½ cup all-purpose flour
1 teaspoon salt
1 egg
about 3 teaspoons water

For the Sauce

4 ounces mushrooms, sliced
1 garlic clove, minced
3 tablespoons homemade beef stock or canned
    beef broth or consomme
¾ pound scallops
juice of half a lemon
1 teaspoon arrowroot
2 tablespoons reduced-sodium soy sauce
¼ cup Chinese cooking wine or mirin
2 teaspoons minced fresh ginger
1 scallion, minced
3 cups chopped raw spinach, stems removed
¼ teaspoon or to taste hot oil

To Complete the Dish

1 tablespoon peanut oil
1 teaspoon or to taste sesame oil

To Prepare the Buckwheat Noodles

1. To make the noodles in a food processor: Pour the flours into the bowl of a food processor. Add the salt and egg. Process, adding drops of water, until the dough can be formed into a ball. Buckwheat flour takes more water than white flours and the dough is more crumbly. Pinch the dough with your fingertips to determine if it will hold together rather than allowing a ball to form in the food processor. To make by hand: Pour the flours and salt into a mixing bowl. Make a well in the center and put the egg in it. Mix together with a fork or your fingertips, adding drops of water, until the dough can be formed into a ball.

2. Pinch off half the dough and work with one half at a time. To knead the dough, set the smooth rollers of the pasta machine as far apart as possible (generally, the

lowest setting, 1, on most pasta machines). Dust the dough with flour and feed it through the rollers. Buckwheat dough is very crumbly and will break apart in the first few rollings. Don't despair; simply fold the dough over and keep rolling, dusting with flour to prevent sticking, until a smooth strip is formed.

3. To roll out the dough: Set the machine to the second notch and feed the strip through the rollers. Repeat, advancing the notch a setting higher after each rolling so the rollers progressively come closer together and the dough gets thinner. Continue until the dough is rolled through the last setting (7).

4. Dust the pasta strip with flour on both sides and let it rest at least 15 but no more than 30 minutes while you make the sauce. Repeat the kneading and rolling steps with the remaining dough.

To Prepare the Sauce

1. Combine the mushrooms, garlic, and beef stock in a 10-inch skillet. "Saute" the mushrooms and garlic over high heat until the stock has evaporated and the mushrooms are limp, about 3 minutes.

2. Add the scallops to the skillet. Season with lemon juice and cover. Cook at high heat, stirring occasionally, until the scallops are opaque, about 3 to 4 minutes.

3. While the scallops cook, dissolve the arrowroot in the soy sauce.

4. Uncover the skillet. Stir in the soy sauce, cooking wine, ginger, and scallion. Stir over medium-high heat until the sauce thickens slightly, about 2 minutes.

5. Remove the skillet from heat. Stir in the spinach. It will wilt slightly from the heat of the sauce. Add a few drops of hot oil to taste. (Sauce may be held, off heat, covered, for up to ½ hour. If you want to hold it longer, cover and refrigerate.)

To Cut and Cook the Pasta and Complete the Dish

1. When the sauce is completed, feed a single pasta strip through the narrow cutting blades of the pasta machine. The noodles are ready to cook immediately, or they may be dried (draped over the back of a chair or on a pasta rack to dry) as long as 2 hours. They will be brittle and may break easily if they are held longer.

2. Bring 6 to 8 quarts of water with the tablespoon of peanut oil to a boil. Set a sieve or colander into the sink. Gently drop the noodles into the water. Stir to prevent them from sticking together. Freshly made noodles will be done (no bright white center when a noodle is pinched apart) in 2 minutes; dried ones in 5 to 6 minutes. Drain the noodles in the colander.

3. Turn the drained noodles into a large bowl. Season the noodles with the sesame oil. Toss with the sauce. Taste and adjust seasoning if necessary. The salad may be served immediately or held chilled, covered with plastic wrap, up to 24 hours before serving.

Yield: 4 servings
+ Calories per serving: 226
Carbohydrate per serving: 31g
Cholesterol per serving: 92mg

+ Dietary fiber per serving: 2g
Fat per serving: 3g
Protein per serving: 20g
Sodium per serving: 5097mg

Tomato Slices with Basil and Extra-virgin Olive Oil

❖

The finest of summer salads is, I think, the simplest. Ripe-to-bursting tomatoes drizzled with best-quality olive oil and a snipping of basil requires no time and no imagination, but is unsurpassed by more elaborate concoctions.

For peak flavor, the tomatoes should be at room temperature, not chilled. A bit of chèvre crumbled over the dressed tomatoes is an added treat.

> *2 large, very ripe tomatoes*
> *1½ tablespoons olive oil, extra-virgin*
> *   recommended*
> *2–3 fresh basil leaves, snipped*
> *⅛ teaspoon salt*
> *freshly ground black pepper to taste*

1. Core the tomatoes and slice them crosswise into ¼-inch-thick slices. Place, slightly overlapping, on individual salad plates or on a small serving platter.
2. Drizzle the tomatoes with the oil, sprinkle with basil, and season with salt and pepper. Serve within half an hour.

Yield: 4 servings
✦ **Calories per serving: 59**
Carbohydrate per serving: 3g
✦ **Cholesterol per serving: 0mg**

Dietary fiber per serving: 1g
Fat per serving: 5g
Protein per serving: 1g
✦ **Sodium per serving: 100mg**

❖ Focus: Osteoporosis ❖ and Calcium

One quarter of American women over the age of 65 suffer from a potentially debilitating weakening of the bones. Osteoporosis, loss of bone matter, is of particular concern to women, for the rate of bone loss accelerates after menopause. Women who check off two or more of the following risk factors—compiled by the University of California, Berkeley Wellness Letter—may well be concerned about the amount of calcium in their diet, their estrogen level, and how much weight-bearing exercise they're getting: At risk are those who:

- smoke,
- exercise infrequently,

- are fair-skinned,
- are small-boned,
- have dieted frequently,
- regularly take three or more drinks,
- have been underweight most of their life.

The first noticeable signs of osteoporosis may be a decrease in height, the beginnings of a humped back, and proneness to fractures, most notably of the hip and spine.

Although the Food and Nutrition Board, a branch of the National Academy of Sciences, currently recommends consuming 800 milligrams of calcium daily (new RDAs are expected in the future), many health experts are urging women of all ages to get 1000 to even 1500 milligrams daily. The chairman of the Food and Nutrition Board believes it is as important for young women as for menopausal women to get enough calcium.

There is some debate, though, about the advisability of popping calcium supplements, which women are doing in ever-increasing numbers. Nay-sayers warn of kidney stones, lowered zinc and iron absorption, wasted calcium if the diet isn't high enough in phosphorous (since calcium can't be put into the bones except as calcium phosphate), constipation, and possible interference with the absorption of needed medicines. They would have us get all our calcium needs from food. Those in favor of calcium supplements suggest that if the mineral isn't supplied in sufficient quantity by the diet—which it frequently isn't—pills may be in order.

Women aren't the only persons who need be concerned about getting enough calcium, however. Adolescent girls, persons with high blood pressure, and persons with family histories of colon cancer might want to consider the mineral more seriously. Teenage girls, for example, frequently stop drinking milk in the perpetual pursuit of slimness. Surveys have shown that calcium intake has dropped 10 percent from the already inadequate level found during the early 1970s. Many doctors are urging women to raise calcium intake during young adulthood as an important preventive measure.

In two studies, calcium has also been shown to have a positive effect on high blood pressure. In a report from Memorial-Sloan Kettering Cancer Center, patients with a family history of colon cancer benefited from increased calcium. Though none of the patients had colon cancer, cells taken from their colons did resemble those from actual cancer victims. After two to three months of increased calcium, the subjects' colon cells returned to a more normal growth pattern.

It seems sensible then to boost the family's calcium intake at the dinner table. Below are valuable, lower-calorie dietary sources of calcium.

FOOD	SERVING SIZE	PER SERVING MILLIGRAMS
Skim milk	1 cup	302
Low-fat yogurt (plain)	1 cup	415
Cheddar cheese	1 ounce	204
Cottage cheese	½ cup	136
Parmesan cheese	1 ounce	390
Swiss cheese	1 ounce	272
Broccoli	1 cup	136
Beet greens, cooked	1 cup	198
Collard greens	1 cup	357
Bean curd	4 ounces	154
Sardines with bones	3 ounces	372
Salmon (canned with bones)	3 ounces	167

❖Thirty-five hundred extra calories are needed to make a pound of body fat. To lose a pound of fat in a week, you need to create a calorie deficit of 500 calories a day, either by eating less, exercising more, or both.❖

CLASS ACT

Seafood Raviolis with Tomato Cream Sauce
Bibb Lettuce Salad with Balsamic Dressing
Mocha Custard

These light-as-down-pillow raviolis filled with shrimp and topped with a creamy but creamless sauce are indeed a class act. They are so good they deserve to be the centerpoint of this menu for six. If you've never made raviolis before, the detailed instructions will help the most inexperienced cook to pasta perfection. A hand-cranked pasta maker is helpful unless you want to roll out the dough by hand. The recipe would also make a distinctive beginning to a more formal meal.

Serve a very simple salad with the raviolis. The one suggested here is Bibb lettuce with a dark, aromatic balsamic vinaigrette. Offer breadsticks if you like, and round out the meal with a do-ahead, cool, and chocolately mocha custard.

❖If you're determined to lose some weight, keep a "food diary" for a few days, writing down *everything* you eat and drink. At the end of the day, roughly compute your caloric intake with the help of a calorie guide (available in paperback). This little exercise may help you cut back on snacking as well as highlighting what you're actually eating. Remember, cheating only hurts you!❖

Seafood Raviolis with Tomato Cream Sauce

❖

This is a wonderful dish, appealing to the eye and deliciously satisfying, but with very little fat. Don't be intimidated by the length of the recipe. It can be accomplished in an hour and a half or the tasks can be spread out over a day or two. The illustrations on the following pages will be helpful as you cut the raviolis. You will need a pasta machine (the hand-cranked, chrome versions are very reliable and relatively inexpensive), but a ravioli attachment, while convenient, isn't a necessity. The raviolis may be made as much as a week or two ahead and frozen, or they may be made early in the day. The tomato cream sauce also can be made early in the day. This recipe easily serves 8 as a first course or six as a main dish.

For the Sauce

4 tomatoes
2 tablespoons unsalted butter
1 large garlic clove, minced
2 tablespoons all-purpose flour
1 cup low-fat or skim milk
4 tablespoons low-fat cottage cheese
2 teaspoons freshly grated Parmesan cheese
½ teaspoon salt
freshly ground black pepper to taste
freshly grated nutmeg to taste
5–6 leaves fresh basil, snipped

For the Ravioli Filling

⅔ pound raw medium shrimp (40–45 to the
    pound), unpeeled
3 scant tablespoons minced shallot

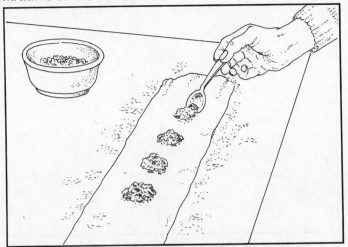

1. Lay the rolled pasta strip on a floured work surface. Working from the midpoint of the pasta to the right, center 6 to 7 rounded teaspoons of shrimp mixture, 1 inch apart.

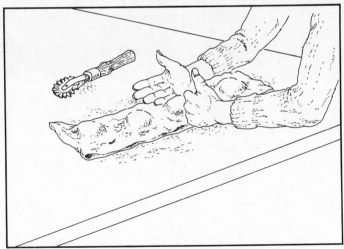

2. Fold the left-hand pasta strip over the right half, encasing the shrimp mixture. Flour the sides of your hands and press the edges of the pasta to form the raviolis.

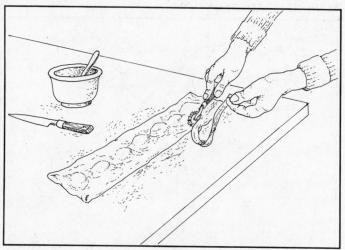

3. Trim the excess dough from the raviolis with a pastry wheel or pizza cutter, leaving a ¼-inch border.

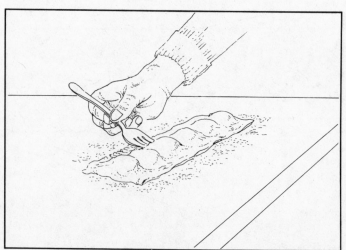

4. To seal the edges of the raviolis, dip the tines of a fork in flour (or use a pastry wheel) and crimp the edges. Then you will cut between the shrimp mounds.

3 tablespoons low-fat cottage cheese
1½ tablespoons freshly grated Parmesan cheese
2 egg whites

For the Spinach Pasta

1½ cups all-purpose flour
1 teaspoon salt
1 egg
¼ cup tightly packed, squeezed dry, cooked
    spinach
1 tablespoon olive oil

To Complete the Recipe

1 tablespoon vegetable oil for the cooking water
1 tablespoon unsalted butter, at room
    temperature
salt and freshly ground black pepper to taste
6–8 whole fresh basil leaves for garnish (optional)
freshly grated Parmesan cheese to pass at the
    table (optional)

To Prepare the Sauce

1. Fill a 2½-quart saucepan three-quarters full of water.
   Bring it to a boil.
2. Meanwhile, core the tomatoes and cut small crosses
   into their bottoms. Drop the tomatoes into the boiling
   water. Blanch the tomatoes 30 seconds for very ripe
   ones, or as long as 1 minute for less ripe tomatoes.
3. Drain and cool the tomatoes under running water.
   Starting at the cross, peel and discard the skin. Quarter
   the tomatoes. Push the seeds out with your thumb and
   discard them. Chop the tomato pulp and set aside.
4. Melt the butter in an 8-inch skillet over medium-high
   heat. Add the garlic and saute, stirring, about 1 minute.
   When the butter is foamy and the garlic is fragrant, stir
   in the flour.
5. Stir the flour over medium heat for 1 minute. Remove

the skillet from the heat and whisk in the milk. Continue to whisk until smooth.

6. Return the skillet to medium-high heat, and whisk the sauce until thickened, about 1 to 2 minutes. Scrape the sauce into the bowl of a food processor.

7. With the machine on, add the cottage cheese, Parmesan cheese, salt, pepper, and nutmeg. Process until very smooth.

8. Add the chopped tomato pulp and pulse machine just to mix; do not puree. Scrape sauce back into the skillet if you are serving it soon; put it into a bowl if you are chilling it. Stir in the basil. Set aside or chill, covered, up to 10 hours.

To Prepare the Ravioli Filling

1. Shell and devein the shrimp. Place the shrimp in the bowl of a food processor.

2. Add the shallot to the shrimp. Pulse the machine just to mince; do not puree the shrimp.

3. Add the cottage cheese, Parmesan cheese, and egg whites to the shrimp. Pulse just to combine. Scrape into a bowl, cover with plastic wrap, and chill until you are ready to make raviolis. (The filling may be chilled for several hours.)

To Prepare the Spinach Pasta

1. To make pasta in a food processor: Pour the flour into the bowl of a food processor. Add the salt, egg, spinach, and olive oil. Process until the dough can be formed into a ball. To make by hand: Mince the spinach. Pour the flour and salt into a mixing bowl. Make a well in the center and put the egg, spinach, and olive oil in it. Mix together with a fork or your fingertips until the dough can be formed into a rough ball.

2. Pinch off a quarter of the dough and work with one quarter at a time. Cover remaining dough with a damp towel. To knead the dough, set the smooth rollers of

the pasta machine as far apart as possible (generally, the lowest setting on most pasta machines). Dust the dough with flour, and feed it through the rollers. Reroll this strip 4 or 5 more times, folding under the ragged edges and dusting the dough in flour, when necessary, to prevent sticking.

3. To roll out the dough, cut the strip so it measures 2½ inches by 7 inches. (Patch it if it tears.) Set the machine to the second notch and feed the strip through the rollers. Repeat, advancing the notch a setting higher after each rolling so the rollers progressively come closer together and the dough gets thinner. After the dough is rolled through the last notch setting it should measure approximately 3½ inches by 36 inches.

4. Lay the pasta strip crosswise on a lightly floured counter. Working from the midpoint of the strip to the right-hand edge place 6 or 7 rounded teaspoonfuls of shrimp filling, roughly 1 inch apart, along the center of the pasta.

5. Dip a pastry brush in water and "paint" around each shrimp mound (this will "glue" the top sheet of pasta to the bottom). Avoid dribbling water on the work surface, if possible, for wet flour is a mess to pick up.

6. Fold the left-hand strip of pasta over the shrimp mounds. Flour the sides of your hands. Press the top pasta sheet to the bottom, with the sides of your hands, pressing out air bubbles. With your fingertips press the dough close to the shrimp filling.

7. With a pizza cutter or pastry wheel, trim the excess dough from the top and bottom edges of the strip, leaving a ¼-inch border between the filling and the edge of the ravioli. Discard the trimming.

8. Dip the tines of a fork (or use a pastry wheel) in flour. Press the tines along the two long sides of the ravioli strip to seal the edges. Seal the ravioli edges with the floured fork tines. Use the pizza cutter or pastry wheel to cut between the shrimp mounds, forming raviolis about 2¼ inches square.

9. Place each ravioli on a floured cookie sheet as it is completed. Cover the raviolis with a damp towel to

keep them from drying out. Repeat steps 2 through 9 until all the dough and filling are used. (Raviolis may be made a week in advance and frozen up to 2 weeks. Cook them without thawing and increase cooking time accordingly. Or make them early in the day and chill, covered with plastic wrap and a damp cloth.)

To Cook the Raviolis

1. Bring 6 to 8 quarts of water to a boil with the added tablespoon of vegetable oil. Put a colander in the sink. Drop the raviolis into the boiling water, and stir gently to prevent them from sticking together. Boil about 5 or 6 minutes (longer for frozen raviolis) or until they are tender.
2. While the raviolis cook, reheat the sauce over medium-low heat, stirring frequently. Add a few drops of milk if the sauce seems too thick. Heat shallow soup bowls on a warming tray, in a microwave oven (add a glass of water), or in a 150-degree oven
3. Drain the raviolis in the colander. Toss with the butter, salt, and pepper. Serve 4 to 5 raviolis per person, and top each serving with 3 tablespoons of sauce. Garnish each serving with a basil leaf. Pass grated Parmesan cheese at the table.

Yield: about 30 raviolis, slightly more than a cup of sauce
✦ Calories per serving: 311
Carbohydrate per serving: 33g
Cholesterol per serving: 136mg

Dietary fiber per serving: 1g
Fat per serving: 11g
Protein per serving: 20g
Sodium per serving: 921mg

❖Despite the current interest in sports, aerobics, and working out, one study estimates only 35 percent of adults in this country exercise regularly.❖

Bibb Lettuce Salad
with Balsamic Dressing

❖

This is a simple yet sophisticated salad dressing that may become a standard at your house as it is at mine. Balsamic vinegar, available at specialty food shops and some supermarkets, is a rich, dark-brown wine vinegar aged in oak casks. (Malt vinegar is a very acceptable substitute.) Walnut oil, also available at specialty stores, is a very light oil. (In a pinch, safflower oil would do.) Keep walnut oil in the refrigerator once it has been opened. The dressing recipe may be doubled and chilled for several days. Bring the dressing to room temperature before serving or zap it for a few seconds in a microwave oven to liquefy the consomme, which will jell under refrigeration.

> *7 tablespoons canned beef consomme or*
> *double-strength homemade beef stock*
> *4 tablespoons walnut oil*
> *2 tablespoons plus 2 teaspoons balsamic vinegar*
> *1 garlic clove, minced*
> *1 round teaspoon Pommery (whole grain)*
> *mustard*
> *1 teaspoon sugar*
> *freshly ground black pepper to taste*
> *1 head Bibb lettuce*

1. Combine the first seven ingredients in a screw-top jar and shake well. The dressing may be held at room temperature up to 2 hours before being served or chilled for several days.
2. Rinse and spin dry the lettuce as much as a day before serving, if desired. (Rinsed lettuce, loosely packed in a plastic bag and chilled at least 2 hours, is wonderfully

crisp.) Toss the lettuce with the dressing no more than 15 minutes before serving.

Yield: 6 servings
✦ **Calories per serving: 73**
Carbohydrate per serving: 3g
✦ **Cholesterol per serving: 1mg**

Dietary fiber per serving: 0g
Fat per serving: 7g
Protein per serving: 1g
✦ **Sodium per serving: 17mg**

Mocha Custard

❖

Light, cool, and chocolatey. Allow a minimum of 2 to 3 hours chilling time before serving.

> *1 cup instant espresso or other strong coffee*
> *1 cup low-fat milk*
> *½ cup evaporated skimmed milk*
> *3 eggs*
> *3 tablespoons sugar*
> *½ cup semisweet real chocolate chips*
> *1 teaspoon Irish whiskey or coffee-flavored*
> *   liqueur (optional)*
> *freshly grated nutmeg to taste*
> *grated unsweetened chocolate (optional)*

1. Preheat oven to 325 degrees. Combine the coffee, low-fat milk, and evaporated milk in a 1-quart saucepan. Scald over high heat.
2. While milk heats, beat the eggs and sugar together in a small bowl until thick and lemon-colored.
3. When a skin forms on the milk, remove the pan from the heat. Gradually pour the milk into the eggs, while beating.
4. Place the chocolate chips and whiskey in a glass measuring cup. Melt in a microwave oven on high power for

about 1½ minutes, or place the cup in a small saucepan with water halfway up the sides and heat over medium-high heat until the chocolate is melted.

5. Stir the chocolate and add it to the egg mixture. Add the nutmeg. Beat until smooth with an electric mixer at slow speed.

6. Pour the mixture into 6 ½-cup custard dishes, a 1-quart souffle dish, or other ovenproof serving dish. Place the custard cups or souffle dish in a baking pan just large enough to hold them. Pour hot tap water into the baking pan to come halfway up the side(s) of the dish(es).

7. Set the baking pan in the middle of the preheated oven. Stir the custard after 10 minutes. Stir again in another 10 minutes. Then cook 25 minutes more (45 minutes all together), or until a knive inserted in the middle comes out with only a little custard on it. (Check custard cups after 35 minutes; they will require slightly less time.) Custard will shake when jiggled. Remove the custard from the oven and the baking pan.

8. Cool the custard at room temperature for about 30 minutes, then refrigerate at least 2 to 3 hours or for as long as 24 hours before serving. Garnish with grated unsweetened chocolate curls or shavings if you wish.

Yield: 4 to 6 servings (analysis based on 6)
✦ Calories per serving: 168
Carbohydrate per serving: 19 g
Cholesterol per serving: 122 mg
Dietary fiber per serving: 0 g
Fat per serving: 8 g
Protein per serving: 6 g
✦ Sodium per serving: 75 mg

❖ Focus: The Importance ❖ of Exercise

Exercise is vital to any weight loss program. Here's why: As you supply your body with less food, the rate at which your body metabolizes the energy supply slows down. What a cruel twist of fate! Just when you can little afford it, your basal metabolic rate (BMR) has been altered by the decrease in nutrients and calories. That explains why you may experience an encouraging weight loss at the start of a diet (actual weight plus water loss) but plateau just when you're feeling hungriest. This natural tendency of the body to conserve energy may decrease your BMR by as much as 15 to 30 percent.

But a recent study has demonstrated that exercise can increase the rate at which the body uses food, so the natural slow-down brought on by dieting need not hinder weight loss. In the study, the subjects' BMR was actually increased by exercise at the end of a two-week period. A rise in the BMR coupled with the calories burned off by exercise and the feeling of well-being brought on by exercise point out how essential exercise is to a successful get-it-off and keep-it-off program.

Exercising shouldn't give you the excuse to eat more, particularly if you're trying to pare off a pound or two. On the contrary, it takes such effort to expend so few calories, as this chart will show, that it's license to little more than a glass of water if weight loss is your goal. These are average calories used per hour by a 150-pound individual. Smaller persons will use fewer calories, larger persons, more. (The figures come from the American Heart Association.)

ACTIVITY	SPEED	CALORIES
Bicycling	6 mph	240
Bicycling	12 mph	420
Jogging	5½ mph	740
Jogging	7 mph	920
Running	10 mph	1280
Swimming	25 yards/minute for an hour	275
Tennis	Singles	400
Walking	3 mph	320
Walking	4½ mph	440

COOKING TO GO

**Vegetable Lasagne with Spinach Noodles
and Three Cheeses**

Romaine Lettuce with Garlic Vinaigrette

"Lasagne" needn't conjure up the greasy ground-meat-and-tomato-sauce version served at many a steam table. This "Cooking to Go" dinner for four offers a lightened version, chock-full of vegetables and bound with a creamy (but low-fat!) white sauce. A pasta machine is needed to make the homemade spinach noodles, but store-bought lasagne noodles would certainly pass. All in all, it's a tempting change from the ordinary that travels well and/or freezes, too.

A quick glance at the ingredient list may deter readers who feel their daily protein quota requires at least a small serving of meat, fish, or poultry. But another glance at the nutritional analysis proves otherwise. A serving of this vegetable lasagne supplies 19 grams of protein, 35 percent of an average woman's needs, a very respectable amount for a single meal. For more on meatless meals see *Focus: Complete Vegetable Protein*, on page 274.

With the lasagne, offer a simple tossed salad with a zingy garlic vinaigrette and crispy croutons prepared without fat. Hearty appetites would appreciate the Garden Goodness Cheese Rolls (page 180) or purchased and heated Italian bread.

Vegetable Lasagne with Spinach Noodles and Three Cheeses

❖

This is a do-ahead, non-meat meal studded with nearly every color of the garden. While instructions are given here for making your own spinach pasta (you'll need a pasta machine), 8 store-bought lasagne noodles would do just fine. Even meat lovers will find nothing wanting in this delicious vegetarian variation of an old standby. Because the dish freezes well, you might consider doubling the recipe.

If you make the single recipe of spinach pasta, there will be a very small amount left over; it's difficult to work with any less than ½ cup of flour when making noodles. Double the noodle recipe and freeze the unused portion if you prefer not to be wasteful.

For the Spinach Lasagne Noodles

½ cup all-purpose flour
1 tablespoon tightly packed, chopped, cooked, and squeezed dry spinach
¼ teaspoon salt
½ of a beaten egg
a few drops olive oil

For the Vegetables

2 leeks, white part only, rinsed and diced
$^1/_2$ cup homemade chicken stock or canned chicken broth
2 small carrots, shredded
$^1/_2$ cup chopped, cooked broccoli
$^2/_3$ cup chopped, cooked spinach

1 red bell pepper, diced
1 cup sliced mushrooms

For the Sauce

1 tablespoon unsalted butter
1 garlic clove, minced
1 tablespoon all-purpose flour
1 cup homemade chicken stock or canned
    chicken broth
1 egg yolk
1 cup low-fat cottage cheese
2 tablespoons freshly grated Parmesan cheese
freshly ground black pepper to taste
freshly grated nutmeg to taste
1 tablespoon arrowroot
1 tablespoon Madeira

To Complete the Recipe

1 tablespoon vegetable oil for the cooking water
2 ounces part-skim mozzarella cheese, grated

To Prepare the Spinach Noodles

1. To make the pasta in a food processor: Pour the flour
   into the bowl of a food processor. Add the spinach,
   salt, and egg. Process, adding the oil, until the dough
   can be formed into a ball. (It is unlikely but possible
   that you'll need to add a few drops of water to make
   the dough form a ball.) To make the pasta by hand:
   Pour the flour into a mixing bowl. Make a well in the
   center and put the spinach, salt, and egg in it. Mix together with a fork or your fingertips, adding drops of
   olive oil, until the dough can be formed into a rough
   ball.
2. Pinch off half the dough and work with one half at a
   time. To knead the dough, set the smooth rollers of a
   pasta machine as far apart as possible (generally, the
   lowest setting on most pasta machines). Dust the

dough with flour and feed it through the rollers. Reroll this strip 4 or 5 times, folding under the ragged edges and dusting the dough with flour, when necessary, to prevent sticking.

3. To roll out the dough: Set the machine to the second notch and feed the strip through the rollers. Repeat, advancing the notch after each rolling so the rollers progressively come closer together and the dough gets thinner. As you roll, dust the dough with flour to prevent sticking. Finally roll the strip through the last notch to make it as thin as possible.

4. Set the strip onto a floured counter. Trim it to approximately 3½ by 11 inches. Repeat steps 2 and 3 with the remaining dough and dough trimmings. (Noodles may be made up to 2 hours ahead and held at room temperature before boiling.)

5. Bring 6 to 8 quarts of water with the tablespoon of vegetable oil to a rolling boil. Carefully drop the noodles into the boiling water. Stir gently to prevent them from sticking together. Boil 3 minutes for homemade noodles, or follow package directions for purchased noodles. Drain and cool under running water. Lay the noodles flat in a single layer on kitchen towels to drain. Pat dry. (The cooked noodles may be held at room temperature, covered with the towels, for up to 2 hours before completing the recipe.)

To Prepare the Filling

1. Combine the leeks with 4 tablespoons of the chicken stock in a 10-inch skillet. Cover, bring to a boil over high heat, and boil for 2 to 3 minutes or until tender, stirring occasionally.

2. Add the carrots, stir, cover, and cook another 2 minutes. Scrape into a bowl.

3. Stir the broccoli, spinach, and red pepper into the bowl with the carrots and leeks.

4. In the same skillet, "saute" the mushrooms over high heat in the remaining 4 tablespoons chicken broth

until the mushrooms are limp and the broth has evaporated, about 4 to 5 minutes. Combine the mushrooms with the other vegetables in the bowl. Set aside. (Vegetable mixture may be made several hours ahead and held, covered, in the refrigerator.)

To Prepare the Sauce

1. In the same 10-inch skillet, heat the butter and garlic over high heat until the butter is foamy, about 1 minute. Stir in the flour, reduce heat to medium, and cook, stirring constantly, until the flour is just golden, about 1 minute.
2. Remove the skillet from the heat. Whisk in the chicken broth. Continue to whisk until smooth.
3. Return the pan to medium heat, and whisk 2 to 3 minutes or until the sauce is smooth and lightly thickened. Pour into a food processor.
4. Add the egg yolk, cottage cheese, Parmesan cheese, pepper, and nutmeg to the sauce in the food processor. Process until smooth. Meanwhile, dissolve the arrowroot in the Madeira.
5. Pour the sauce back in the skillet. Place the skillet over medium-high heat. Stir in the Madeira. Stir until thickened, about 2 to 3 minutes. Taste and adjust seasoning. (Sauce may be made several hours ahead and held, covered, in the refrigerator.)

To Assemble

1. Preheat the oven to 350 degrees. Coat an 8-inch-square baking pan with cooking spray. Film the bottom of the pan with a few tablespoons of the sauce.
2. Mix half of the sauce with the vegetables, and set the remaining sauce aside for the top. Cut the noodles in half across. Place two noodle halves in a single layer over the sauce. (The noodles should cover the bottom.) Smooth half of the vegetable and sauce mixture over the noodles. Top with a second noodle layer. Smooth the remaining vegetable mixture on top. Cover with

the third noodle layer. Smooth the remaining sauce on top. Top with the grated mozzarella. (Casserole may be made ahead to this point and frozen for up to a month without flavor loss or chilled up to 8 hours before baking. Add 20 minutes to the baking time for a frozen casserole, or 5 minutes for a chilled casserole.)

3. Bake the casserole in the upper third of the oven for 35 minutes or until it is bubbly and lightly browned. If necessary, broil briefly to brown the top before serving. Let the casserole rest 5 to 10 minutes before you cut it into fourths to serve.

Yield: 4 servings
✦ Calories per serving: 280
Carbohydrate per serving: 32g
✦ Cholesterol per serving: 121mg

✦ Dietary fiber per serving: 3g
Fat per serving: 10g
Protein per serving: 19g
Sodium per serving: 555mg

Romaine Lettuce with Garlic Vinaigrette

❖

A creamy "Italian" type dressing best suited to romaine, chicory, and salad bowl lettuces, this salad is the perfect accompaniment for Vegetable Lasagne or anytime a garlicky dressing is in order.

For the Dressing

1 garlic clove, minced
1 egg
1 teaspoon Dijon mustard
2 tablespoons lemon juice
3 tablespoons freshly grated Parmesan cheese

¼ cup canned beef consomme or homemade
  beef stock
½ cup olive oil, extra-virgin recommended

For the Salad

2 slices bread, white or whole-wheat
½ head romaine lettuce, rinsed and dried
a few leaves salad bowl lettuce, rinsed and dried
½ cup shredded red cabbage
a few rings Bermuda onion
½ cucumber, sliced

To Prepare the Dressing

1. Place the garlic, egg, mustard, lemon juice, and cheese
   in the bowl of a food processor or blender. With the
   machine on, gradually add the consomme, then the oil.
   Transfer the dressing to a screw-top jar and keep
   chilled. It will keep up to 1 week in the refrigerator.

To Prepare the Salad

1. Cube the bread by stacking the two slices and making 5
   lengthwise cuts, and then 5 crosswise cuts.
2. Spray an 8-inch nonstick skillet with cooking spray.
   Add the bread cubes and toss them over medium-high
   heat until lightly browned, about 5 to 6 minutes. Reduce heat as necessary to prevent burning. Remove the
   croutons from the pan and set aside. (Croutons also
   can be oven baked, as on page 145.)
3. Combine the remaining ingredients in a salad bowl.
   Dress with just enough garlic vinaigrette to moisten.
   Garnish the salad with the croutons.

Yield: 1 cup dressing;
    4 salad servings
✦ Calories per serving: 112
  Carbohydrate per serving: 11 g
✦ Cholesterol per serving: 16 mg

Dietary fiber per serving: 1.5 g
Fat per serving: 8 g
Protein per serving: 3 g
✦ Sodium per serving: 115 mg

QUICK EATS

Grilled Shrimp
Angel Hair Pasta with Chèvre
Steamed Broccoli

Time constraints brought on by nightly meetings, juggled schedules, and the like don't have to mean boring, hurried meals. Here's a savvy, flavorful dinner for two (the recipes are easily doubled to serve four) to cook up in about twenty-five minutes—maybe less.

Grilled Shrimp

Buy the freshest, largest shrimp you can for this quick dinner treat. It would also make a simply delicious first course or luncheon dish. The shrimp may be broiled as well as grilled. Cooking times will differ greatly from stove to stove and grill to grill, so use suggested times as a guide only. You will need 2 10-inch bamboo skewers.

> *2 raw jumbo shrimp (about 5 to the pound),*
> *   unpeeled*
> *juice of ½ a lemon*
> *1 tablespoon safflower oil*
> *1 small garlic clove, minced*
> *2 lemon wedges for garnish*

1. Cover the skewers with water and soak them for 20 minutes.

2. Meanwhile, shell and devein the shrimp. Butterfly the shrimp with a single cut on the underside of the shrimp from tip to tail. Be careful not to cut all the way through the shrimp.
3. Combine the lemon juice, oil, and garlic.
4. Push a skewer through the center of each shrimp, working from tail to tip. Marinate the shrimp in the oil mixture at room temperature for 10 minutes or in the refrigerator, covered, for up to 6 hours.
5. Grill the shrimp over low coals, basting with the marinade and rotating often, for about 12 to 15 minutes or until shrimp are firm (but not dried out) and pink. To broil: Place the oven rack about 4 inches from the broiler. Broil the shrimp, basting frequently, about 2 minutes on each side. Serve the shrimp on the skewer with the lemon wedge on the side.

Yield: 2 servings
Dietary fiber per serving: 0g
✦ Calories per serving: 100
Fat per serving: 7g
Carbohydrate per serving: 2g
Protein per serving: 7g
✦ Cholesterol per serving: 57mg
✦ Sodium per serving: 53mg

Angel Hair Pasta with Chèvre

❖

Quick, easy, and good. The angel hair noodles may be homemade (see page 198; but the recipe makes more than you'll need here) or purchased. Chèvre is available from fancy produce stores. Select a young, mild chèvre such as Banon or St. Chevalier. Tiny cooked green peas would be a colorful addition.

½ pound purchased or homemade angel hair noodles or very thin pasta

3 ounces mild chèvre, at room temperature
4 tablespoons low-fat milk
1 tablespoon minced fresh parsley
1 tablespoon unsalted butter, at room
temperature
¼ teaspoon salt
freshly ground black pepper to taste

1. Boil the pasta according to package instructions or follow instructions for cooking fresh angel hair pasta on page 201.
2. While the pasta cooks, prepare the sauce. Combine the chèvre, milk, and parsley in a food processor and process until smooth. Or by hand, combine the chèvre, milk, and parsley in a bowl, and mix with a fork or beater until smooth.
3. Drain the pasta. Toss with the butter, salt, and pepper. Then toss with the cheese sauce. The pasta may be held in a double boiler for 30 minutes or so, but add a few more drops of milk to keep it moist.

Yield: 2 servings
Calories per serving: 604
Carbohydrate per serving: 88g
✦ **Cholesterol per serving: 50mg**

Dietary fiber per serving: 0g
Fat per serving: 17g
Protein per serving: 24g
Sodium per serving: 613mg

Steamed Broccoli

❖

Broccoli is the wonder kid of the vegetable world. High in vitamins A and C, and the minerals iron, calcium, and potassium, it also contains appreciable amounts of fiber. This member of the much-touted cruciferous vegetable family (which includes Brussels sprouts, cabbage, and cauliflower) is now believed, by some researchers, to be a cancer fighter. Broccoli is available all year 'round and is at its peak from October to May, an otherwise bleak season for the fresh produce counter. If the stems are peeled with a swivel-bladed vegetable peeler and sliced into thin rounds or sticks they're every bit as good as the flowerets. Steaming the broccoli makes the most of the water-soluble B vitamins and the heat-sensitive ascorbic acid. Generally, one 2-pound bunch serves 4.

1 stalk broccoli (about ½ pound)
1 tablespoon lemon juice
2 teaspoons unsalted butter, at room temperature
⅛ teaspoon salt
freshly ground black pepper to taste

1. Place 1 inch of water in a 2½-quart saucepan. Fit a collapsible steaming basket in the saucepan. Cover the pan and bring it to a boil.
2. Meanwhile, separate the flowerets from the stalk. Slice the flowerets into roughly 2- to 3-inch bite-size pieces. Peel the stalk (the leaves, which are very high in vitamin A, may be added to the flowerets if you wish). Slice the stalk lengthwise into quarters. Slice the quarters in half lengthwise again. Cut the stick shapes into 2- or 3-inch lengths.
3. Place the broccoli flowerets and stems into the steamer. Cover the pan and return it to a boil. Steam 6 to 7 minutes, occasionally stirring the vegetables from the bottom to the top. The broccoli is done when a stem is tender but still crisp when pierced with a fork.
4. Lift the steamer from the saucepan and turn the broccoli into a serving bowl. Season with the lemon juice, butter, salt, and pepper, and serve. Leftover broccoli reheats nicely in a microwave oven (about 45 seconds at high power depending on the amount) with a little added water.

Yield: 2 servings
✦ Calories per serving: 61
Carbohydrate per serving: 6g
✦ Cholesterol per serving: 10mg
✦ Dietary fiber per serving: 1.3g
Fat per serving: 4g
Protein per serving: 3g
✦ Sodium per serving: 177mg

❖ Focus: ❖
Exercise and Longevity

A recent study of 17,000 Harvard College alumni proved what many exercise gurus have long touted—that vigorous exercise does indeed lengthen life, on the average about two years, or as much as if all cancer were wiped out.

The study found that men between the ages of 35 and 54 who jogged at a moderate pace only 3 hours a week or walked briskly 20 miles a week—expending at least 2000 calories by exercising in the seven days—could expect to live an additional 2½ hours for every hour they spent in vigorous exercise.

Men over the age of 50 benefited most from exercise; those who were physically fit had an almost 50 percent lower death rate than their sedentary peers.

❖Orange juice poured over cut-up fruit for a salad will help retard loss of vitamin C.❖

DINNER IN THE KITCHEN

❖ Dinner in the Kitchen ❖

Much as we might like to, few of us sit down to elegantly prepared and served meals every night of the week. Indeed, in most busy households such occasions are peppered—sparsely at that—during the year, and casual, albeit predictable, meals are the norm. Not that predictability is unappealing—the success of the fast food mega-industry attests to that—unless predictability includes cooking habits that overuse saturated fats and pay little heed to other nutritional guidelines.

The meals—somehow "menu" sounds far too more formal—in this "Dinner in the Kitchen" section are intended for those casual, everyday times when cooking chores get squeezed between other obligations and a bit of blessed free time. We'd like something good to eat, and we'd like to serve healthy foods too, but often there just isn't time to fuss nor the energy to bother.

These are the times to put the lower fat and calorie concepts in *The Enlightened Gourmet* and *Gourmet Light* to work for you. Don't reach for the oil, butter, or margarine when sauteing those onions; opt instead for chicken broth, a nonstick skillet, and cooking spray. Thicken the stew with arrowroot, not flour. Enrich the soup with dry milk powder or low-fat milk and a bit of arrowroot, not cream. Save the butter for the table; use cholesterol-free oils in cooking. Think legumes, whole wheat breads, and fresh vegetables instead of slabs of fatty meat or greasy fried chicken. Offer a fresh, instead of frozen, vegetable. (The freshness factor does more than a hollandaise could ever do.) Modifying your standard, everyday recipes takes more resolve than anything else. Once you've decided to cook more healthily, the doing isn't so tough. For those times when you'd like to try something new and different for family or other informal gatherings, try some of the recipes in this "Dinner in the Kitchen" section.

Here you'll find mussels or eggs as the main course, oatmeal muffins, a cornbread loaf, and whole wheat breadsticks. There are recipes using legumes like lentils, white beans, and kidney beans. Taken out of context, many of the recipes, particularly a few of the desserts, would do a more formal meal proud. As a group, these menus are meals for family and friends who join you in the kitchen.

❖ Focus: Health Food ❖ or Junk Food?

Some foods have an undeserved "good-for-you" image. Nutrition-savvy consumers have to be good label readers if they want to avoid empty-calorie foods, foods high in saturated fats, or other foods with a built-in health risk factor. Don't be duped by these innocent appearing "natural" or so-called "light" products:

Granola cereals or some others with a homey "100% natural" label: These breakfast cereals promote a health food image that is unwarranted when the calories and total fat values are weighed. A serving of a representative brand of granola cereal has a teaspoon of added fat; a serving of another "all-natural" cereal (remember there's nothing unnatural about fat or sugar) has a teaspoon and a half of added fat, while a bowl of cornflakes has an insignificant amount. And cornflakes are less fattening, ounce for ounce.

Fruit bars: These are indeed made with fruit—and lots of sugar. Supplying less than 2 percent of the RDA of vitamins, fruit bars are a weak second to the real thing. An orange, for instance, supplies more than 100 percent of the RDA for vitamin C.

Ten percent fruit juice sodas: These are indeed made with fruit juice and 90 percent sugar and water.

Croissants: This seems obvious, but one company does market a frozen croissant as "Deliciously light." It's not the company's fault, of course, that "light" has come to be associated with lower calorie, but no one can deny that it has. And at 109 calories with an added teaspoon and a half of fat per roll, a croissant cannot be considered low calorie or low in fat. (By comparison, a slice of white bread has about 1/5 teaspoon of fat.)

Cholesterol-free, lactose-free frozen desserts (ice cream substitutes): Certainly a boon for lactose intolerant people, these may not be right for cholesterol or calorie counters. Check the label for the kind of oil used in processing, and avoid those that are high in saturated fats like coconut oil. One brand supplies 345 calories in a ¾ cup serving, second only to a popular premium brand of ice cream.

❖The hardest part about losing weight is making up your mind. The way you look has to be more important to you than how much you eat. But you can eat well and still be thin, as this book tries to show.❖

SOME LIKE IT HOT

Shrimp and Crab Gumbo

White Rice*

Tossed Salad with Raspberry Vinaigrette

The recent culinary obsession with all things American has caused a celebration of regional cuisines like Creole and Tex-Mex. One fingerprint of Creole cookery, the gumbo, is particularly well suited to the interests of health-conscious cooks. Heavy on vegetables and light on often fatty meats, gumbos—a dish out of Africa by way of the West Indies—are highly personal renditions of a few basic ingredients: tomatoes, onions, and garlic with a little meat, poultry, or shellfish simmered with Cajun spices and served on rice. What the nutritionists term "complex carbohydrates" amounts to "good ol' eatin' " if spicy, hot foods appeal to you.

Unlike lots of slow-cooked concoctions, gumbo is a jiffy affair—about 35 minutes or so are all that are required. In fact, if it overcooks and okra has been used in it, a gummy, too heavy stew is the unhappy result.

Serve this shrimp and crab gumbo for six with simply boiled white rice (follow package instructions or your favorite recipe), crusty French bread for hearty appetites, and a tossed salad (recipe included or use your personal favorite). If hot foods (hot in seasoning that is) don't appeal to you but the other ingredients do, go easy on the Creole Spice Mix.

❖ Focus: Low-Calorie Staples ❖

Keeping the following food items and equipment on hand will help you pare unneeded calories from your daily cooking:

Lemons: Use lemons where you might use salt (on poultry and fish), or oils (on veal or salads), or butter (on vegetables). Use the zest on pasta.

Canned consomme: Use it to replace about half the oil in your standard salad dressing.

Canned chicken and beef broth: Don't be without them for the "sauteing" of onions, garlic, and the like; for cooking mushrooms; or anytime a recipe calls for cooking, not browning, a food in a few tablespoons of butter or other fat.

Plain yogurt: Use yogurt in place of mayonnaise. Stir a teaspoon of arrowroot into ½ cup of yogurt to use in place of cream.

Low-sugar ketchup: Use the recipe on page 352 with yogurt and lemon for a quick low-calorie salad dressing. Use it anytime to replace commercially prepared ketchup.

Mustards: Get exotic with mustard. It's a low calorie replacement for mayonnaise, and a delicious spread on grilling chicken and meats. Spread it liberally on crisp bread (the dark brown crackers; one brand is Wasa), top with a thinly sliced chicken breast, and top with another mustard-coated cracker. Wrap the sandwich tightly in foil and refrigerate up to 24 hours—the crackers will soften like bread.

Arrowroot: Use arrowroot for thickening; it has fewer than one-third of the calories of flour.

Fresh ginger in sherry: the ginger is terrific grated on grilling chicken or fish, and the sherry is excellent as a deglazing liquid after pan-sauteing of meats.

A scale: Weigh those meat portions until you can spot a 3-ounce serving.

Parchment paper: Use for steaming of chicken, fish, and vegetables without added fats.

Cooking sprays: Use them on nonstick skillets to get truly fat-free cooking without sticking.

Freshly grated Parmesan cheese: At 20 calories per tablespoon, it's a terrific way to add flavor and calcium to vegetables and salads, without adding lots of fat.

Parsley: Parsley keeps fresh in a tall glass of water in the refrigerator for several days. Use to delight the eye as well as add flavor without calories.

Vinegars: There are so many wonderful vinegars on the market, make use of them often for flavor without calories. Try a few drops on greens such as spinach instead of butter; use with a little broth to deglaze a skillet after pan-frying meat or poultry; use to enliven staid, ordinary salad dressings.

Fresh herbs: Grow a few fresh herbs; the most basic are thyme, rosemary, tarragon, and basil. All are very simple to care for and most can be brought in for the cold months. Cooking with fresh herbs rather than dried ones (particularly if a container of dried herbs never gets tossed unless it's empty) is as dramatic a difference as garden fresh vegetables are to their canned or frozen counterparts. With fresh herbs, you'll be less inclined to coax out flavor with butter and other fats.

Shrimp and Crab Gumbo

Once a regional dish, gumbo has traveled north and west beyond the Mason-Dixon line to newfound popularity nationwide. A frequent ingredient of this tomato-based stew is okra, a pod-shaped vegetable available from late spring to early fall. Okra, a good source of calcium, has a mucilaginous quality when it is cut, which makes it useful for thickening soups and stews, but it can become unpleasantly slimy if overcooked. Plan accordingly and reheat leftovers as briefly as possible. Another thickener in the gumbo pot—although some purists would decry using both at once—is filé powder. An Indian invention, filé powder is made from the leaves of a sassafras tree. It is available at specialty food shops. It too can become stringy when overcooked, so it is added when the gumbo is completely cooked and has been removed from the heat.

Like most stews the ingredients and the proportions listed below are suggestions. You'll have more Creole Spice Mix than you need for this recipe because it is difficult to make in smaller batches. A teaspoon added to the cooking water of new potatoes or green beans is quite good, or you may sprinkle it on any grilled fish or meat. It keeps indefinitely in a screw-top jar in a dark, cool spot.

For the Creole Spice Mix

1 tablespoon sweet paprika
¾ teaspoon dried red pepper flakes
1 teaspoon ground black pepper
½ teaspoon dried oregano
¼ teaspoon onion powder
¼ teaspoon celery salt
1 teaspoon ground dried thyme

For the Gumbo

1 large onion, diced
1 green bell pepper, diced
1 celery rib, diced
2 garlic cloves, minced
1¾ cups homemade chicken stock or canned
    chicken broth
3 tomatoes, blanched, peeled, and seeded (see
    page 177) or 2 cups canned tomatoes,
    seeded, with their juice
5 ounces trimmed okra, sliced
1 8-ounce bottle clam broth
2 tablespoons tomato paste
2 tablespoons snipped fresh chives
2 teaspoons or to taste Creole Spice Mix

¾ pound mussels (about a dozen), cleaned and
    debearded (see page 206)
½ pound large raw shrimp, shelled and deveined
6 ounces crab meat, fresh or frozen and thawed
1 teaspoon filé powder

1. Combine all the ingedients for the Creole Spice Mix in
   a screw-top jar. Cover and shake well to combine. Set
   aside.
2. Combine the onion, green pepper, celery, garlic, and 4
   tablespoons of the chicken stock in a 4-quart or larger
   saucepan. Cover and bring to a boil over high heat. As
   soon as a boil is reached, lower the heat to medium
   and simmer, covered, until the vegetables are tender,
   about 6 to 7 minutes.
3. Stir in the tomatoes, okra, the remaining 1½ cups
   chicken stock, clam broth, tomato paste, chives, and 2
   teaspoons Creole Spice Mix. Cover and reduce heat to
   medium-low so the liquid just simmers. Simmer 20 to
   25 minutes, stirring occasionally.
4. Uncover the pan and add the mussels. Cover, increase
   heat to medium-high, and cook 1 minute. Add the
   shrimp and crab. Cook over medium heat just until the
   shrimp are pink and the mussels have opened, about 2
   minutes.
5. Taste and adjust seasoning. Remove the pan from the
   heat and stir in the filé powder. Let the gumbo stand,
   covered, 2 to 3 minutes before serving it over white
   rice.

Yield: 6 servings
✦ Calories per serving: 146
Carbohydrate per serving: 13g
✦ Cholesterol per serving: 103mg

Dietary fiber per serving: 1g
Fat per serving: 2g
Protein per serving: 19g
✦ Sodium per serving: 406mg

Tossed Salad with Raspberry Vinaigrette

❖

For meals such as this one where the salad should complement and cool, not overpower or take precedence, here is a very basic tossed salad. The dressing will keep up to 4 days in the refrigerator.

For the Salad

> 6 cups prepared assorted greens, such as spinach, red leaf lettuce, Bibb lettuce, and romaine
> ½ bunch of watercress or arugula, if desired
> 1 carrot, grated
> 1 apple, such as Granny Smith or McIntosh, cored and diced

For the Dressing

> 1½ tablespoons olive oil
> 3 tablespoons safflower oil
> 2 tablespoons fruity vinegar such as raspberry or white wine vinegar
> 2 tablespoons canned beef consomme or homemade chicken stock
> freshly ground black pepper to taste

1. Tear the greens into a salad bowl. Roughly chop the watercress or tear the arugula. Mix with the greens. Grate the carrot onto the greens, then toss the apple with the greens. (The salad may be prepared to this point up to 2 hours before serving. Keep chilled, covered with plastic wrap.)

2. Combine the dressing ingredients in a screw-top jar. Shake well and chill. Just before serving toss it with the greens.

Yield: 6 servings
✦ Calories per serving: 89
Carbohydrate per serving: 6g
✦ Cholesterol per serving: 0mg

Dietary fiber per serving: 1g
Fat per serving: 7g
Protein per serving: 1g
✦ Sodium per serving: 28mg

❖You'll more likely stick to an exercise program if you start with another person. Each can reinforce the other on those inevitable days when you simply don't want to do it. Once you get the habit of exercise and begin to see and feel the results, you'll make yourself carry on—but a little help from a friend is really useful in the beginning.❖

FARM FRESH

Vegetable Frittata with Two Cheeses

Sesame and Chive Dressing for Tossed Greens

**Tomato Slices with Basil
and Extra-virgin Olive Oil**

Orange Pot de Crème

This is a simple, calcium-rich supper for two (or double the frittata to serve four). Its success lies in the freshness of the eggs and the ripeness of the tomatoes. The remaining ingredients you are likely to have on hand, making this an easy "do."

It may seem odd to serve both a salad and sliced tomatoes in the same menu, but richly red, sun-warmed tomatoes (they are much less flavorful if they are icy cold) are better complemented with a mere drizzle of good olive oil and a snippet of fresh basil, than obscured beneath a strong salad dressing. (The recipe is in another menu, on page 217.) My only exception to this purely personal preference is to serve them with a dab of good homemade (low-cal of course) mayonnaise. If you prefer the tomatoes tossed with the greens, consider adding another vegetable to this menu. Honey Glazed Carrots (see page 317), or Steamed Broccoli (page 242), asparagus would all do nicely, as would parslied new potatoes.

Capping the meal is an extremely easy orange custard. Make it early in the day to allow ample chilling time. The recipe serves four, even though the menu is designed for two. Leftovers will keep up to two days, chilled with plastic wrap.

With eggs as the basis of the frittata as well as of the dessert, this is not a menu for cholesterol watchers. It is, however, recommended for those who watch their fat content and desire more calcium.

Vegetable Frittata with Two Cheeses

❖

When we're in the mood for something quick and not too heavy, a frittata (a sort of Italian omelet) is just perfect. Because this is a good way to use up a little of this or a smidgen of that, consider the following ingredients and their proportions as guidelines only. Most anything from yesterday's leftover ear of corn on the cob to those wilted scallions will be revived and delicious in this homey meal.

4 tablespoons homemade chicken stock or
  canned chicken broth
1 leek, white part only, diced
1 garlic clove, minced
1 tablespoon safflower oil
2 small zucchini (about 4 ounces total), sliced
  thinly
4 eggs
1 tablespoon low-fat milk or low-fat plain yogurt
½ tomato, diced
1 ounce fontina cheese, grated
½ ounce feta cheese, crumbled
salt and freshly ground black pepper to taste

1. Preheat the oven to 350 degrees. Coat an 8-inch oven-proof skillet with cooking spray. Add the chicken stock and bring it to a boil over high heat. Add the leek and garlic. Cover the skillet and cook the vegetables over medium-high heat, stirring often, until the leek is tender and the liquid has evaporated, about 4 minutes. Uncover the skillet, if necessary, to evaporate the liquid.
2. Add the safflower oil and the zucchini. Cover the skillet and cook the zucchini slices over medium-high heat, stirring often, until they are tender, about 5 minutes.

3. Meanwhile, break the eggs into a small bowl. Add the milk and beat with a fork until light.
4. Uncover the pan. Add the beaten eggs. In about 30 seconds, when the bottom has set, add the tomato and cheeses. Reduce the heat to medium. Cover and cook, turning the pan to ensure even heat, 5 minutes, or until the frittata has set.
5. Slide the skillet into the top third of the hot oven. Bake 10 to 12 minutes or until the center of the frittata is no longer runny but still soft.
6. Remove the skillet from the oven. Free the frittata by running a flexible-bladed, thin spatula between the rim of the pan and the edge of the frittata, and then under the frittata to free the bottom. The frittata may be served, cut in wedges, from the skillet or inverted onto a serving platter and then cut in wedges.

Yield: 2 servings
✦ **Calories per serving: 310**
Carbohydrate per serving: 10g
Cholesterol per serving: 505mg

Dietary fiber per serving: 1g
Fat per serving: 23g
Protein per serving: 17g
✦ **Sodium per serving: 368mg**

Sesame and Chive Dressing for Tossed Greens

❖

This is a distinctive, hearty dressing ideal with peppery greens such as watercress or arugula and soft-leafed lettuces. Try Bibb, Boston, or red leaf. This salad is untraditional but good with the Chinese Steamed Chicken with Mushrooms and Broccoli on page 284.

1 egg
1 tablespoon lemon juice

1 tablespoon tarragon vinegar
2 teaspoons Dijon mustard
1 small garlic clove, minced
2 to 3 drops hot oil, available at Oriental or
    specialty food markets
3 tablespoons peanut oil
½ teaspoon sesame oil, available at Oriental and
    specialty food markets
3 tablespoons beef consomme or homemade beef
    stock
2 tablespoons snipped fresh chives
1 tablespoon sesame seeds

1. Combine the egg, lemon juice, vinegar, mustard, garlic,
   and hot oil in the bowl of a food processor or a
   blender. Process for 30 seconds.
2. Combine the peanut oil, sesame oil, and beef consomme in a 1-cup measure. With the machine running,
   slowly dribble the liquids into the egg mixture.
3. Add the chives and sesame seeds and pulse the machine just to combine. Keep the dressing covered and
   chilled. It will keep up to 4 to 5 days.

Yield: 1 cup
✦ **Calories per tablespoon: 33**
Carbohydrate per tablespoon: 0g
✦ **Cholesterol per tablespoon: 15mg**
Dietary fiber per tablespoon: 0g
Fat per tablespoon: 3g
Protein per tablespoon: 1g
✦ **Sodium per tablespoon: 33mg**

Orange Pot De Crème

Traditionally, a pot de crème is a rich chocolate dessert
made with lots of eggs, sugar, and rich milk or cream. But
this *Enlightened Gourmet* version is sugarless, sweetened
with the fructose of oranges, and low in fat while calcium

rich. It's made in a minute, mixed right in the baking dish if you like, or it can be baked in individual molds. Prepare this dessert at least 2½ hours before serving to allow for chilling. It is terrific served with a spoonful of leftover sauce from Glazed Gingered Oranges on page 89.

> 2 eggs
> ½ cup dry skim milk powder
> 1 cup skim milk
> 1 6-ounce can frozen orange juice concentrate,
>   without added sugar, thawed
> 1 tablespoon orange-flavored liqueur such as
>   Triple Sec or Grand Marnier
> 2 oranges, for garnish (optional)
> 4 mint leaves, for garnish (optional)

1. Preheat the oven to 300 degrees. In a 1-quart souffle dish, ovenproof casserole, or bowl, beat the eggs until slightly thickened. Beat in the dry milk powder and milk. Beat until smooth. Beat in the orange juice and liqueur.

2. If you are using individual molds, divide the mixture among 4 ½-cup ramekins, or use a single 1-quart souffle dish. Place the molds or souffle dish in an 8-inch baking pan filled with 2 inches of hot tap water. Slide the baking dish with the mold(s) into the bottom third of the preheated oven.

3. Bake 1 hour for the souffle dish—about 35 minutes for the ramekins—or until a knife inserted slightly off center comes out with just a tiny bit of custard on it. The custard will shake slightly when the mold is jiggled. Remove the custard from the oven and the baking pan. Cool on the counter about ½ hour, then chill uncovered at least 1½ hours but preferably longer.

4. Pot de crème may be served as is or garnished very attractively with the oranges. Working over a bowl to catch the juices, peel off all the skin including the white membrane of the oranges. Free the orange sections by cutting between the membranes. Chill the orange sections in the juice, if desired. At serving time,

place 5 sections of orange pinwheel-fashion around the custard(s), which may be unmolded or not. Place a mint leaf or even a tiny flower blossom in the center.

Yield: 4 servings
+ **Calories per serving: 217**
Carbohydrate per serving: 34g
Cholesterol per serving: 125mg

Dietary fiber per serving: 0g
Fat per serving: 3g
Protein per serving: 12g
+ **Sodium per serving: 145mg**

❖ Focus: ❖
Too Much of a Good Thing

The notion that "a little is good for me, so more must be better" doesn't always hold true for vitamins and minerals. (See *Focus: Tracing Vitamin Poisoning*, page 329.) Not that there's anything wrong with vitamins or minerals as they occur naturally in food. But when all the daily needed vitamins amount to no more than an eighth of a teaspoon and vitamin supplements can be purchased in grossly exaggerated quantities—sometimes as much as 200 times the daily recommended amount—the potential for harm is clear.

Consider the case of a 57-year-old man who had been diagnosed as severely anemic. He was about to undergo chemotherapy for his "preleukemia" when it was discovered he had been taking 30 times the RDA of zinc for 2 years. The University of Missouri Health Services Center, where he was treated, concluded that his illness had been caused when the massive amounts of zinc interfered with his normal absorption of copper—a mineral needed to prevent the kind of anemia he had.

While a rare case, it does serve as a reminder that the body's biochemistry is a balanced one that can be thrown out of sync with too much meddling.

Too much calcium, for example, can interfere with the absorption of iron. An overdose of iron in persons with too high an absorption level can damage the liver and pancreas. High doses of vitamin E can lessen the body's ability to form vitamin A from its precursor, carotene, which is found in vegetables. And high doses of vitamin C may also alter the absorption of copper.

Determining how much of a vitamin or mineral might cause harm is considerably less precise than figuring an RDA value. Much depends on the individual, how long the overdose has continued, and how large it is. In addition, a dose that risks one person's health may not affect another's.

It all adds up to one more vote for moderation.

❖Losing weight, even maintaining desirable weight, takes a lot of mental energy. You have to be prepared to think about food in terms other than taste. You have to take the time (and have the knowledge) to seek out low-calorie choices and use cooking methods that maximize taste while skimping on fat. Habits that caused the weight gain to begin with have to be broken, and new habits must be made. Weight loss is just a dream if old eating patterns creep back.❖

A QUICK FIX

Mussels in Black Bean Sauce
Boiled Rice*
Spinach with Sesame Oil

When time is as tight as your waistband, it's *no* time for a hasty sandwich. That leads to the "I-deserve-this" snacks, which lead to an even tighter waistband. Instead, develop a series of quick meals that are tasty and interesting, yet easy on the clock. Then you'll know you've eaten and eaten well, making treats less tempting and more resistible.

This "Quick Fix" menu for four is such a meal. The lengthiest preparation is cleaning the mussels, a job that will be shortened if you can buy cultivated rather than "wild" mussels. Boil up a little rice to serve with the mussels and wilt some vitamin-A-iron-and-fiber-rich spinach in a hot pan. This low-fat meal ranks high on both taste and speed scales.

❖ Focus: Does What We Eat ❖ Really Matter?

One might well ask, "Does good nutrition really make a difference? What evidence is there that what I eat will have any effect on my health?" There are, of course, no guarantees in life and certainly none that state if you eat this, that, or the other thing, you won't die of a particular disease. But the USDA did attempt to estimate the cost of malnutrition in the United States. The agency suggests that improved nutrition alone could reduce illness and death from heart disease by 25 percent, from respiratory and infectious diseases by 20 percent, from cancer by 20 percent, and from diabetes by as much as 50 percent. Further, the Senate Committee on Nutrition felt improved nutrition could lessen the cost and suffering of anemia, obesity, alcoholism, allergies, dental decay, arthritis, and osteoporosis. Substantial sums, to say nothing of human discomfort, could be saved with better nutrition. It may be America's most valuable underutilized resource.

Mussels in Black Bean Sauce

❖

This is an interpretation of a recipe from Nina Simonds, a wonderful Chinese cook whose book and articles in *Gourmet* and other cooking magazines have done much to demystify and popularize that often healthy cuisine. You'll need a small jar of fermented black beans (actually soybeans) available at Oriental markets, many larger supermarkets, and specialty shops. You also will find Chinese cooking wine and hot oil in these shops. Clams or shrimp may be substituted for the mussels. (For more on mussels, see page 206.) This is indeed "A Quick Fix," an ideal meal when saving time (and calories) is paramount.

5 dozen mussels, about 4 pounds
4 tablespoons fermented or salted black beans
1 large or 2 small garlic cloves, minced
2 scallions, minced
2 tablespoons minced fresh ginger
2½ cups homemade chicken stock or canned
  chicken broth
2 tablespoons reduced-sodium soy sauce
3 tablespoons Chinese cooking wine

a few drops hot oil
2 teaspoons cornstarch
2 tablespoons chicken broth or water or Chinese
    cooking wine
1 tablespoon safflower oil

1. Soak the mussels in a big bowl, covered with water. Add a handful of cornmeal (theory has it the mussels ingest the cornmeal, forcing them to expel grit and sand) and let them rest at least 20 minutes or as long as 2 hours.
2. Lift the mussels from the bowl to a colander (don't pour, or all the sand will be washed back into them). Rinse them thoroughly in the colander. Then pull off the beard—the black threadlike strings—with a small knife or your fingers. Try to slide the top and bottom shells in opposite directions between your thumb and index finger. Discard any shells that move easily, are open, or full of mud. Rinse the mussels again under lots of running water. Drain.
3. Place the black beans in a strainer and rinse under running water to remove most of the salt. Drain and chop. Mix the beans with the minced garlic, scallions, and ginger in a small bowl. Set aside.
4. Combine the chicken stock, soy sauce, wine, and hot oil. Set aside.
5. Dissolve the cornstarch in the 2 tablespoons of stock or water. Set aside.
6. Heat a wok or 12-inch skillet over high heat for about 1 minute or until it is very hot. Add the oil and black bean and scallion mixture. Stir-fry until fragrant, about 15 seconds.
7. Add the chicken stock mixture and heat over high heat until it is boiling. Add the cleaned mussels and cover. Cook, shaking the pan and stirring occasionally, until the mussels have opened, about 5 to 6 minutes. Be careful not to overcook the mussels or they will become tough.
8. Uncover the pan and stir in the dissolved cornstarch. Reduce heat to medium. Cook the sauce, stirring, until

it is lightly thickened. Serve in shallow soup bowls with rice as a side dish, or scoop the rice into the bottom of the soup bowl and put the mussels and sauce on top.

Yield: 4 servings
✦ Calories per serving: 222
Carbohydrate per serving: 10g
✦ Cholesterol per serving: 82mg

Dietary fiber per serving: 0.8g
Fat per serving: 9g
Protein per serving: 27g
Sodium per serving: 868mg

Spinach with Sesame Oil

❖

Spinach is a handy vegetable, but somewhat maligned. Quite versatile, it is good cooked with a range of other flavorings from tomatoes to onions. It also is a crispy addition to the salad bowl. A half cup is very low in calories (21), provides more than 100 percent of an adult's daily vitamin A requirement, and is a decent source of iron, calcium, and fiber.

1 tablespoon peanut oil
1 scallion, minced
1½ to 2 pounds fresh spinach, washed
¼ teaspoon sesame oil, available at specialty food
shops or Oriental markets
a few drops hot oil, available at specialty food
shops or Oriental markets

1. Heat the peanut oil in a 12-inch nonstick skillet over high heat until hot. Add the scallion, reduce heat to medium-high, and stir-fry for 30 seconds.
2. Add the spinach with the water that clings to its leaves to the skillet. Cover and cook the spinach over medium-high heat until it is wilted, about 1 to 2 minutes.

3. Remove the skillet from the heat, season it to taste with sesame oil and hot oil, and serve.

Yield: 4 servings
✦ Calories per serving: 83
Carbohydrate per serving: 8g
✦ Cholesterol per serving: 0mg
✦ Dietary fiber per serving: 7g
Fat per serving: 5g
Protein per serving: 7g
✦ Sodium per serving: 179mg

❖Avoid "mindless munchies." If you want to eat less, then make every mouthful count. Cook and eat delicious yet fat-stringent food. Don't eat on the run if you can help it. If you must, at least choose something relatively light. Make a rule not to snack from the box or whatever, and never to eat unless the food is on a plate and you are sitting at the table.❖

SIMPLE, NOT PLAIN

Chicken Paillards with Fresh Herb Salsa

Lentils with Parsley and Scallions

Roasted Asparagus "Al Forno"

Here's a meal that is simple—in thought—but not plain in taste. Boneless, skinless chicken breasts are perked up with a fresh herb sauce that heightens but doesn't mask their flavor. Grilled, or pan sauteed, these paillards take only a few minutes to cook. Equally quick are roasted asparagus. Yes, roasted asparagus spears. A technique used by a popular Rhode Island restaurant, high temperature oven-cooking concentrates the sugars yet leaves a crisp, brilliantly green vegetable. You might try the same idea with thin sliced potatoes, or green beans (see page 286).

Rounding out this midweek supper are lentils. Unlike many of their cousins, these good-for-you legumes cook up in little more than half an hour's time—ten minutes if presoaked.

Simple needn't be synonymous with plain or predictable. This menu serving two proves otherwise.

❖ Focus: Grilling Chicken ❖

Come summer Saturdays, the sum of my cooking creativity seems to amount to: How shall we do the chicken on the grill this time? Like most families we harbor a few idiosyncrasies when it comes to grilled chicken. We don't like heavy, sugary barbecue sauces, we do like really moist meat, and we do like—no love—the crispy, crunchy, browned skin that the grill turns out so right. Imagine then my husband's horror when I mentioned that the chicken—the first of the season yet—would go on the grill without the health-threatening (it's high in saturated fat and calories) but delicious skin! A culinary skeptic of the "Show me" school, he found, much to his surprise, that the skinless chicken was just as good as the old way. Here are a few tips for delicious, grilled, skinless chicken:

1. Shake the skinned chicken pieces in a plastic bag with about ½ cup of bread crumbs and a couple table-spoons of flour; add salt and pepper to taste. An added teaspoon of dried rosemary, oregano, tarragon, or thyme (not all at once) is compatible with chicken.
2. Combine the following in a 1-cup measure for a basting sauce: a tablespoon or so of safflower oil, the juice of 1 lemon, ½ cup dry white wine, a crushed clove of garlic, a tablespoon of Dijon or Pommery mustard, and a shake or two of curry powder if you like. Whisk with a fork and use to baste chicken as it cooks.
3. Cook the chicken over very slow coals, or the lowest setting if you are using a gas grill. While grill temperatures will vary, I find 55 to 65 minutes for cut-up chicken to be about right.
4. Turn the chicken frequently, and twist it as it cooks to ensure even cooking.
5. Partially precooking the chicken in a microwave oven before browning it on the grill makes for very tender chicken. Shake the chicken with the bread crumbs after microwaving.
6. Use mesquite or other woods for interesting flavors. I doubted mesquite offered any real flavor after various tries in restaurants until I used it myself with a covered grill. When the chips are soaked about 20 minutes (water is fine, though spirits or juices can be tried) and the cover is used throughout the cooking, mesquite does indeed impart a distinctive yet subtle flavor. Cherry, apple, and hickory woods are good, too.

Chicken Paillards with Fresh Herb Salsa

❖

This is a quick and tasty dish for the warmer months of the year when the kitchen herb patch is in full bloom (though dried proportions are included). A chicken paillard is the breast boned, skinned, and cooked without fat. The Fresh Herb Salsa recipe can be halved, as it provides more than is needed for just these paillards. But it keeps for a little more than one week and is so versatile, you might like to have it on hand. Try a spoonful on grilled or baked white fish or stirred into hot vegetables such as green beans, or use it as a dip for crudités.

You may grill or pan saute the paillards as you wish.

For the Fresh Herb Salsa

1 red bell pepper
¼ cup chopped sweet onion, such as Vidalla or
    Bermuda
½ cup minced fresh parsley
1 tablespoon snipped fresh tarragon or ½
    teaspoon dried tarragon
6 to 7 fresh sage leaves or ½ teaspoon dried sage
1 tablespoon snipped fresh chives
1 garlic clove, minced
dried red pepper flakes to taste
2 tablespoons olive oil, extra-virgin recommended
5 tablespoons homemade chicken stock or
    canned chicken broth
1 tablespoon balsamic vinegar
¼ cup plain low-fat yogurt

For the Chicken Paillards

2 chicken breasts, boned and skinned
2 teaspoons safflower oil for pan sauteing

To Prepare the Salsa

1. Combine all the salsa ingredients except the yogurt in the bowl of a food processor. Process until the mixture is well blended; the herbs should still be coarse, not pureed.
2. Add the yogurt and pulse the machine just to combine. Store the mixture in the refrigerator in a covered container. It will keep slightly longer than a week.

To Prepare the Chicken

1. To saute the chicken breasts: Coat an 8- to 10-inch skillet with cooking spray and place the pan over high heat. Add a film of safflower oil. When the oil is hot, add the chicken and brown. When lightly browned, about 2 minutes, reduce the heat to medium and coat the top side of each breast with a tablespoon of fresh herb salsa. Continue to cook the chicken 2 minutes more, with the pan covered. Uncover the pan, flip the breast over, and again film the pan with safflower oil. Return the heat to high, if necessary, to brown the other side. When browned, about 1 to 2 minutes, coat the top side of each breast with another tablespoon of salsa. Re-cover the pan, reduce the heat to medium, and continue to cook about 1 to 2 minutes until the paillards are firm but not hard when pressed. Transfer paillards to a serving platter.
2. To grill the chicken: place the breasts over the hot coals (or heating element). Coat the top surface of each breast with a tablespoon of herb salsa. Twist the breasts as they cook to guarantee even heat. When they are browned on one side and partially cooked, about 4 minutes, flip them over. Coat the remaining side with another tablespoon of herb salsa. Cook, twisting the

paillards from time to time, until they are firm but not hard when pressed. Serve the paillards hot from the grill with another spoonful of herb salsa, if desired.

Yield: 1 cup Fresh Herb Salsa;
2 servings chicken with
2 tablespoons each of salsa
✦ Calories per serving: 306
Carbohydrate per serving: 3g

✦ Cholesterol per serving: 73mg
Dietary fiber per serving: 0g
Fat per serving: 20g
Protein per serving: 27g
✦ Sodium per serving: 67mg

Lentils with Parsley and Scallions

❖

Unlike lots of legumes (see *Focus: Beans* on page 337), lentils are relatively quick cooking. If soaked for about an hour, they'll cook up in a mere 10 minutes. If they are set to simmer with no presoaking, plan on 30 to 35 minutes. A staple in Middle Eastern cooking, lentils are compatible with parsley, scallions, shallots, garlic, and mint (not all together!). An excellent source of vegetable protein, lentils make a little meat or chicken go a long way. Lentils are also a good source of carbohydrates and fiber, and contribute fair amounts of potassium (aids water balance in body tissues) and phosphorus (good for bones and teeth). They're delicious too. Try the red ones if they are available; they have great color.

½ cup lentils
2 tablespoons minced fresh parsley
1 tablespoon minced scallion
1 teaspoon safflower oil
2 teaspoons unsalted butter, at room temperature
¼ teaspoon salt
lots of freshly ground black pepper to taste

1. If you wish, soak the lentils in water that covers them by 2 inches for 1 hour; drain. Place the lentils in a 2½-quart saucepan with 2 cups of fresh water. Cover and bring to a boil over high heat.
2. Reduce the heat so the liquid just simmers. Simmer the lentils until they are tender (determine by munching a few), about 10 minutes for soaked lentils, or 30 to 35 minutes for unsoaked lentils. Drain.
3. Toss the lentils with the parsley, scallions, oil, butter, and salt. Mix well to combine. Add pepper and taste for seasoning adjustment. Serve hot. Lentils may be reheated in a microwave oven at high power for 1½ minutes, if needed.

Yield: 2 generous servings
Calories per serving: 219
Carbohydrate per serving: 29g
✦ **Cholesterol per serving: 10mg**

✦ **Dietary fiber per serving: 2g**
Fat per serving: 7g
Protein per serving: 12g
✦ **Sodium per serving: 310mg**

Roasted Asparagus "Al Forno"

❖

A fine restaurant in Providence, Rhode Island, named "Al Forno" (meaning "from the oven") runs many of its vegetables through very high heat ovens. Asparagus come out crisp yet tender and superbly flavored with very little added fat and no salt. This simple recipe is my adaptation of their unique technique.

½ pound asparagus, peeled
1 teaspoon olive oil, extra-virgin recommended
2 lemon wedges
freshly ground black pepper to taste

1. Preheat the oven to 500 degrees. Place the asparagus on a baking sheet in a single layer, not touching. Drizzle with the oil.
2. Roast the asparagus in the upper third of the oven, turning occasionally, until the spears are tender when pierced with a fork. This will take about 8 to 10 minutes, depending on the thickness of the spears.
3. Place the asparagus on a serving platter. Garnish with lemon wedges and pass a pepper mill at the table.

Yield: 2 generous servings
✦ Calories per serving: 49
Carbohydrate per serving: 6g
✦ Cholesterol per serving: 0mg

Dietary fiber per serving: 1g
Fat per serving: 3g
Protein per serving: 4g
✦ Sodium per serving: 3mg

❖ Focus: Complete Vegetable ❖ Protein

If your diet includes animal foods—meat, poultry, fish, and dairy—there's very little chance of a protein deficiency. But if you do serve or would like to serve more vegetable meals that exclude meats, it's best to rely on concentrated sources of plant proteins, such as legumes and whole-grain products, and to supplement with small amounts of animal proteins such as low-fat cheeses and milk. Here's why.

The body builds protein from units called amino acids. There are 20 such acids; the body produces 11, and 9 must come from food. If any single amino acid is missing—known as the limiting amino acid—the body can't form protein, the "building block" of life.

All animal foods, except gelatin, contain all 9 essential amino acids, making them excellent protein sources. Vegetables, however, have a limiting amino acid. (Soybeans and nuts do contain all the amino acids, but not in sufficient quantity for growth.) For the body to synthesize protein from vegetable foods then, they must be paired so all 9 amino acids are present at the same meal. An example is rice and beans (see Hoppin' John, page 158), where the limiting amino acid in the rice is compensated for by the black-eyed peas and vice versa.

Vegetable protein can also be boosted by adding a bit of animal protein. Chili's a good example; predominately kidney beans, with a little meat, it makes for a nutritionally complete meal as does fettucine with clam sauce, or cereal and milk. We really don't need meat or other animal foods to stay healthy, but it does make good sense to heed a little nutritional science.

❖Skipping meals is a pretty ineffective way to achieve permanent weight loss. 1) It doesn't modify the habits that contributed to the weight gain to begin with, and 2) you'll be so hungry and self-righteous about not eating that it's far easier to be tempted into snacking on high-calorie foods, like cheese and crackers or chips.❖

OVERNIGHT
SUCCESS

Veal and Artichoke Ragout
Apple, Walnut, and Roquefort Salad
Buttered Egg Noodles*
Spiced Pumpkin Rum Chiffon

Veal is considered such a luxury by most people that its presence in this "Dinner in the Kitchen" section may seem odd until the recipe is closely read. Inexpensive veal chunks and a package of frozen artichoke hearts are the prime ingredients of this do-ahead stewlike recipe. Double the Veal and Artichoke Ragout if you like; half may be frozen, providing an easy meal for a hurried day. Or cook the dish a day before serving, keeping it chilled and covered for up to twenty-four hours. Like many dishes where the flavors must mingle and marry, this is a true "overnight success."

Salads are a natural with stews. This menu, which serves four, offers a delightful salad of walnuts, apples, and Roquefort cheese. The dressing will keep under refrigeration for up to five days; toss it with the salad just before serving. Serve the ragout and salad with packaged egg noodles, though heartier appetites might enjoy another vegetable. The Roasted Green Beans (page 286), Lentils with Parsley and Scallions (page 272), or a saute of summer squash would complement the meal nicely. If dinner is not dinner without dessert, try the Spiced Rum Pumpkin Chiffon. It too is best made a day ahead, and will provide a dessert for yet another meal.

Veal and Artichoke Ragout

A simple dish, low in fat but heavy on satisfaction and welcome in cool weather. For a change, serve with lentils (page 272) tossed just before serving with a diced tomato for color. Select a casserole dish that can be placed on direct heat as well as in the oven to reduce the number of cooking dishes.

> 1¼ pounds boneless veal for stew, trimmed of
>   any fat
> 1 tablespoon safflower oil
> 1 tablespoon all-purpose flour
> ¼ teaspoon salt
> freshly ground black pepper to taste
> 3 tablespoons brandy
> 6 tablespoons dry white wine or vermouth
> 2 large or 3 medium shallots, chopped
> 1 large garlic clove, minced
> 1 teaspoon fresh thyme or ½ teaspoon dried
>   thyme
> 4 tablespoons balsamic vinegar
> 1 tablespoon brown sugar
> 1 cup homemade chicken stock or canned
>   chicken broth
> 1 9-ounce package frozen artichoke hearts
> 1½ teaspoons arrowroot

1. Preheat the oven to 375 degrees. Cut the veal into bite-size chunks if necessary. Pat the meat dry on paper towels.
2. Coat a 12-inch nonstick skillet with cooking spray. Add the oil and place the skillet over high heat. When it is hot, add the meat cubes so they are in a single layer and not touching. (Saute the meat in two batches if necessary.) Saute the meat over high heat, stirring frequently with a wooden spoon, until the cubes are browned on all sides, about 4 minutes.

3. Reduce the heat to medium. Sprinkle flour, salt, and pepper over the meat and stir to combine.
4. Scrape the meat into an ovenproof 1½-quart casserole. Return the skillet to medium-high heat. Add the brandy. Ignite and stir with a wooden spoon for about 30 seconds to loosen particles from the skillet. Only a glaze—a very thin film on the bottom of the pan—should remain.
5. Add the wine, shallots, and garlic to the skillet, stirring frequently. Reduce the heat to medium, if necessary, to prevent burning. Cook the shallots and garlic until tender, about 1 minute.
6. Add the thyme, vinegar, and brown sugar to the shallots and garlic. Over medium heat stir to combine for 1 minute. Pour the mixture over the meat in the casserole.
7. Reserving 1 tablespoon of chicken stock, stir the remaining stock into the casserole. Cover the dish and bake it for 45 minutes in the middle of the preheated oven.
8. Remove the casserole from the oven. Stir in the artichoke hearts. Re-cover the dish and reduce the oven temperature to 300 degrees. Return the casserole to the middle of the oven for 45 more minutes.
9. When the meat is tender, dissolve the arrowroot in the reserved tablespoon of chicken stock. Transfer the meat and artichoke hearts with a slotted spoon to a serving platter or bowl. Stir the dissolved arrowroot into the casserole juices. Set the casserole over high heat (pour the juices into a skillet if your casserole would break over direct heat) and stir until the juices are lightly thickened, about 1 minute. Return the meat to the casserole dish to serve, or pour the juices over the meat on a serving platter.

Yield: 4 servings   Dietary fiber per serving: 1g
✦ Calories per serving: 381   Fat per serving: 18g
Carbohydrate per serving: 18g   Protein per serving: 30g
Cholesterol per serving: 145mg   ✦ Sodium per serving: 325mg

Apple, Walnut, and Roquefort Salad

One of my favorite salads, a double portion with a hunk of crusty bread makes a great, light dinner.

For the Dressing

2 tablespoons sesame oil, available at Oriental or specialty food markets
2 tablespoons olive oil, extra-virgin recommended
¼ cup canned beef consomme or homemade beef stock
1 tablespoon plus 1 teaspoon lemon juice
3 drops or to taste hot oil, available at Oriental or specialty food markets
2 tablespoons minced fresh chives

For the Salad

torn greens including red leaf lettuce, arugula if available, and Bibb
2 ounces crumbled Roquefort cheese, room temperature
1 ounce roughly chopped shelled walnuts
1 apple, Granny Smith or McIntosh recommended, cored and chopped

1. Combine all the dressing ingredients in a small bowl. Blend with a fork and chill. It will keep in the refrigerator for up to 5 days.
2. Toss the greens in a large bowl. Sprinkle with the cheese, walnuts, and apple. Just before serving add the dressing and toss.

Yield: 4 generous servings
Calories per serving: 248
Carbohydrate per serving: 8g
✦ **Cholesterol per serving: 14mg**

✦ **Dietary fiber per serving: 2g**
Fat per serving: 22g
Protein per serving: 6g
✦ **Sodium per serving: 266mg**

Spiced Rum Pumpkin Chiffon

❖

This recipe is for pumpkin and spice lovers. The unorthodox dry milk powder whipped with the egg whites contributes body without the fat calories of whipped cream.
This dessert may be made the day before serving; plan on
at least 3 to 4 hours chilling time if it is to be served the
day it's made. Although the menu is for four, this dessert
serves 6 or even 8. The leftovers will keep in the refrigerator for 2 or 3 days, covered with plastic wrap.

> 2 envelopes unflavored gelatin
> ½ cup apple juice or cider
> 1 tablespoon cornstarch
> 1 cup low-fat or skim milk
> 1 tablespoon dark brown sugar
> 4 tablespoons molasses
> 2 eggs, separated
> ½ teaspoon ground cinnamon
> 1 teaspoon freshly grated fresh ginger
> freshly grated nutmeg
> ½ cup canned or fresh, mashed, cooked pumpkin
> a pinch of salt
> 1 tablespoon sugar
> 2 tablespoons instant dry milk powder
> 2 teaspoons dark rum

1. Soften the gelatin in the apple juice in a 1-quart saucepan; let stand 1 minute. Then stir over medium heat for
   1 minute until the gelatin is dissolved. Set aside.
2. Dissolve the cornstarch in the milk in a 2½-quart saucepan. Stir over medium-high heat until lightly thickened, about 2 minutes. Stir in the brown sugar and
   molasses and remove the pan from the heat.
3. Beat the egg yolks in a small bowl until frothy. Whisk

into the milk-cornstarch over medium-high heat until the mixture is thickened, about 2 to 3 minutes.

4. Remove from heat and beat in the cinnamon, ginger, nutmeg, pumpkin, and dissolved gelatin. Turn into a bowl and chill until the mixture mounds slightly when dropped from a spoon, between 1 hour and 3 hours, depending on the refrigerator.

5. Beat the egg whites with the pinch of salt until soft peaks form. Beat in the sugar and continue to beat until stiff peaks form. Beat in the milk powder and rum. Fold into the pumpkin mixture. Divide among 6 to 8 parfait glasses and chill at least 3 to 4 hours.

Yield: 6 to 8 servings
✦ **Calories per serving: 95**
Carbohydrate per serving: 15g
Cholesterol per serving: 70mg

Dietary fiber per serving: 0g
Fat per serving: 2g
Protein per serving: 4g
✦ **Sodium per serving: 115mg**

❖ Focus: ❖
The Difference in Fats

"Saturated," "monounsaturated," and "polyunsaturated" are terms that refer to the chemical makeup of fats. If a fat molecule were a sports stadium and every seat was taken it would be a saturated fat, monounsaturated if a few seats were empty, and polyunsaturated if many seats were empty.

Polyunsaturated fats tend to help the body get rid of cholesterol, saturates tend to raise cholesterol, and monounsaturates are neutral.

When vegetable oils are processed to make them firm, as for some margarines, those imaginary seats in the stadium are filled with hydrogen atoms. This hydrogenation makes a more saturated fat. When buying margarines, look for those with liquid vegetable oil as the first ingredient, or buy the softest margarine available. Read more about the different fats and oils on page 145.

Let this brief chart be a guide to fats.

POLYUNSATURATES	MONOUNSATURATES	SATURATES
corn oil	almonds	butter
cottonseed oil	olive oil	lard
fish	avocados	chocolates
grapeseed oil	peanut butter	palm oil
margarine (most)	cashews	coconut oil
mayonnaise	walnuts	cheese
safflower oil	peanut oil	poultry skin
sesame oil		meat
		milk
		egg yolk

❖Coriander is an herb that supplies both seeds and green, lacy leaves (also known as cilantro or Chinese parsley). Much used in Mexican, Indian, and Oriental cooking, its pungent taste and distinctive odor may take some getting used to. Very easy to grow in a small kitchen herb garden, coriander is a natural with tomatoes and fruits such as apples and pears.❖

CHOPSTICKS

**Chinese Steamed Chicken with Mushrooms
and Broccoli**

Chinese Noodles

Roasted Green Beans

Steaming foods is an excellent cooking method for the calorie-conscious, because flavors intensify and sauces are superfluous. It's also quick and requires no special equipment, though an inexpensive wok and bamboo steamer come in handy. In this quick dinner for two, boneless chicken breasts pair with mushrooms and broccoli in a typically Chinese-style duo. Half an hour—certainly no more than forty-five minutes—is all that's needed from the first chop of the knife to the first click of the chopsticks. Served with the steamed dish are fresh Chinese noodles (store-bought) and unique high-heat-roasted green beans.

If you've never eaten with chopsticks before, give it a try. My husband and I started using them several years ago when we were trying to eat more slowly. For a while, a very short while, perhaps we did eat less and linger over each mouthful longer. But you get good, very quickly. Hunger is a great incentive.

If Chinese noodles aren't available at your market, use spaghetti or substitute a simple boiled rice.

Chinese Steamed Chicken with Mushrooms and Broccoli

❖

Fragrant with ginger and nearly fat-free, this is a recipe you'll reach for often. A wok and bamboo steamer work best, but a similar arrangement can be fashioned by placing a cake rack on 4 inverted ramekins in a deep electric skillet that has a cover.

> 2 chicken breasts, skinned and boned
> 3 ounces mushrooms, sliced
> 1 cup broccoli flowerets
> 1 teaspoon minced fresh ginger
> 1 small garlic clove, minced
> 2 tablespoons water
> 2 tablespoons reduced-sodium soy sauce
> 2 tablespoons Chinese cooking wine or rice wine,
>   or 1 tablespoon dry wine plus 1 tablespoon
>   dry sherry
> 1 tablespoon cornstarch
> 2 teaspoons peanut oil
> ¼ teaspoon sesame oil, available at Oriental and
>   specialty food markets
> 1 recipe Chinese Noodles (see next page)

1. Slice the chicken on the bias into 1-inch-wide pieces. Set aside.
2. Combine all the remaining ingredients except the noodles in a medium-size bowl. Stir to combine as well as to dissolve the cornstarch. Add the chicken pieces to the bowl. Stir well to combine.
3. Tear off a sheet of aluminum foil about 20 inches long. Pour the chicken mixture onto the center of the foil. Spread it out so the meat is as nearly as possible in a

single layer. Roll the foil closed, keeping the package as flat as possible. (Recipe may be prepared to this point and kept chilled up to 4 hours.)

4. Bring 2 cups of water to a boil over high heat in a wok fitted with a bamboo steamer. When a boil is reached, place the foil package in the steamer. Cover and steam, adjusting heat if necessary, for 15 minutes.

5. Remove the foil package from the steamer using tongs and an oven mitt. Arrange the Chinese Noodles on a serving platter. Open the chicken package and pour the contents over the noodles.

Yield: 2 servings
+ Calories per serving: 245
Carbohydrate per serving: 11g
+ Cholesterol per serving: 68mg

Dietary fiber per serving: 1g
Fat per serving: 7g
Protein per serving: 31g
Sodium per serving: 674mg

Chinese Noodles

❖

Look for fresh Chinese noodles in the produce section of most large supermarkets. They are delicious and easy to prepare. An opened package of noodles will keep in the refrigerator for 2 to 3 days.

4 ounces fresh Chinese noodles
1 teaspoon minced scallion
½ teaspoon minced fresh ginger
2 teaspoons peanut oil
1 teaspoon reduced-sodium soy sauce

1. Fill a 2½-quart saucepan three-quarters full with water. Cover and bring to a boil over high heat. When the water is boiling, remove the cover and add the noodles. Boil, stirring occasionally, for 3 minutes.

2. Drain the noodles. (Noodles may be cooked as much as 1 hour in advance and left to drain. Reheat by dousing with 2 to 3 quarts boiling water.)
3. Return the drained noodles to the saucepan. Combine with the scallion, ginger, oil, and soy sauce. (The seasoned noodles may be held in a double boiler up to 45 minutes over low heat, or held off the heat, covered, for up to 1 hour. Reheat gently before serving.) Serve warm.

Yield: 2 servings
Calories per serving: 320
Carbohydrate per serving: 33g
✦ **Cholesterol per serving: 7mg**

Dietary fiber per serving: 0g
Fat per serving: 18g
Protein per serving: 8g
✦ **Sodium per serving: 97mg**

Roasted Green Beans

❖

Borrowing again from Al Forno Restaurant in Providence, Rhode Island (see Roasted Asparagus, page 273), these green beans are remarkably well flavored. Try them with other entrees such as the Vegetable Frittata with Two Cheeses (page 257) or the Curried Cod with Couscous (page 288).

½ pound fresh green beans
2 teaspoons olive oil, extra-virgin recommended
fresh lemon juice to taste
freshly ground black pepper

1. Preheat oven to 500 degrees. Prepare the beans for cooking by lining up several beans and cutting across the tips. Realign and cut across the bottom ends. Repeat until all the beans are "tipped and tailed." Spread the beans in a single layer on a baking sheet.

2. Drizzle the beans with the oil. Roast the beans in the middle of the preheated oven, turning 2 or 3 times, until they are tender, about 5 or 6 minutes.
3. Transfer the beans to a serving dish. Season with lemon juice and pepper.

Yield: 2 generous servings
✦ Calories per serving: 76
Carbohydrate per serving: 8g
✦ Cholesterol per serving: 0mg

✦ Dietary fiber per serving: 2g
Fat per serving: 5g
Protein per serving: 2g
✦ Sodium per serving: 7mg

❖ Focus: Natural ❖ Vitamins—Are They Better?

To the body, or a scientist, a vitamin is a vitamin is a vitamin. Whether it originates in a test tube and is labeled ascorbic acid or in an orange and commonly called vitamin C, biochemically the synthetic and the natural vitamin are identical. Some "natural" vitamin products—with their implied superiority—are in fact mostly synthetic with a small amount of vitamin from a natural source added. Ascorbic acid with rose hips or B vitamins in a yeast base are predominately manufactured nutrients, no better than a generic, synthesized vitamin, which in turn is no better or worse than a natural vitamin. The only counter to this rule is vitamin E, which is somewhat different chemically, and hence less effective when manufactured.

❖Chilling will congeal the bit of fat in canned broth, making it easy to spoon off.❖

PURSE PLEASER

Curried Cod with Couscous
Tahini Dressing for Mixed Greens
Banana Bread with Wheat Germ

This casual meal for four or five provides dividends for another day with leftovers of salad dressing (which will keep a week and make a great spread on pita or as a dip for raw vegetables) and banana bread. It is a meal that pairs some very familiar foods with some unknown (to many people) foods, such as couscous and tahini. Both are available at large supermarkets and specialty food shops. It's not a meal to fuss over or devote a lot of time to, but it is rather unique and certainly more than satisfying. Make the banana bread a day ahead for best flavor and slicing. Much of the curried cod may be put together a few hours in advance. Roasted Green Beans, on page 286, are particularly good with this menu if another vegetable is your pleasure.

Curried Cod with Couscous

A casual dish for those who like curries and grains, this is easily prepared, thanks to the quick-cooking couscous available at specialty food shops and some large supermarkets. Couscous is a staple of North African Mediterranean countries where this semolina wheat "paste" lends its name to an entire dish, a spicy mutton stew.

Quick-cooking couscous involves little more than opening a box and boiling some water. A good source of fiber with a rich, wheat, almost nutty flavor, it is ready in a mere 10 minutes. Here, it melds deliciously with low-fat curried fish. Inexpensive "junk" white fish, such as cusk, cod cheeks, or chowder fish, is ideal for this spicy, full-flavored meal. Pass a small bowl of chutney for added flavor.

> 1 cup chopped mild onion, such as Spanish or Vidalla
> 2 celery ribs, chopped
> 2 small or 1 large garlic clove, minced
> 2 cups homemade beef stock or canned beef consomme
> 2 8-ounce bottles clam juice
> 2 tablespoons pine nuts
> 1 tablespoon safflower oil
> 1 tablespoon minced fresh ginger
> 1 tablespoon curry powder or more to taste
> 2 apples, cored and chopped (Granny Smith recommended)
> 2 tablespoons all-purpose flour
> ½ cup dry white wine (a Chardonnay is excellent)
> 3 tablespoons golden raisins
> ⅔ cup peas, fresh or frozen
> 1 tablespoon unsalted butter
> 1 cup quick-cooking couscous
> 1 pound white fish fillets or chunks such as cod, monkfish, haddock, or cusk, cut into bite-size pieces
> chutney to pass at the table (optional)

1. Combine the onion, celery, and garlic with ½ cup of the beef stock and 1 bottle of the clam juice in a 12-inch skillet. Cover, and bring to a boil over high heat. Then reduce the heat so the liquid just simmers, and cook until the onion and celery are tender, about 20 minutes.
2. While the vegetables cook, place the pine nuts in a

heavy-bottomed 8-inch skillet. Place the skillet over high heat and toast the nuts, shaking the pan frequently until the nuts are golden, about 2 minutes. Watch carefully as pine nuts burn readily. Remove the nuts from the pan and set aside.

3. Uncover the vegetable pan and add the oil, ginger, and curry powder. Cook over medium heat for 1 minute, stirring.

4. Stir in the apple and flour. Stir over medium heat 1 more minute.

5. Add the remaining bottle of clam juice and the wine. Stir over medium heat until the sauce is free of lumps, about 3 to 4 minutes.

6. Stir in the raisins, peas, and pine nuts. (Recipe may be made to this point and held on the stove up to 1 hour, or chilled and held several hours before completing. If you do hold it, more liquid, either broth, wine, or clam juice, may be needed to thin the sauce.)

7. Cover the skillet and simmer over very low heat, stirring frequently, 10 to 15 minutes.

8. While the curry simmers, put the remaining 1½ cups beef stock with the butter in 2½-quart saucepan. Bring it to a boil, then stir in the couscous, cover the pan, and remove it from the heat. Let it rest 5 minutes while you complete the dish.

9. Uncover the curry skillet and add the fish. Stir, re-cover, and set the skillet over medium-low heat until the fish is tender, about 5 minutes. Fluff the couscous with a fork. Serve the curry with the couscous. Pass chutney at the table, if desired.

Yield: 4 to 5 servings (analysis based on 5)
+ **Calories per serving: 300**
  Carbohydrate per serving: 33g
+ **Cholesterol per serving: 60mg**
+ **Dietary fiber per serving: 2g**
  Fat per serving: 8g
  Protein per serving: 23g
+ **Sodium per serving: 453mg**

Tahini Dressing
for Mixed Greens

❖

Tahini is to the Middle East as peanut butter is to the United States. A rich, thick paste made from sesame seeds, it's most familiar to Americans in a dip known as hummus, a gutsy blend of lemon, garlic, chick peas, and tahini served with wedges of pita bread. Here, tahini lends its nutty heft to a salad dressing that is excellent with hardy greens; try spinach, shredded cabbage, shredded iceberg, watercress, and chicory. A few slices of apple would add color and tang. Tahini dressing will keep in the refrigerator for over a week, but it does thicken with chilling. Thin, if desired, with lemon juice and/or chicken stock or even water. Left thick, it's a wonderful spread for pita bread, run under the broiler until bubbly and browned, or as a dip for raw vegetables. Tahini paste may be purchased at specialty food shops and some large supermarkets. Stir or whirl the paste in a food processor before using it if the oil has separated. Keep unused tahini chilled if you use it infrequently.

⅓ cup tahini paste
⅓ cup lemon juice
2 small garlic cloves, minced
½ cup homemade chicken stock or canned
    chicken broth
2 tablespoons minced fresh parsley
2 tablespoons minced scallion
¼ teaspoon cumin (optional; makes the dressing
    "hot")

1. Combine all the ingredients in the bowl of a food processor or blender and combine until smooth. Scrape

into a container. The dressing is ready to use; cover and chill the remainder.

Yield: 1 cup
✦ **Calories per tablespoon: 33**
Carbohydrate per tablespoon: 2g
✦ **Cholesterol per tablespoon: 0mg**
Dietary fiber per tablespoon: 0g
Fat per tablespoon: 3g
Protein per tablespoon: 1g
✦ **Sodium per tablespoon: 7mg**

Banana Bread
with Wheat Germ
❖

This familiar dessert bread is a simple variation on one a friend gave me. It is best made a day ahead and allowed to rest after cooling, tightly sealed in plastic wrap. Cut thin slices for calorie control!

1 egg
½ cup brown sugar
½ cup white sugar
3 tablespoons vegetable oil
4 small or 3 large very ripe bananas, peeled and
    mashed
1½ cups all-purpose white flour
1 teaspoon baking soda
1 teaspoon baking powder
½ teaspoon salt
½ cup whole wheat flour
⅓ cup wheat germ
½ cup chopped walnuts (optional)

1. Preheat the oven to 350 degrees. Coat 2 small loaf pans or 1 regular loaf pan with cooking spray.
2. In the bowl of a food processor or in a large mixing bowl, beat the egg until frothy.

3. Beat the sugars with the egg until thick and smooth. Beat in the oil and bananas. Mix until smooth.

4. Sift together the white flour, baking soda, baking powder, and salt. Add to the banana mixture and stir just to combine.

5. Stir in the whole wheat flour, 4 tablespoons of the wheat germ, and walnuts. Stir just to combine.

6. Pour the batter into the prepared pan(s). Sprinkle the top(s) with the remaining wheat germ. Bake the bread in the lower third of the oven until a toothpick inserted slightly off-center comes out clean. This will take about 35 minutes for small pans, 45 to 50 minutes for a large pan.

7. Allow the bread to cool in the pan(s) for 30 minutes, then transfer to a rack and cool until room temperature (if you can resist it!). Wrap in plastic wrap and chill for easy slicing or store at room temperature.

Yield: 1 large loaf (15 thin slices)
Calories per slice: 185
Carbohydrate per slice: 31g
✦ **Cholesterol per slice: 16mg**

Dietary fiber per slice: 1g
Fat per slice: 6g
Protein per slice: 4g
✦ **Sodium per slice: 128mg**

❖ Focus: Whole Grains ❖

Whole grains are the relatively unprocessed seeds of grasses. While not a mainstay of the American diet, grains such as rice, corn, and millet make up a significant portion of the world's diet. Grains are low in fat, high in carbohydrate, and supply moderate, though incomplete (see *Focus: Complete Vegetable Protein*, page 274) amounts of protein. The corn products supply vitamins A and C, and most grains are good sources of some of the B vitamins. Some, like kasha and millet, are excellent sources of iron, a nutrient many women don't get enough of. And many of these grains are good sources of fiber.

From a culinary point of view, whole grains provide variety and interest in place of the standard starches. For those interested in reducing their fat intake, grains paired with beans (see *Focus: Beans* page 337) can replace some of the meat in the daily diet without jeopardizing nutrition.

Here are some uncommon grains with tips on how to cook and serve them:

Barley: Perhaps best known in the perennial winter favorite, Barley and Mushroom Soup, barley is a delicious grain that deserves more attention. Most commonly available as pearl barley (the bran has been removed), it comes in coarse, medium, or fine depending on your preference. Use it as a side dish (see page 39) or stir it into soups and stews as a thickener.

Buckwheat or Kasha: This doesn't come from a grass so it isn't a true grain, but it is generally used as such. Buckwheat groats—designating a grain that's been hulled and broken up like grits—are boiled (1 cup buckwheat to 2 cups water, simmer 15 to 20 minutes, and they will double in volume) and mixed with onions and other vegetables for flavoring. Buckwheat flour is used in noodles (see pages 214–15), pancakes, and some breads.

Corn including Cornmeal, Grits, and Masa Harina: Well known in America, cornmeal is a basic found in cornbread, spoonbread, hush puppies, corn fritters, Indian Pudding, and so on. Grits are a way of life in the South where they show up at breakfast and dinner. Masa Harina is a cornflour treated with lime and much used in Tex-Mex and Mexican cooking. When the Pilgrims' wheat crop failed, the Indians showed them how to grow what the English came to call "corn," a generic term for grain or anything else very small. With the current surge of culinary chauvinism, corn is now probably America's most promoted grain.

Millet: A very high-quality protein grain relatively unknown in the western world. Millet has little flavor, making it a perfect foil for the highly spiced dishes of Africa.

Oats: This most nutritious of cereal grains is also now thought to be a cholesterol fighter. Oats come in different grinds and require different cooking times; check the labels. Use in muffins, breads, and as a cereal.

Rice: (See page 112 for information on white and

brown rice). Wild rice is not a true cereal grain but is treated as such. Wild rice is expensive because it has so far defied commercial cultivation. It grows where it wants in precious amounts. To keep this rare plant from extinction, many states have passed regulations making it illegal to harvest the wild rice in any way other than the inefficient Indian method of thwacking the plant with a stick. Some of the rice falls in the boat and some of it into the water, hopefully to sprout new plants. A basic way to cook wild rice is to add 1 cup of rice to 4 cups of boiling water. Cover and simmer 30 to 40 minutes or until tender.

Wheat: The only cereal grain rich in gluten, the property needed to make light, airy breads. Most wheat is eaten as flour, but whole grains are also processed. Bulgur (also known as wheat pilaf and given numerous spellings) comes in three grinds. It requires only a soaking to soften, making it extremely quick and easy to cook with. It is most often used in tabouli salads (see page 328). Wheat germ is highly perishable due to its high oil content. Very high in protein and fiber, it is used as a condiment sprinkled on salads, yogurt, and the like, or a few tablespoons can be stirred into bread batters (see page 288).

Most whole grains, unlike dried beans, are subject to spoilage either from insects or—for the higher fat types—rancidity. Once a package is opened, transfer it to a tightly covered canister. If the grain has a high fat content, like wheat germ, store it in the refrigerator.

❖Poppy seeds have more flavor if toasted in a 350-degree oven for 15 minutes. Shake the pan from time to time.❖

PICNIC PACK

Ham and Bean Salad
Whole Wheat Oatmeal Muffins
Fresh Fruit and Cheese

As wholesome as the out-of-doors, this picnic or backyard spread for four (easily more if the salad is doubled) is little effort. The ham and bean salad only gets better after a few hours in the refrigerator, and is easily mixed together in the morning. Make the muffins then too if you like; they'll stay moist up to twenty-four hours if wrapped tightly in foil. And the dessert is a hundred-percent no-cook non-effort.

Of particular nutritional interest are the many forms of fiber offered here. Beans, oatmeal, All-Bran cereal, whole wheat flour, and fruit are all significant and taste-appealing sources. For more on fiber see *Focus: There's Fiber...*, on the next page.

In addition to fiber, there's also plenty of protein. Although the salad calls for only a half-pound of meat, the beans and cheeses contribute important amounts of this "building block" nutrient. For calorie and fat control, increase the proportion of beans and deemphasize the animal proteins.

There is much room for such "play" in these recipes; they are the sort where you may let your creativity run. The salad easily plays host to a variety of other ingredients; kielbasa or other sausages, grilled zucchini, bits of red onion, grated and cooked corn, and a smattering of fresh thyme or basil would all lend their individual spunk. The muffins could be altered with wheat germ, nuts, raisins, a few tablespoons of millet, molasses instead of brown sugar, or half a mashed banana substituted for a bit of the buttermilk. Cooking's a lot more fun—and the results a little uncertain—when it's spontaneous. Believe me, we've laughed (and groaned) our way through a few spontaneous creations at my house!

❖ Focus: There's Fiber, and ❖ then, again, There's Fiber

Fiber, what our grandparents called "roughage," has been the subject of considerable attention in both the popular and scientific press. Once considered important only as a sort of system "regulator," it is now widely touted as a cancer preventative, weight-loss aid, and cholesterol reducer. But just what is fiber? Does it all work the same in the body and have all the claims been justified?

Definitions first. Fiber is the blanket name given several kinds of undigestible residues from plant foods. Some labels list "crude fiber" values and others "dietary fiber." Crude fiber is the term given the residue of a food sample after the lab has treated it with a solvent. Crude fiber values are really of limited use, since they may account for as little as one-seventh of the actual total dietary fiber of a food. Dietary fiber is the term given food residues that are not broken down by enzymes and absorbed into the bloodstream—in other words, what's left in the intestine after digestion. These residues are several different kinds of compounds found in the cell walls of plants. Therefore there is fiber, and then, again, there is fiber.

Basically all the compounds of dietary fiber fall into two categories, either Type I fiber or Type II.

TYPE I: acts like a sponge, absorbing many times its weight in water. Cellulose is an example of a Type I fiber. Found in wheat bran, whole-grain breads, and cereals, this fiber may help prevent colon cancer by removing carcinogens and by reducing the level of bile acids. It also helps to relieve some digestive problems and helps prevent constipation.

TYPE II: acts chemically to reduce or prevent some substances from being absorbed into the bloodstream. Pectin is an example of a Type II fiber. Found in fruits, vegetables, nuts, brown rice, barley, and oats, this type of fiber may help to lower the level of LDL cholesterol (the bad kind) without decreasing the amount of HDL cholesterol (the good kind). It does less to keep the system "regular" than Type I, however.

The benefits of both types of dietary fiber have been shouted from the rooftops in the last year. Here is a quick glance at the suspected benefits, with the most substantiated claims first. Remember, not all the tests are conclusive, not all the facts are in . . .

- Fiber relieves constipation.
- Fiber may help prevent diverticulosis, a disorder of the large intestine.
- Fiber has been implicated in the reduction of serum cholesterol, one of the chief risk factors in heart disease.
- Fiber may be instrumental in preventing colon cancer.
- Fiber may have an effect on high blood sugar levels of diabetics.
- Fiber may help with weight-loss or maintaining ideal weight by satisfying the appetite without adding lots of calories.

Health experts theorize the average American eats between 5 and 10 grams of dietary fiber a day, but ideally should be consuming at least twice that amount. It stands to reason that if lowering cholesterol is your health goal, you should be eating more Type II fiber—the fruits, vegetables, barley, oats, and brown rice. If you have a family history of colon cancer or wish to guard against constipation, eating more wheat bran, whole-grain breads, and cereals—the Type I fiber—might be in order.

Can you eat too much fiber? If the diet is nutritionally poor to begin with, too much fiber could interfere with the body's ability to absorb zinc, iron, magnesium, and calcium, but this shouldn't be a problem if you eat a wide variety of foods. Intestinal gas is another possible adverse effect; adding fiber gradually to the diet should overcome the problem.

This chart will help you spot high-fiber foods, and help you calculate your daily intake. Nutritionists recommend eating about 25 grams of fiber daily. Remember, fruits and vegetables eaten raw and with the peel generally have more fiber.

FOOD	SERVING SIZE	GRAMS OF FIBER
All-Bran cereal	½ cup	12.6
peanuts	3 ounces	8.0
Grape Nuts cereal	½ cup	7.5
corn	1 medium ear	5.2
raspberries	½ cup	4.6
bran muffin	1 medium	4.2
apple	1 medium	4.0
pear	1 medium	4.0
potato (baked)	1 medium	3.9
broccoli (cooked)	½ cup	3.8
banana	1 medium	3.0
spaghetti	3 ounces	3.0
brown rice	½ cup	2.4
beets (cooked)	½ cup	2.1
carrot (raw)	1 medium	1.8
strawberries	½ cup	1.6
whole wheat bread	1 slice	1.3
celery (raw)	1 stalk	1.1

❖To keep mint from taking over the herb garden, plant it pot and all. The pot will help confine the roving roots.❖

Ham and Bean Salad

❖

Here are ham 'n' beans as you've never had them before, in a do-ahead, even-better-the-second-day salad. Ideal for the picnic basket or a hot summer evening meal, this salad is easily put together in the cooler morning hours or up to 24 hours before serving. A practical way to introduce legumes to a meat-and-potatoes family, the proportion of animal proteins may be increased or decreased to suit your tastes. If meat is omitted altogether, the salad makes an excellent side dish or entree if it is served with a complementing protein such as milk.

The beans may be soaked the night before, or quick-soaked in the morning. If you want to omit the soaking and cooking and prefer to used canned (drained and rinsed) beans such as cannellini (white kidney beans) or red kidney beans, or a mixture of the two for more color, you should omit steps 1 and 2.

> 1½ cups dry small white beans or white kidney
>   beans
> 1 Chinese eggplant or ½ pound regular eggplant
> 2 teaspoons safflower oil
> 8 ounces ready-to-eat ham, trimmed of any fat
>   and diced (about 1⅓ cups)
> 4 ounces cherry tomatoes, halved
> 2 ounces mild cheddar cheese, diced
> ¼ cup fresh minced parsley
> 2 scallions, minced
> ⅓ cup fresh lemon juice
> 4 tablespoons olive oil, extra-virgin recommended
> 2 tablespoons homemade beef stock or canned
>   beef broth
> 2 teaspoons Pommery or other whole-grain
>   mustard
> 1 large garlic clove, minced
> ½ teaspoon salt

a few drops hot pepper sauce to taste
lots of freshly ground black pepper
several lettuce leaves (including watercress or
arugula if desired) to line serving platter

1. To soak beans overnight: Place the beans in a large bowl. Cover with 6 cups water. Drain and continue the recipe at step 2 in the morning or after 8 hours. To quick-soak beans: Place the beans in a 2½-quart saucepan. Cover with 6 cups water. Cover the pan and bring it to a boil over high heat and let it boil for 2 minutes. Remove the pan from the heat. Let the beans rest, covered, for 1 hour. Drain and continue.

2. Place the beans in a 2½-quart saucepan. Cover beans with about 5 cups fresh water. Cover the pan and bring the beans to a boil over high heat. When a boil is reached, reduce the heat and simmer the beans until the skins ripple and break when a few beans are held in a spoon and blown on. This will take about 30 minutes for small white beans, and as long as an hour for larger beans. Drain the beans and pour them into a large bowl.

3. While the beans simmer, prepare the eggplant. Cut the Chinese eggplant in half the long way; cut regular eggplant in ½-inch-thick slices. Chinese eggplant doesn't need salting; regular eggplant does. To salt the eggplant, liberally sprinkle the slices with kosher or regular salt on both sides and let the slices rest on paper towels for 20 minutes. Thoroughly rinse the eggplant and pat dry. To grill either kind of eggplant (if grilling is convenient): Brush eggplant with half the safflower oil. Grill one side (the flesh side of Chinese eggplant) over low coals about 5 to 6 minutes. Baste top with remaining safflower oil. Turn over and grill the other (the skin side of Chinese eggplant) for another 4 to 5 minutes or until the flesh is tender when pierced with a fork. Remove from the coals and cool a few minutes. Slice the eggplant into large bite-size pieces and add to the bowl with the beans. To broil: Preheat the broiler. Place the eggplant slices on a baking sheet. Brush the top side

with half the safflower oil. Position the sheet about 4 inches from the broiler. Broil until the eggplant is lightly browned, about 3 to 4 minutes. Turn the slices over, brush again with the remaining oil, and broil until the under side is browned, about 3 to 4 minutes, and the slices are tender when pierced with a fork. Remove and cool slightly. Quarter the slices and add to the bowl with the beans.

4. Add the ham, tomatoes, cheese, parsley, and scallions to the beans and eggplant. Stir to combine.

5. In a small bowl or jar or a measuring cup, combine the lemon juice, olive oil, beef stock, mustard, garlic, salt, hot pepper sauce, and black pepper. Mix with a fork and pour over the salad. Toss to combine.

6. The salad may be served at once or chilled (covered with plastic wrap) up to 24 hours before serving. Bring it to room temperature before serving to enhance its flavor. To serve, line a serving platter with lettuce. Mound the salad over the lettuce.

Yield: 4 entree servings	✦ Dietary fiber per serving: 18g
Calories per serving: 535	Fat per serving: 25g
Carbohydrate per serving: 50g	Protein per serving: 30g
✦ Cholesterol per serving: 42mg	Sodium per serving: 1287mg

Whole Wheat Oatmeal Muffins

❖

These tasty little treats are a snap to prepare and are good warm or cold. I used the All-Bran cereal with extra fiber, then worried that the NutraSweet (aspartame) in that product, which turns bitter when heated, would ruin the muffins. It didn't! We (our kids too, joy of joys!) found them quite delicious. Make them in tiny muffin cups for more calorie-conscious servings. Try the leftovers at breakfast, split and toasted under the broiler, then spread with a bit of butter and sprinkled with cinnamon sugar.

> 1 cup quick-cooking (not instant) oatmeal
> ½ cup All-Bran cereal
> 1½ cups skimmed buttermilk
> 2 tablespoons margarine at room temperature
> 2 tablespoons brown sugar
> 1 egg
> 1 cup whole wheat flour
> 1 teaspoon baking powder
> 1 teaspoon baking soda
> ⅞ teaspoon salt
> cinnamon and sugar

1. Soak the oatmeal and bran cereal in the buttermilk in a medium-size bowl for 45 minutes to 1 hour.
2. Preheat the oven to 400 degrees. In another medium-size bowl with an electric beater or in the bowl of a food processor, cream together the margarine and brown sugar. Then beat in the egg.
3. Stir in the flour, baking powder, baking soda, and salt. Stir just to combine. (Overmixing makes tough bread products.) Stir in the oat-buttermilk mixture. Stir just to combine.
4. Coat 2 6-cup medium-size muffin tins with cooking spray. Fill the cups two-thirds full of batter. Sprinkle the tops of the muffins with the cinnamon-sugar mixture.
5. Bake in the middle of the preheated oven for 15 to 20 minutes or until a toothpick inserted slightly off center in a muffin comes out clean. Serve warm, or cool and wrap in plastic wrap and then foil. Muffins will stay moist at room temperature or chilled up to 24 hours.

Yield: 12 medium-size muffins
✦ Calories per muffin: 113
Carbohydrate per muffin: 18g
✦ Cholesterol per muffin: 20mg
✦ Dietary fiber per muffin: 3g
Fat per muffin: 4g
Protein per muffin: 4g
Sodium per muffin: 311mg

Fresh Fruit and Cheese

❖

This oldest of desserts is remarkably satisfying, to say nothing of nutritious and simple, but with the good news there is bad. First, on the up side of things, is the satiability factor. A dessert of fresh fruit and cheese staves off hunger. Fructose, the natural sugar in fruit, takes longer to digest than sucrose (table sugar), so it "stays with you" longer than, say, a cookie. Cheese, relatively high in fat, also takes some time to digest, because fats are metabolized more slowly than either proteins or carbohydrates.

Another advantage for the cook who has a million things to do, is the ease of preparation of this dessert. Finding a good cheese store is all there is to it. Cheeses should be cut to order or, at the very least, cut frequently. The quality of the cheeses is more important than how many varieties the store carries. Delicate cheeses should be stored away from strong ones, and customers should be free to sample.

On the down side of things, the nutrition-minded menu planner will need to plan carefully when offering a fruit and cheese dessert. Planning is necessary in order to keep the lid on fats—unfortunately often high in most cheeses. Cheeses labeled "part-skim" are indeed lower in calories, but not enormously; about 10–20 calories an ounce less is the extent of it. Do choose cheeses made from milk, not cream, and skim milk when possible. As a rule the softer, more fluid cheeses like Brie and Camembert have a higher water content and therefore lower calorie level (and fewer important minerals like calcium) than hard cheeses like cheddar. Other lower calorie cheeses are goat cheese, lappi, Neufchâtel (this mixes easily with flavorings), Port du Salut, Sapsago, and string cheese—but remember this is not to say they are low calorie. Ranging from about 80 to 100 calories an ounce, these are foods to eat with discretion. An ounce of cheese isn't much to look at, but it is a concentrated source of calories and fats. Weigh a typical bite of cheese to shock yourself into portion control. Plan on no more than an ounce of cheese per person and perhaps one serving of fruit. (For more information on cheese, read *Focus: The Low-Down on Cheeses* on the next page.)

While there are several imitation and low-calorie cheeses on the market, for my money they can stay there; I'd never bring them home.

Fruits to serve depend, of course, on what's available. Generally speaking, tart apples such as Granny Smiths are excellent when served crisp and cold with cheeses. Pears, at room temperature for best flavor, are terrific. And no one would quibble with a handful of grapes or some sweet cherries in season. The lucky few to whom calorie is a meaningless word will welcome crackers or biscuits. English graham biscuits (a brand name is Wheatolo) are marvelous with fruit and cheese.

Cheeses (other than cottage or farmer's cheese) are best served at room temperature. But they should be kept well chilled half an hour or so before serving to discourage spoilage. Buy cheese in small quantities, as cut pieces never store as well as larger ones.

❖ Focus: The Low-Down ❖ on Cheeses

Cheeses are delicious, convenient, and come with a good-for-you reputation, but many are quite high in saturated fats and sodium. Let this little chart be your guide for cooking and snacking.

SODIUM: mg/oz	FAT: grams/oz	CALORIES/oz
LOW SODIUM: 0–99		
Farmer's, no salt added	3	40
MODERATE SODIUM: 100–199		
Swiss	8	107
Mozzarella, whole milk	6	80
Neufchâtel	7	74
Jarlsberg	7	100
Mozzarella, part-skim	5	79
Port du Salut	8	100
Ricotta, part-skim (½ cup)	10	171
MODERATELY HIGH SODIUM: 200–299		
Tilsit, whole milk	7	96
Creamed cottage cheese (½ cup)	5	120
HIGH SODIUM: 300–399		
Feta	6	75
Romano	8	110
VERY HIGH SODIUM: 400+		
Parmesan	7	111

SUMMER BREEZE

Chicken and Broccoli Salad
Molded Rice Ring with Chinese Mayonnaise
Strawberries with Strawberry Cream

Not even Escoffier would want to spend time in a sweltering kitchen when cooling summer breezes beckon, yet it is pleasant to sit down to a well-cooked, appetizing, light meal when the sun sets. This menu for four, which might more appropriately be a "Dinner on the Porch" rather than a "Dinner in the Kitchen," lets you enjoy your day and still serve a refreshing and delicious dinner.

"Summer Breeze" features the common combination of rice and chicken in a little different style. Key to both is a homemade mayonnaise flavored with sesame oil and other Oriental ingredients. Once the mayonnaise is done—a quick job in either a food processor or blender—the rice ring and chicken and broccoli salads can easily be made in less than an hour's time. While the chicken salad may be served immediately, the rice needs a good three hours to chill so it will unmold nicely. Both can be made early in the day and kept refrigerated until dinner time. Dessert is a simple affair—long stemmed strawberries with a creamy dipping sauce. Plan on ten minutes for its preparation. This, too, may be whipped up in the morning, but let the strawberry cream come to room temperature for maximum flavor.

Chicken and Broccoli Salad

❖

Can chicken salad have personality? It may seem an odd thought, but in this case, it is apt. See for yourself with this do-ahead meal. Remember to remove the salad from the refrigerator about a half an hour before dinner. The hot oil and sesame oil are available at Oriental markets and specialty food shops.

a 1-inch-long piece of ginger root, peeled and
   sliced
1 scallion, chopped
3 chicken breasts (with skin and bones are fine)
1 large stalk broccoli, about 12 ounces
1 red bell pepper
¾ cup Chinese Mayonnaise (page 310)
¼ teaspoon salt
a few drops hot oil, to taste
¼ teaspoon sesame oil
1 recipe Molded Rice Ring (page 310)
lettuce to line serving platter
5 to 6 cherry tomatoes, halved (optional)

1. Fill a 10- or 12-inch skillet three-quarters full of water. Add the ginger and scallion. Cover and bring to a boil over high heat. Meanwhile, if you are using a whole chicken breast, make a 4-inch-long cut through the breast along the top length of the breastbone so it will lie flat. Add the chicken breasts, skin side down, to the skillet.

2. Re-cover the pan and return the water to a boil. When a boil is reached, immediately reduce the heat so the liquid just simmers. Simmer the chicken for 10 minutes. Turn the breasts over and simmer for another 5 to 8 minutes or until the flesh is springy but not too soft when pressed. Remove the pan from the heat and

let the chicken rest in the hot liquid, covered, for 5 more minutes. Then cool the chicken on a plate. (Chicken may be microwaved if desired, but it tends to be juicier if cooked traditionally.)

3. Cut the flowerets from the broccoli stalk. (Reserve the stalk for another use.) Cut the flowerets into bite-size pieces.

4. Transfer the chicken from the cooking liquid to a plate to cool. Strain the cooking liquid into a 2½-quart saucepan. Discard the ginger and scallion. Add enough water to the cooking liquid in the saucepan to make the pan three-quarters full.

5. Cover the pan and bring the liquid to a boil over high heat. Uncover, add the broccoli, and boil until it is tender when pierced with a fork, about 5 to 6 minutes. Drain.

6. Cut the red pepper in half the long way. Remove the seeds and whitish membrane. Flatten the pepper halves with the palm of your hand. Place on a baking sheet and slide under the broiler. Broil until blackened and charred, about 5 to 6 minutes, turning the sheet occasionally to ensure even cooking. Transfer the peppers to a paper or plastic bag. Roll the bag tightly closed and put into the freezer to cool.

7. Discard the skin from the chicken. Lift the meat from the bones with your fingers. Chop the meat into fairly large bite-size pieces and put them into a large bowl. Add the drained broccoli to the bowl.

8. Remove the peppers from the freezer. Peel off and discard the blackened skin from the peppers and slice them into ¼-inch-wide strips. Add the pepper strips to the chicken and broccoli.

9. Add the mayonnaise, salt, hot oil, and sesame oil to the chicken mixture. Stir carefully to combine. Taste; adjust seasoning if necessary. (Salad may be made ahead to this point and chilled, covered, up to 12 hours before serving.)

10. Tuck lettuce leaves around the outside of the un-molded rice ring. Decorate with halved cherry toma-

toes if desired. Scoop the salad into the center of the mold.

Yield: 4 servings
Calories per serving: 439
Carbohydrate per serving: 8g
✦ **Cholesterol per serving: 106mg**

✦ **Dietary fiber per serving: 2g**
Fat per serving: 34g
Protein per serving: 27g
✦ **Sodium per serving: 367mg**

Molded Rice Ring
with Chinese Mayonnaise

❖

This is an attractive and simple way to serve a chilled rice salad. For variety, mold the rice in individual ramekins if desired. While designed to be served with the Chicken and Broccoli Salad for this "Summer Breeze" menu, the rice ring would be very nice for a picnic (keep it well chilled) or as a side dish with a simple grilled chicken breast. Make the mold early in the day or at least three hours before serving. The cooking wine, rice vinegar, sesame oil, and hot oil are available at Oriental markets and specialty food shops.

For the Rice

1 cup converted white rice
1½ cups homemade chicken stock or canned
*   chicken broth*
1 cup water
¼ teaspoon salt
¼ cup fresh minced parsley
1 tablespoon slivered almonds

For the Chinese Mayonnaise

1 egg
1 tablespoon Chinese cooking wine

2 teaspoons rice vinegar or white wine vinegar or
     distilled white vinegar
1 tablespoon lemon juice
1 teaspoon Dijon mustard
⅔ cup peanut oil
1 teaspoon sesame oil
a few drops hot oil to taste

1. Combine the rice, chicken stock, water, and salt in a 2½-quart saucepan. Cover and bring it to a boil over high heat. Once a boil is reached, reduce the heat so the liquid just simmers. Cook the rice until all the liquid is absorbed, about 16 minutes.

2. While the rice cooks, make the mayonnaise. Combine the egg, cooking wine, vinegar, lemon juice, and mustard in the bowl of a food processor or in a blender. Process a few seconds to combine.

3. With the machine running, very slowly dribble in the peanut oil. Add the sesame oil and hot oil. Set the mayonnaise aside.

4. When the rice is tender, remove it from the heat, uncover, and let it cool until tepid.

5. Stir the parsley and almonds into the rice. Combine the rice with ¼ cup of the Chinese Mayonnaise, reserving the remaining mayonnaise for the Chicken and Broccoli Salad on page 308 (or chill for some other use).

6. Coat a 1-quart ring mold with cooking spray. Pack the rice into the mold. Smooth the top with a spatula. Cover the mold with plastic wrap. Refrigerate the rice at least 3 hours or as long as 12 hours before serving.

7. Run a flexible-bladed spatula around the outer and inner rims of the ring mold to free the rice. Place a serving platter upside down over the rice mold. Invert. Lift mold from the rice and garnish as described on pages 309–10.

Yield: 4 servings
Calories per serving: 184
Carbohydrate per serving: 40g
✦ **Cholesterol per serving: 0mg**

Dietary fiber per serving: 0g
Fat per serving: 1g
Protein per serving: 4g
✦ **Sodium per serving: 160mg**

Strawberries with Strawberry Cream

❖

Almost a "no-recipe" recipe, this simple dessert is quite elegant if jumbo strawberries with long stems are available. Diners either dip their share of scarlet beauties into a communal pot of strawberry cream or are given individual servings. Lacking long-stemmed strawberries, simply slice ripe berries into pretty glass bowls and top with a healthy spoonful of strawberry cream.

> 2 ounces Neufchâtel cheese, at room temperature
> 3 tablespoons orange juice
> ½ cup crushed (fresh or frozen) strawberries
> zest of 1 orange
> 1 tablespoon orange liqueur, such as Triple Sec or Grand Marnier (optional)
> 1 pint fresh strawberries

1. In the bowl of a food processor or in a bowl with an electric mixer, combine the cheese, orange juice, and crushed strawberries until smooth. Stir in the zest and liqueur. (Cream may be made up to 8 hours before serving. Keep covered and chilled, but bring it to room temperature before serving.)
2. To serve, either spoon the strawberry cream over sliced berries, or arrange long-stemmed strawberries around a small glass bowl of the strawberry cream.

Yield: 4 servings
✦ Calories per serving: 77
Carbohydrate per serving: 10g
✦ Cholesterol per serving: 11mg

✦ Dietary fiber per serving: 2g
Fat per serving: 4g
Protein per serving: 2g
✦ Sodium per serving: 58mg

FAST TRACK

Chicken Breasts with Green Peppercorn Sauce
Herb Roasted Potatoes
Honey Glazed Carrots

Learning to cook lighter meals that don't skimp on flavor means changing some old habits. Throughout this book, you've been coached to reach for the chicken broth; to smatter, not slather the butter; to use cholesterol-free oils whenever possible; and to use arrowroot instead of flour for thickening. You've traded the sour cream container for one of yogurt, the cream carton for a milk carton, and all but thrown the mayonnaise away. Highly fatty meats have been replaced with skinless chicken and ocean-fresh fish. You've served more vegetable-rich meals with small servings of animal protein. You've seen the emphasis placed on fresh ingredients and found that good food is just that: it doesn't need a lot of doctoring. You've been cutting back on fats, but have still enjoyed delicious meals because you've made conscious choices when shopping and cooking.

"Fast Track," a menu for four, holds another little trick for the weight- and health-conscious cook. In the Chicken Breasts with Green Peppercorn Sauce recipe you'll learn how to make a "cream" sauce that never sees cream. Dishes that deep-fat fry or cover chicken with a cream and butter sauce obliterate the calorie advantage of skinned poultry while augmenting its somewhat bland flavor. Here is the best of both worlds—pound-saving chicken with a mouth-filling yet body-sparing sauce.

With the chicken are Herb Roasted Potatoes, a deliciously simple way to enjoy potatoes without the butter they absorb like sponges. Kids are particularly partial to these, so you might like to have the herb mixture on hand.

Add some color with Honey Glazed Carrots and you'll have a meal that will help speed your way on the fast track to health.

❖ Focus: Heart Disease ❖
Risk Factors

One result of all the research that has gone into determining the causes of heart disease is the identification of risk factors. It is important to remember that none of these factors *cause* the disease, rather they happen in association with it. They are:

- Elevated blood cholesterol and triglyceride concentrations,
- High blood pressure,
- Cigarette smoking,
- Diabetes mellitus,
- Obesity,
- Lack of physical activity.

Chicken Breasts with Green Peppercorn Sauce
❖

Here is a peppery, piquant sauce for those who'd rather eat a bowl of cereal than a bland, plain chicken breast. The sauce preparation is a snap, but if you'd rather, it can be prepared several hours ahead and held, covered, in the refrigerator. Green peppercorns are packed in brine and sold in specialty food shops, an opened jar or can will keep for weeks in the refrigerator, or months in the freezer.

For the Chicken Breasts

4 chicken breasts, boned and skinned
juice of half a lemon
⅛ teaspoon salt
freshly ground black pepper to taste

For the Green Peppercorn Sauce

4–6 raw spinach leaves
1 tablespoon unsalted butter
1 tablespoon all-purpose flour
½ cup homemade chicken stock or canned
    chicken broth
2 tablespoons low-fat cottage cheese
¼ teaspoon salt
1 teaspoon or to taste drained green peppercorns

1. Preheat the oven to 450 degrees (unless you prefer to microwave the chicken). Place the chicken breasts in an ovenproof dish just large enough to hold them. Season them with the lemon juice, salt, and pepper. Cover the dish with foil and bake in the lower third of the oven until chicken is firm when pressed, but still juicy, about 12 to 16 minutes. To cook the chicken in a microwave oven: Season it as described above, cover with plastic wrap, and cook it at high power for about 3 minutes.
2. While the chicken cooks, prepare the sauce. Rinse the spinach and place it in an 8-inch skillet with the water that clings to its leaves. Cover and bring to a boil over high heat. Boil just until the spinach is wilted, about 1 to 2 minutes. Scrape the spinach into a food processor.
3. Over high heat melt the butter in the same skillet until foamy, about 1 minute. Stir in the flour. Cook, stirring, over medium-high heat until very lightly browned, about 45 seconds to 1 minute.
4. Remove the skillet from the heat. Whisk in the chicken broth until smooth. Return the skillet to medium-high heat and stir until the sauce thickens, about 2 to 3 min-

utes. Scrape the sauce into the food processor with the spinach.

5. Add the cottage cheese, salt, and peppercorns to the food processor. Process until flecks of spinach remain in a light green sauce. (If you decide to make the sauce several hours ahead, hold it, covered, in the refrigerator, and reheat over low heat, stirring often, just before serving.)

6. Remove the chicken from the oven. Pour the cooking juices into the sauce and pulse the machine to combine. Place a chicken breast on each plate, and spoon the sauce on top.

Yield: 4 servings
✦ **Calories per serving: 185**
Carbohydrate per serving: 3g
✦ **Cholesterol per serving: 81mg**

Dietary fiber per serving: 0g
Fat per serving: 6g
Protein per serving: 28g
✦ **Sodium per serving: 349mg**

Herb Roasted Potatoes

❖

You might like to double or even triple the herb mixture and keep it handy in the refrigerator—making this pleaser even snappier to prepare.

1 tablespoon freshly grated Parmesan cheese
1 tablespoon sesame seeds
1 tablespoon minced fresh parsley
1 teaspoon minced garlic
¼ teaspoon paprika
¼ teaspoon dry mustard
¼ teaspoon salt
freshly ground black pepper to taste
2 large baking potatoes (1 pound), scrubbed but
    not peeled
1 tablespoon safflower oil

1. Preheat the oven to 400 degrees. Combine the cheese, sesame seeds, parsley, garlic, paprika, mustard, salt, and pepper.
2. Cut the potatoes in half the long way, then cut each half in quarters, also the long way. Place the potatoes in a 7- by 11-inch baking dish. Brush the potatoes with half the oil, and sprinkle with half the herb mixture.
3. Bake in the upper third of the oven for 20 minutes. Turn potatoes over, brush with the remaining oil, and sprinkle with the remaining herb mix. Bake another 20 minutes or until potatoes are tender when pierced with a fork. Broil 4 to 5 minutes to brown, if necessary.

Yield: 4 servings
+ **Calories per serving: 140**
Carbohydrate per serving: 20g
+ **Cholesterol per serving: 1mg**

Dietary fiber per serving: 0g
Fat per serving: 5g
Protein per serving: 3g
+ **Sodium per serving: 175mg**

Honey Glazed Carrots

❖

Rich in vitamin A and ever-present in many a refrigerator, carrots are as handy a fresh vegetable as you'll find. Buy carrots with the tops attached, if possible, for they are infinitely tastier, but twist off and discard the tops before storing them. For variety, add a teaspoon of chopped fresh mint or dill.

4 to 5 carrots, peeled
5 tablespoons homemade chicken stock or
    canned broth
1 tablespoon unsalted butter
2 teaspoons honey
½ teaspoon salt
a few gratings fresh nutmeg
freshly ground black pepper to taste

1. Slice the carrots into thin sticks or rounds either by hand or in a food processor. Place them in a 1-quart saucepan and add the remaining ingredients.
2. Press aluminum foil right on top of the carrots, then cover the pan. (Carrots may be prepared to this point and held 1 to 2 hours at room temperature.)
3. Place the pan on high heat. When steam escapes, lower the heat to medium-high. Cook 18 to 20 minutes, shaking the pan by the handle from time to time. Serve the carrots hot.

Yield: 4 servings
✦ **Calories per serving: 78**
Carbohydrate per serving: 13g
✦ **Cholesterol per serving: 8mg**

Dietary fiber per serving: 1g
Fat per serving: 3g
Protein per serving: 1g
✦ **Sodium per serving: 328mg**

❖Eggplant, a.k.a. the mad apple, was once believed to cause insanity.❖

TURKEY REDUX

Curried "Cream" of Turkey Soup
Whole Wheat Bread Sticks
Strawberry Parfait

More than other dishes, a bowl of hot soup always seems to equal more in taste than the sum of its parts. Nowhere is this truer than with a sparse turkey carcass and a few humble carrots and onions. Simmered together with a judicious drift of herbs, a pinch of this, and a dab of that, and you've got a bowl of good eating, nearly one hundred percent fat free plus chock-full of the foods nutritionists champion.

And what's more appropriate with soup than hot homemade bread? "Turkey Redux" offers a simplified breadstick recipe that requires only one rising and has a rich whole wheat taste.

Unlike most other menus in *The Enlightened Gourmet*, both the soup and bread recipes serve more than the standard four, six, or eight persons. It makes good use of time to work in big batches here, for the leftovers freeze very nicely. The finish is a cool and smooth Strawberry Parfait, a gelatin-thickened dessert that needs an hour's chilling time before it is served. It serves four generously and is easily doubled for eight.

Curried "Cream"
of Turkey Soup

❖

The Yankee thrift in me used to cringe when I threw out a turkey carcass, yet I long ago tired of traditional turkey soup. This soup is a little variation with my ever popular curry powder. It is thick and rich but not fattening, and looks spectacular when served from a hollowed out pumpkin. A carcass from a 12-pound turkey yields 10 to 12 cups of stock. Freeze the remaining turkey stock for another soup or use whenever a recipe calls for chicken stock. Leftover soup may be frozen up to 2 months or chilled up to 3 days. Chilled soup will thicken, so thin it with a little stock or milk.

For the Turkey Stock

1 meaty turkey carcass, without skin
water to cover
4 medium onions, chopped
3 celery ribs, chopped
2 carrots, chopped
½ cup minced fresh parsley
1 teaspoon salt
freshly ground black pepper to taste

For the Soup

6 cups turkey stock
4 small onions, chopped
3 carrots, chopped
3 celery ribs, chopped
½ cup minced fresh parsley
¾ cup brown or white (not instant or converted)
    rice

1 medium apple, cored, peeled, and chopped
1 bay leaf
1 teaspoon salt
freshly ground black pepper to taste
2 cups low-fat or skim milk
1½ tablespoons or to taste curry powder
1 cup fresh or frozen peas

To Prepare the Turkey Stock

1. Roughly chop the turkey carcass into fourths. Place the bones in a 15-quart stockpot and cover with fresh, cool water. Add the remaining ingredients listed under turkey stock.
2. Cover and bring to a boil over high heat. When a boil is reached, reduce the heat so the liquid just simmers. (Stock should not boil or it will be cloudy.) Half cover the pot and simmer for 3 to 4 hours.
3. In the sink place a strainer over a bowl large enough to hold the stock. Pour the stock through the strainer. Cool the solids in the strainer until you can pick the meat from the bones.
4. Add the meat to the stock. Hold the strainer over the stock and press the solids with the back of a wooden spoon to extract the juices. Discard the solids in the strainer. The stock is now ready to use. Or it may be chilled and held up to 24 hours before using, or frozen up to 4 months before using. Boil chilled or frozen stock 5 minutes before using it.

To Prepare the Soup

1. Combine the turkey stock, onions, carrots, celery, parsley, rice, apple, bay leaf, salt, and pepper in a 12-quart or larger stockpot. Cover and bring to a boil over high heat.
2. When a boil is reached, half cover the pot and reduce the heat so the liquid just simmers. Simmer 1 hour, stirring occasionally. Remove the bay leaf.

3. Puree the soup in batches in a food processor or blender. Return the pureed soup to the stockpot.
4. Stir in the milk and curry powder over medium heat. Whisk until well blended. Taste for seasoning adjustment.
5. Stir in the peas and simmer until they are tender, about 15 minutes. The soup is ready to serve, or it may be kept warm up to 1 hour before serving.

Yield: 8 to 10 servings
      (analysis based on 10)
✦ Calories per serving: 129
   Carbohydrate per serving: 26g
✦ Cholesterol per serving: 2mg

✦ Dietary fiber per serving: 3g
   Fat per serving: 1g
   Protein per serving: 5g
✦ Sodium per serving: 295mg

Whole Wheat Bread Sticks

❖

Making bread sticks needn't be a chore. These are table-ready in about three hours. Leftovers wrapped tightly in plastic and then in foil stay fresh in the refrigerator up to 3 days or up to 6 months in the freezer. For variety, brush the risen breadsticks with an egg wash just before baking, then sprinkle with sesame, poppy, or caraway seeds.

>   2 packages (¼ ounce) dry yeast
>   3 tablespoons warm (105–115 degrees) water
>   ½ teaspoon sugar
>   1 cup skimmed buttermilk
>   2 tablespoons honey
>   3 tablespoons margarine
>   1 teaspoon salt
>   1½ cups all-purpose flour
>   1½ cups whole wheat flour
>   additional whole wheat flour for work surface

1. Put the yeast, water, and sugar in a glass measuring cup. Let rest about 10 minutes or until foamy and at least doubled in volume.

2. Scald the buttermilk and honey in a small saucepan on the stove over high heat or in a microwave oven. Set aside to cool slightly. Melt the margarine in a small saucepan over medium heat on the stove or in a microwave oven. Set aside to cool slightly.

3. When the liquids are still warm but not hot and the yeast has doubled, sift the salt and white flour into a large bowl. Mix the liquids into the flour with a wooden spoon. Mix in enough whole wheat flour to make a stiff dough. (You may use slightly more or less than the 1½ cups specified. Let the consistency of the dough be your guide, not the recipe.)

4. Sprinkle the work surface with whole wheat flour, and turn the dough out onto it. Knead the dough until smooth and elastic, about 3 minutes.

5. Shape the dough into a ball. Return it to the bowl and cover the bowl with a kitchen towel. Leave the bowl in a warm place for about 10 minutes.

6. Turn the dough out onto the work surface and knead again for about 3 to 4 minutes.

7. Spray 2 large baking sheets with cooking spray. To shape the dough into breadsticks follow one of the following methods. For twisted breadsticks: Roll, stretch, and pat the dough into a rough rectangle about 7 by 11 inches. Cut the dough crosswise into ¼-inch-wide strips. Twist two strips together to form a breadstick. Pinch the ends together and place the breadstick crosswise on the baking sheet. Continue until all the dough is formed. Place the breadsticks 2 inches apart on the baking sheet. The dough may be rerolled as often as necessary. For twirled breadsticks: Follow the twisted breadstick instructions but cut the dough into ½-inch-wide strips. Hold either end of the breadstick in your fingers. Twist the dough in opposite directions, which will make the stick twirl. Place the breadstick on the prepared baking sheets. Repeat until all the dough

is formed. The dough may be rerolled as often as necessary.
8. Cover the breadsticks loosely with a kitchen towel.
   Place the sheets in a warm spot to rise until the breadsticks have about doubled in size, which will be
   roughly 2 hours. (They may be held as long as 4 hours
   before baking, if desired.)
9. Preheat oven to 375 degrees. Bake the breadsticks in
   the middle of the oven for 12 to 15 minutes or until
   golden brown and cooked through. Serve warm.

Yield: about 19 breadsticks
Calories per breadstick: 94
Carbohydrate per breadstick: 16g
✦ Cholesterol per breadstick: 1g

Dietary fiber per breadstick: 4g
Fat per breadstick: 2g
Protein per breadstick: 3g
Sodium per breadstick: 160mg

Strawberry Parfait

❖

Neufchâtel cheese is much like cream cheese but with
lowered fat and more protein. It combines beautifully
with strawberries and orange in this do-ahead dessert.

1 package unflavored gelatin
2 tablespoons orange juice or water
3 ounces Neufchâtel cheese, at room temperature
1 6-ounce can orange juice concentrate
½ cup skimmed evaporated milk
12 ounces fresh or frozen strawberries, no sugar
    added
4 tablespoons orange liqueur, such as Grand
    Marnier or Triple Sec
2 tablespoons sugar
finely grated rind (zest) of an orange (optional)

1. Soften the gelatin in the 2 tablespoons of orange juice in a 1-cup measure. Place the cup in a 1-quart saucepan filled with 2 inches water and place the saucepan over high heat. Stir the gelatin frequently until it has dissolved, about 2 to 3 minutes. Remove the pan from the heat.

2. Combine the cheese with the orange juice concentrate and the evaporated milk in a food processor or blender. Process until smooth. Add the gelatin and process until well blended. Scrape the mixture into a bowl.

3. Coarsely puree the strawberries with 3 tablespoons of the liqueur, leaving the fruit slightly chunky. Fold half the berries into the cheese mixture in the bowl.

4. Divide the cheese-strawberry mixture among 4 parfait or champagne glasses. Cover and chill until set, about 1 hour. They also can be held chilled up to 24 hours.

5. Combine the remaining berries with the sugar and the remaining tablespoon of liqueur. Chill, covered, until serving time.

6. To serve, top each parfait with a tablespoon of the strawberry sauce, garnish with the orange zest, and pass the remaining sauce at the table.

Yield: 4 to 6 servings
    (analysis based on 6)
Calories per serving: 189
Carbohydrate per serving: 30g
✦ **Cholesterol per serving: 12mg**

Dietary fiber per serving: 1g
Fat per serving: 4g
Protein per serving: 5g
✦ **Sodium per serving: 83mg**

❖A single kiwifruit has twice as much vitamin C as several types of oranges.❖

CHILL FACTOR

Chilled Potato and Watercress Soup
Tabouli Salad with Shredded Chicken
Pita Bread*

Summer's swelter is gently cooled by this "Chill Factor" menu for four (dinner-size servings) or six (lunch servings). Neither dish will keep you in the kitchen very long—as important a consideration for summer meal planning as any—and both can, in fact should, be done several hours before serving to allow for the chill factor to do its work. To keep things easy, dress up store-bought pita bread with a sprinkle of poppy or sesame seeds and toast lightly under a broiler for a little added crunch. If a dessert seems mandatory, cut up fresh fruits and marinate them in orange juice and/or champagne for the perfect ending to a perfect summer day.

Chilled Potato and Watercress Soup

A reduced-fat version of the ever popular vichyssoise, this quickly put together soup packs pizzazz with the dual tang of watercress and yogurt. Make it a day ahead or at least 4 hours before serving if it is to be served chilled, or enjoy it warm. It is pretty when served in glass dishes.

5 cups homemade chicken stock or canned broth
1 tablespoon safflower oil
1 large onion, chopped
1 bunch watercress (about 4 ounces)
3 potatoes, peeled and sliced
½ cup plain low-fat yogurt
½ teaspoon salt
dash of cayenne pepper
paprika for garnish

1. Combine ½ cup of the chicken stock with the oil in a 2½-quart saucepan. Cover and place over high heat. When the stock begins to boil, add the onion. Cover and reduce heat to medium-high. Cook, stirring occasionally, until the onion is limp, about 6 to 7 minutes.
2. Meanwhile, remove and discard the stems from the watercress. Roughly chop the leaves. Uncover the saucepan, add the watercress, and stir well to combine.
3. Add the remaining stock and the potatoes. Cover and return heat to high. When the stock begins to boil, reduce the heat to low and cook for 30 minutes or until the potatoes are tender.
4. Remove the saucepan from the stove. Puree the soup in batches in a food processor or in a blender. Pour the pureed soup into a bowl or refrigerator container.
5. When the soup is pureed, stir in the yogurt, salt, and cayenne. Chill for at least 4 hours or as long as 24 hours.
6. Taste, and adjust seasoning just before serving. Chilling tends to weaken flavors, so additional cayenne or salt may be in order. Garnish each serving with a sprinkle of paprika.

Yield: 1½ quarts; 6 1-cup servings
✦ Calories per serving: 155
Carbohydrate per serving: 28g
✦ Cholesterol per serving: 1g

Dietary fiber per serving: 1g
Fat per serving: 3g
Protein per serving: 5g
Sodium per serving: 242mg

Tabouli Salad with Shredded Chicken

❖

Bulgur wheat, also known as wheat pilaf, is the key ingredient of this cold salad from the Middle East. Made from partially cooked wheat berries, bulgur comes in three grinds, fine, medium, or coarse. Typically, tabouli is a vegetarian concoction, but here shreds of chicken breast have been tossed in. The salad is just as delicious without the chicken, and with other goodies, such as cucumbers, which your garden or a produce stand might yield.

> 1 cup bulgur wheat, fine or medium grind
>   preferred
> 2 cups boiling water
> 2 chicken breasts
> 2 scallions, green part only, chopped
> ¾ cup chopped fresh parsley
> 1 large tomato, chopped
> ¼ cup lemon juice
> 1 to 2 tablespoons chopped fresh mint
> 1 teaspoon salt
> 1 teaspoon chopped fresh coriander (optional)
> lettuce to line serving bowl (optional)

1. Place the bulgur wheat in a medium-size bowl and pour the boiling water over it. Set aside for ½ hour.
2. Place the chicken skin side down in a skillet just large enough to hold it and cover with water. Cover with the pan lid and place the skillet over high heat.
3. When steam escapes from under the lid, reduce the heat so the liquid just simmers. Simmer 15 to 18 minutes. Transfer the chicken to a plate to cool.
4. When the chicken is cool enough to handle, discard the skin and bones. Dice or shred the chicken meat and add it to the softened bulgur wheat.

5. Add the remaining ingredients to the bowl. Stir well to combine. Chill at least 1 hour or up to 24 hours before serving. Taste, and adjust seasoning just before serving, as chilling weakens flavors.

Note: If the salad is served from a platter or bowl, line it with lettuce leaves.

Yield: 4 entree servings
    (6 or more side dish servings)
✦ Calories per serving: 302
    Carbohydrate per serving: 37g
✦ Cholesterol per serving: 68mg

✦ Dietary fiber per serving: 2g
    Fat per serving: 2g
    Protein per serving: 33g
    Sodium per serving: 679mg

❖ Focus: ❖
Tracing Vitamin Poisoning

It's ironic that in this, perhaps the best fed country in the world with an abundant and varied food supply, vitamins are causing health problems. Not from a deficiency due to overprocessed food or undernourished soil, but from an excess. In the honest pursuit of health, some Americans are poisoning themselves, and the FDA wants to know about it.

The FDA pulled together a panel of experts to discuss potential problems associated with oversupplementation. The panel fears that 5 to 10 percent of the population is "megadosing" on single-nutrient vitamin pills (the concern is not with a "supermarket" multi-vitamin in sensible dosages but single-dose, highly exaggerated pills), such as B6, C, and A, in the age-old hope that certain diseases or even learning disabilities may be prevented, cured, or at the least, alleviated. Before the FDA can control the potency of vitamin over-the-counter supplements, however, it must first document cases of toxicity.

A decade ago, the FDA had placed the lid on large doses (10,000 I.U. and 400 I.U. respectively) of vitamin A and D, prohibiting their sale except as prescription drugs. But in 1977 a court ruled that the vitamins weren't drugs because they were sold as dietary supplements and therefore were not subject to regulation. Now, in an effort to prove that too much of a good thing can be harmful, the FDA wants doctors to monitor vitamin supplementing and report toxic cases to the agency.

Many people wrongly think vitamins will restore energy. While vitamins are important in helping the body convert food to energy, they have no caloric value themselves, so they supply no energy. Others feel there is no danger from ingesting too much of the water-soluble vitamins (the B vitamins and C), for it is believed that when the cells reach the saturation point the excess vitamins are metabolized and excreted while only the fat-soluble vitamins (A, D, E, and K) are stored. Instances of toxicity due to water-soluble vitamins are harder to document, but not without incidence. High doses of vitamin C can cause gastrointestinal disturbances, contribute to kidney stones, and interfere with some prescription drugs. Proponents of vitamin C megadosing suggest daily dosages of 1000 milligrams will help prevent colds and prolong the life of cancer patients. A study at the University of Toronto concluded that vitamin C could not prevent colds but might reduce the symptoms when taken in a daily dose of 250 milligrams (found in 16 ounces of orange juice). Higher doses provided no extra benefit. Researchers at the Mayo Clinic could not substantiate claims that vitamin C in any way enhanced the lives of cancer victims.

Vitamin B6 has been advocated for premenstrual syndrome. But doctors' reports have been gathering evidence of damaged nerve systems in takers of 2000 milligrams or more over a period of time. Large doses of niacin, another B vitamin, can cause liver damage and skin rashes. Prolonged intake of vitamin A in high doses can cause headaches, bone pain, and damage to the liver. Excessive vitamin D can cause kidney damage.

This is not to say that such cases are rampant or that no one should supplement his or her diet with vitamins. Persons convalescing from surgery or serious illness, pregnant and lactating women, the elderly, and children with very poor eating habits are some of the groups who may require vitamins.

Nor is this to suggest that vitamin toxicity is a common occurrence. But the FDA wants to make sure it doesn't become common.

❖Hard, dull-skinned nectarines have been picked too young and won't sweeten as they gain color.❖

POTLUCK

Minestrone Soup
Moist Cornbread Loaf
Buttermilk Dressing for Tossed Salad

This is a simple supper that will feed a few or many (up to eleven), depending on your needs. While unpretentious, it offers novelty in the deliciously moist cornbread loaf (easily doubled if you're feeding more than eight) and the appetite-satisfying comfort of a familiar soup and salad. Although there is no meat, chicken, or fish in the menu, the cornmeal combined with the kidney beans provide complete protein. Make the soup when time suits you; having a batch in the freezer for a rainy day is nearly as good as money in the bank.

Minestrone Soup

There are probably as many variations of minestrone soup as there are snowflakes in this world. Here is mine, which is a favorite with my fussy sons. Soups seem better when they are made in big batches; this one makes a hefty 4 quarts plus. Leftovers freeze nicely for up to 6 months.

> 2 tablespoons olive oil
> 1 large Spanish onion, diced
> 1 garlic clove, minced
> 3 quarts homemade beef stock or canned beef
>   broth

3 carrots, diced
2 small potatoes, peeled and diced
1 19-ounce can red kidney beans
1 6-ounce can tomato paste
4 cups loosely packed shredded cabbage
1 teaspoon dried oregano
1 bay leaf
½ teaspoon dried thyme or 1 teaspoon fresh
    thyme
a few drops hot pepper sauce to taste
⅔ cup macaroni elbows or other pasta
½ pound zucchini (about 3 small), sliced in
    ½-inch-thick rounds
⅔ cup fresh or frozen peas
½ cup minced fresh parsley
freshly grated Parmesan cheese to pass at the
    table

1. Heat the oil in a 6-quart or larger saucepan over high heat. When it is hot add the onion and garlic. Reduce the heat to medium and cook, stirring often, for 6 to 7 minutes or until the onion is soft and transparent but not browned.
2. Add the stock, carrots, potatoes, beans (undrained), tomato paste, cabbage, oregano, bay leaf, thyme, and hot pepper sauce. Half cover and simmer for 2 hours.
3. Uncover and add the macaroni. Cover and simmer for 20 minutes.
4. Add the zucchini, peas, and parsley. Cover and simmer 20 to 30 minutes more.
5. Remove the bay leaf (if you can find it). Serve the soup hot. Pass grated Parmesan cheese at the table.

Yield: 11 1½-cup servings
✦ Calories per serving: 172
Carbohydrate per serving: 31g
✦ Cholesterol per serving: 0mg

✦ Dietary fiber per serving: 7g
Fat per serving: 3g
Protein per serving: 7g
✦ Sodium per serving: 208mg

Moist Cornbread Loaf

❖

This is a moist and airy cornbread loaf, although it is made entirely of cornmeal with no added flour. Leftovers are delicious sliced and lightly toasted under the broiler.

> ¾ cup yellow cornmeal
> 2 tablespoons freshly grated Parmesan cheese
> 1 teaspoon salt
> 1 teaspoon dry mustard
> ½ cup boiling water
> 1 tablespoon safflower oil
> 2 eggs, separated
> ½ cup skim or low-fat milk
> 2 teaspoons baking powder
> ½ teaspoon cream of tartar

1. Coat a 4½-inch by 8½-inch loaf pan with cooking spray. Line the bottom with wax paper and coat the wax paper with cooking spray. Preheat oven to 400 degrees. Position an oven rack in the middle of the oven.
2. Place the cornmeal, cheese, salt, and mustard in a medium-size bowl. Stir a few times to combine. Pour in the boiling water and mix well with a wooden spoon. Stir in the oil.
3. Beat the egg yolks until frothy. Beat the yolks into the cornmeal mixture.
4. Stir the milk and baking powder into the cornmeal mixture.
5. Beat the egg whites with a hand-held electric mixer or egg beater until soft peaks form. Add the cream of tartar and continue to beat until stiff peaks form.
6. Fold the whites into the cornmeal mixture. Turn the batter into the prepared loaf pan.
7. Bake the loaf in the middle of the preheated oven until puffed and golden brown, about 35 minutes. Free the bread from the pan by running a flexible-bladed spat-

ula between the bread and the pan. Invert the bread onto a serving platter and peel off the wax paper. Serve hot.

Yield: 8 slices
✦ **Calories per slice: 91**
Carbohydrate per slice: 10g
Cholesterol per slice: 70mg

✦ **Dietary fiber per slice: 1g**
Fat per slice: 4g
Protein per slice: 4g
Sodium per slice: 429mg

Buttermilk Dressing for Tossed Salad

❖

This creamy change from vinaigrette salad dressings gets its zip from a packaged dried herb and spice blend. I use Mrs. Dash, a salt-free brand with lots of lemon, but there are several similar seasonings on the market shelves. This is a calcium-rich, low-fat, hearty dressing that does best with "sturdy" greens, such as romaine, shredded red cabbage, cucumbers, green peppers, and the like. It is particularly good with arugula and watercress, both peppery greens that are well complemented by the tang of the dressing. This will thicken as it chills; thin it with a bit of skim milk or buttermilk.

Packaged dry buttermilk powder, now available at many markets, works well here. Follow package directions to reconstitute. Should you buy a quart of buttermilk, however, and wonder what to do with the remainder, try the Strawberry-Buttermilk Sherbet (page 195), the Whole Wheat Bread Sticks (page 322), or the Whole Wheat Oatmeal Muffins (page 302–3).

½ cup low-fat cottage cheese
⅓ cup low-fat plain yogurt

⅓ cup skimmed buttermilk
2 tablespoons mayonnaise
2 teaspoons dried herb blend such as Mrs. Dash
*   or Vegit*

1. Combine all the ingredients in a food processor or blender and process until smooth. Cover and chill; it will keep up to one week.

Yield: 1⅓ cups
✦ **Calories per tablespoon: 19**
Carbohydrate per tablespoon: 1g
✦ **Cholesterol per tablespoon: 1g**

Dietary fiber per tablespoon: 0g
Fat per tablespoon: 1g
Protein per tablespoon: 1g
✦ **Sodium per tablespoon: 36mg**

❖Ripen mangoes at room temperature in a paper bag poked with a few holes. Sprinkle the flesh with lime juice for a snack or dessert rich in vitamin A with a fair amount of potassium.❖

MEMORY LANE

Black Bean Soup

Apple Salad

Oatmeal Softies

It's unfashionably heavy, unfashionably hearty, and distinctly old-fashioned. This is Depression Era food, preprocessor food, and as far from the "toy" food of Nouvelle Cuisine as you can get. Nutritionally it's tops, long on complex carbohydrates while short on fats, and chock-full of fiber sources from the beans to the apples to the oats.

But forget all that just this once and content yourself in a culinary trip down memory lane with this homestyle meal. Serve ten to twelve with the soup, or freeze the leftovers. The salad is designed for five to six servings; if fewer people pull up a chair to your table, the leftovers are just as good the second day. On the other hand, it's easily doubled when there's a crowd for company.

This is a completely do-ahead meal, convenient for carting away for the weekend or for stocking the freezer when there's a bit of spare time for cooking.

❖ Focus: Beans ❖

Legumes (plants that bear seeds in pods) and particularly the pulses (the dried seeds of the pod, beans and peas) are among the oldest and most nutritious of foods. Once more than mere food, beans were used by ancient Greeks as ballots. A black bean spelled guilt or a "no" vote, while a white bean signaled agreement or suspected innocence. Other cultures used beans to ward off toothache and smallpox. And Scottish witches rode beanstalks not broomsticks. That folklore should sprout up around legumes is no coincidence. After all, dried beans and peas are dietary staples in countries where, from choice or necessity, little rice, grain, or meat are eaten.

Short of prescribing the bean cure for toothache, many modern-day health experts do recommend that beans be included as part of a nutritious diet. Dried beans are good sources of protein and water-soluble fiber. If eaten often, according to the *Journal of Clinical Nutrition*, legumes can lower blood cholesterol counts. How many servings of beans is often? In an experiment 20 men were fed a ¼ pound of dried beans daily for 21 days. Nineteen percent showed a decrease in cholesterol levels and 24 percent showed a decrease in LDL (the "bad") cholesterol. (See *Focus: Cholesterol*, page 42, for more on LDL cholesterol.)

In addition to being good for your heart, beans are an excellent, nearly complete source of protein, though they must be eaten with a dairy product (a glass of milk), or grain or seed (as in red beans and rice), or a small amount of meat (as in chili con carne) to furnish all the protein units needed for growth. Beans vary in nutrients from variety to variety, but they are generally strong suppliers of phosphorus (aids in bone growth and strong teeth) and iron (helps form blood). And they are good suppliers of some of the B vitamins. Beans are also excellent sources of the complex carbohydrates we hear so much about. They also are inexpensive.

An unpleasant side effect of beans is flatulence. Most cookbooks suggest an overnight soaking of the beans, followed by a good rinse and cooking in fresh water to reduce the problem and soften the beans for cooking. Leached out during soaking are oligosaccharides, a carbohydrate that causes gas to form during digestion. Pouring off that soaking water, and cooking with fresh, even a second change of cooking water, may help to remove more of the offending catalyst. Not all beans need soaking, however (see below), and sometimes an overnight soak simply isn't feasible. Both the overnight and the short soak are outlined in the recipes for beans.

Bean Types

Adukis or Adzuki Beans: A small reddish bean used in Oriental cooking. Has a pleasant, sweet flavor that goes well with grains, and is sometimes used in Oriental cakes.

Black Beans: Creamy flesh, strong, meaty flavor. Black beans are used in soups (see next page), for black bean sauce, and are a staple in Mexican cooking.

Black-Eyed Peas: Also known as a cowpea, the black-eyed pea is important in India and here in America's South. It is particularly good in salads and mixed with rice (see page 158). Black-eyed peas are relatively quick to cook, and require no soaking, like other soft beans such as lentils and green or yellow split peas.

Chick Peas or Garbanzos: Extremely hard, round, yellow beans that require an overnight soaking to soften, these beans are primarily used in Spanish and Arab cooking. They have a nutty flavor and are tasty in curries, soups, and salads.

Great Northern Beans: A kidney-shaped white bean used in soups, the French cassoulet, salads (see page 300), and as a side dish.

Kidney Beans: A dark red kidney-shaped bean used in Mexican cookery, as a side dish, in chili, soups, and stews.

Lentils: A small, flat round bean that varies in color from brown to green to orange. Like other soft beans, lentils don't need to be soaked. Popular as a side dish (see page 272), in soup, and in salads.

Lima Beans: Broad, flat, light green bean. An excellent flavored bean, good as a side dish and in casseroles or in soups.

Navy or Small White Beans: Much like Great Northerns but smaller. Sometimes used for Boston Baked Beans or as one would use Great Northerns.

Split Peas: Small, flat beans, green or yellow in color. Used in soups.

Pinto Beans: Pink or brown-speckled medium-size beans. Common in Spain, Mexican, and Tex-Mex food. Good mixed with rice.

Red Beans: Oval-shaped and dark red, red beans are commonly mixed with rice.

Soy Beans: A leading source of protein for many of the world's people, soybeans come in two varieties, vegetable type or field type. The vegetable type may be cooked when fresh and eaten like limas. Field soybeans are dried and ground into flour or used to make oil or a myriad of other uses.

Black Bean Soup

❖

A steaming bowl of black bean soup will chase away the iciest chill and satisfy the greatest hunger, all for a reasonable calorie count with minimal fat. If 4 quarts of soup would overwhelm your freezer space, cut the recipe in half. Black beans are generally available at health food stores.

2 pounds black beans
2 tablespoons safflower oil
¾ cup homemade chicken stock or canned broth
4 cups (about 3 large) sliced onions
3 garlic cloves, minced
3 carrots, diced
2 pork or ham hocks
1 tablespoon ground cumin
2 teaspoons salt
¼ teaspoon hot pepper sauce
1 teaspoon dried oregano
1 tablespoon fresh coriander, chopped (optional)
1 tablespoon fresh thyme or 1 teaspoon dried
    thyme

*1 tablespoon dried herb blend such as Mrs. Dash
   (optional)*
1 tablespoon cider vinegar
1 tablespoon dry sherry per serving (optional)

1. The beans may either be soaked overnight or quick-soaked in the morning. To soak the beans overnight: Rinse the beans and pour them into a 15-quart stockpot. Add water to cover them by 3 or 4 inches, cover the pot, and let rest for 8 to 12 hours. Drain and rinse the beans. To quick-soak the beans: Rinse the beans and pour them into a 15-quart stockpot. Cover them with water by 3 or 4 inches. Place the pot over high heat, cover, and bring to a boil. Boil the beans for just 2 minutes. Remove the pot from the heat and set aside for 1 hour. Drain and rinse the beans.
2. Combine the oil and chicken stock in the 15-quart stockpot. Place over high heat. Add the onions and garlic and stir to combine. Cover. When the liquids boil, reduce the heat to medium-high and cook, stirring occasionally, until the onions are transparent, about 8 to 10 minutes.
3. Add the carrots and stir to combine. Re-cover the pot and cook over medium-high heat for 6 to 7 minutes or until the carrots are tender.
4. To the stockpot add the beans, 6 quarts of water, and all the remaining ingredients except the vinegar and sherry. Stir to combine. Place the stockpot over high heat. Bring the mixture to a boil, skimming off the scum that rises to the surface with a slotted spoon. As soon as a boil is reached, reduce the heat so the liquid just simmers. Simmer, uncovered, for 5 hours or until the liquid has evaporated by about one-third. Stir the soup occasionally as it simmers.
5. Transfer the ham hocks to a plate to cool. When cool, pick off the meat, and return it to the soup. Discard the bones and fat.
6. The soup is now ready to serve, or it may be frozen for up to 8 months. To serve, heat until steaming, stirring

often. Stir in the vinegar and taste for seasoning adjustment. Either stir the sherry into the soup at the serving point or let each person stir in his or her own.

Yield: 10 to 12 servings
   (analysis based on 12)
✦ **Calories per serving: 307**
   Carbohydrate per serving: 52g
✦ **Cholesterol per serving: 1mg**

✦ **Dietary fiber per serving: 20g**
   Fat per serving: 4g
   Protein per serving: 18g
   Sodium per serving: 421mg

Apple Salad

❖

A crisp, clean salad, with the fresh hint of mint. Double the recipe if necessary. If you make the salad ahead, combine the apples and walnuts with the dressing and press plastic wrap right on top of them to prevent them from turning brown during storage. Cover the bowl again with foil or a plastic bag, and press it right onto the surface.

> *3 apples, McIntosh recommended, cored but*
>   *unpeeled*
> *½ cup plain low-fat yogurt*
> *1 tablespoon lemon juice*
> *the finely grated rind (zest) of 1 lemon*
> *1 tablespoon mayonnaise*
> *1 tablespoon chopped fresh mint leaves*
> *1 teaspoon brown sugar*
> *2 tablespoons chopped walnuts*
> *lettuce leaves to line the plates*
> *mint leaves for garnish (optional)*

1. Dice the apples and place them in a medium-size bowl.
2. Combine the yogurt, lemon juice, lemon zest, mayonnaise, chopped mint, and brown sugar in the bowl of a food processor or a blender. Process until smooth.

3. Combine the dressing with the apples and the walnuts. Stir to combine. (Salad may be made to this point and held, refrigerated and covered, up to 4 hours before serving.)
4. Line individual salad plates, or a single serving platter, with lettuce leaves. Mound the apple salad on top. Garnish with mint leaves.

Yield: 6 servings
✦ Calories per serving: 86
Carbohydrate per serving: 13g
✦ Cholesterol per serving: 1mg

✦ Dietary fiber per serving: 2g
Fat per serving: 4g
Protein per serving: 2g
✦ Sodium per serving: 27mg

Oatmeal Softies

❖

There's no pretending this is a low-calorie cookie, but at least it does rate high on the fiber scale with oats, whole wheat flour, carrots, and wheat germ among the ingredients. Kids eat them with delight; just don't mention their nutritional worth. Store the cookies in an airtight tin with wax paper between the layers.

¾ cup margarine
½ cup brown sugar
¼ cup granulated sugar
⅓ cup real maple or maple-flavored syrup
1 egg
¼ cup low-fat milk or skimmed buttermilk
1 teaspoon vanilla extract
1 cup whole wheat flour
½ teaspoon salt
1 teaspoon baking soda
1 teaspoon cinnamon
2 small carrots (or 1 medium), shredded
2 cups quick-cooking (not instant) oats
½ cup wheat germ (honey crunch preferred)

1. Preheat the oven to 375 degrees. Position the oven racks in the middle of the oven. In a medium-size bowl with an electric beater or in the bowl of a food processor, beat together the margarine, sugars, and syrup until creamy.
2. Add the egg, milk, and vanilla. Beat until smooth.
3. Stir in the flour, salt, soda, and cinnamon. Stir just to combine. Stir in the grated carrots. Then stir in the oats and wheat germ.
4. Coat cookie sheets with cooking spray. Drop the batter by the teaspoonful onto the cookie sheets about 2 inches apart.
5. Bake the cookies in the middle of the preheated oven for 10 to 12 minutes or until they are golden brown. Watch closely that the bottoms don't burn. Cool, then store the cookies in an airtight container.

Yield: 4 dozen cookies
✦ Calories per cookie: 69
Carbohydrate per cookie: 9g
✦ Cholesterol per cookie: 5mg

Dietary fiber per cookie: 0.6g
Fat per cookie: 3g
Protein per cookie: 1g
Sodium per cookie: 70mg

❖There are 4 tablespoons of sugar in a 12-ounce can of soda.❖

THE BASICS

❖ The Basics ❖

Unlike commercially prepared broths, homemade stocks are strong with flavor and thickening power but not with salt. While making them is a lengthy process, it's not time spent at the stove so much as a clean-up chore. And if you have large enough pots and ample freezer space, a single cooking session can provide enough stock for weeks.

Stocks must be made from uncooked bones, for these contain collagen that breaks down in the presence of heat, lending richness and density to the stock. Previously cooked bones have lost most of this all-important ingredient, so they contribute little. When boning chicken breasts, simply stash the bones in a plastic bag in the freezer until enough have accumulated to make a decent batch of stock. Short of boning your own chicken, some stores sell chicken backs and wings; be sure to remove the skin, though. Some stores even sell chicken bones, and it seems likely that others would willingly give them away if you ask for them.

Beef bones are harder to come by. Ask for marrow bones (the soft center contains lots of collagen) and buy them whenever you see them. The bones will keep indefinitely in the freezer until the cooking spirit strikes. Veal bones are also highly prized for making stock. Buy them whenever available.

Fish racks, or skeletons, are easy to come by if you have ready access to a fish market that cleans its own fish. Ask for the rack of white, non-oily fish such as haddock or cod. Sole racks are very bony, and fatty fishes may make too strong a stock for general purposes.

All stocks are perishable and should be chilled as soon as possible. If a stock is not used within a day, freeze it. Use various sized containers including ice cube trays (pop the solid cubes into a plastic bag for long-term storage). If a stock has been refrigerated for longer than 24 hours (but not frozen), boil it a good minute before using.

For those without the inclination, space, or equipment to make stock, this section also contains a recipe for boosting the flavor and thickness of canned broth. Also included are a basic tomato sauce and a chunky ketchup recipe.

Chicken Stock

❖

5-6 pounds uncooked chicken bones (saved from
    boning breasts, or buy wings and backs)
2-3 carrots, sliced (no need to peel)
2 medium onions, sliced
2 celery stalks, sliced
4 quarts water
1 cup dry white wine (optional)
a small handful fresh parsley stems, chopped
freshly ground pepper to taste
1 bay leaf
1 garlic clove, halved

1. A rich, brown chicken stock is made like the beef stock (see next page), by browning the bones and vegetables in a 400-degree oven for about 40 to 50 minutes. Strain away and discard the fat. Place the browned bones and vegetables in a stockpot, cover with water, add the wine, and bring to a boil. Continue at step 3.
2. A "white" stock is made by putting unroasted bones and vegetables in a 12-quart stockpot, cover with the water, and add the wine. Bring to a boil.
3. Reduce heat to a simmer and skim off the scum that rises to the surface with a slotted spoon. Repeat the skimming two or three times until most of the scum is removed.
4. Add the parsley, pepper, bay leaf, and garlic. Half cover the pan and simmer about 4 hours, adding more water if the volume falls more than a quart below the original level.

5. Wring out an old kitchen towel or a piece of cheese-cloth in water and line a strainer with it. Pour or ladle the stock through the strainer.
6. If using the stock immediately, pour what you need into a degreaser (a gadget with the spout coming off the bottom, not the top) to complete the defatting, or refrigerate until a pancake of fat forms. Scrape off the fat and freeze the stock in plastic containers of varying sizes.

Yield: about 3 quarts
+ Calories per cup: 21
Carbohydrate per cup: 4g
+ Cholesterol per cup: 0mg

Dietary fiber per cup: 0g
Fat per cup: 0g
Protein per cup: 1g
+ Sodium per cup: 20mg

Beef Stock

❖

8 pounds uncooked beef bones, marrow bones
    highly recommended
3 carrots, sliced (no need to peel)
3 small to medium onions, sliced (no need to
    peel, the skins add color)
3 celery stalks, sliced
7 quarts water
1 cup red wine (optional)
a small handful fresh parsley stems, chopped
freshly ground pepper to taste
1 bay leaf
1 garlic clove, halved

1. Put the bones in a large roasting pan with the carrots, onions, and celery, and roast about 40 to 50 minutes in a 400-degree oven, or until the bones and vegetables are beginning to brown.

2. Strain away and discard the fat. Put the bones and vegetables in a 12-quart stockpot, cover with water, add the wine, and bring it to a full boil.
3. Reduce heat to a simmer and skim off the scum that rises to the surface with a slotted spoon. Repeat the skimming two or three times until most of the scum is removed.
4. Add parsley, pepper, bay leaf, and garlic. Half cover the pan and simmer about 8 hours, adding more water if the volume falls more than a quart below the original level.
5. Wring out an old kitchen towel or a piece of cheesecloth in cold water and line a strainer with it. Pour or ladle the stock through the strainer.
6. If using the stock immediately, pour what you need into a degreaser to complete the defatting, or refrigerate the stock. A pancake of fat will form that is easily scraped off. Freeze stock in plastic containers of various sizes.

Yield: 3½ to 4 quarts
✦ Calories per cup: 18
Carbohydrate per cup: 4g
✦ Cholesterol per cup: 00mg

Dietary fiber per cup: 0g
Fat per cup: 0g
Protein per cup: 1g
✦ Sodium per cup: 20mg

Enriched Quick Commercial Beef or Chicken Broth

❖

½ pound uncooked beef or chicken bones
3 unpeeled carrots, sliced
1 onion, chopped
1 tablespoon oil (optional)
1 quart canned beef or chicken broth

½ cup red or white wine (optional)
1 bay leaf
1 garlic clove, halved
freshly ground black pepper to taste
a small handful fresh parsley stems, chopped

1. If dark color is desired, brown the bones and vegetables in the oil in a covered skillet over high heat for about 6 minutes. Deglaze the skillet with 2 tablespoons wine (from the ½ cup).
2. For a "white" stock simply put all the ingredients in a 2½-quart saucepan, half cover, and simmer 30 minutes.
3. The stock may be used immediately after straining and discarding bones, vegetables, and herbs.

Yield: 3½ cups	Dietary fiber per cup: 0g
Calories per cup: 24	Fat per cup: 0g
Carbohydrate per cup: 5g	Protein per cup: 1g
Cholesterol per cup: 0g	Sodium per cup: 227mg

Fish Stock

❖

This delicate stock must be frozen if not used within 24 hours.

1 fish rack (skeleton) weighing about 1½ pounds
    from a white-fleshed, nonoily fish such as
    haddock or cod, innards removed and rack
    rinsed
6 cups water
2 cups dry white wine (optional)
1 small onion, chopped
1 small carrot, chopped
1 bay leaf

1. Put the fish rack (don't shy away from using the head, as it contains lots of collagen, which melts into gelatin) in a heavy pot, preferably nonaluminum if using the wine, and add the water and wine.
2. Bring to a boil, reduce the heat so the liquid just simmers, and skim off the scum with a slotted spoon. When most of the scum is removed, add the remaining ingredients and half cover pot. Simmer for 40 minutes.
3. Rinse out an old kitchen towel or a piece of cheesecloth in water, line a strainer with it, and pour or ladle stock through. Store in the refrigerator, or freeze if the stock is not used within 24 hours.

Note: Bottled clam juice is a very acceptable substitute in recipes calling for fish stock. Dilute the bottled product with ¼ cup dry white wine or vermouth to 8 ounces clam juice, and omit salt from the recipe.

Yield: about 1 quart
✦ **Calories per cup: 33**
Carbohydrate per cup: 8g
✦ **Cholesterol per cup: 0g**

Dietary fiber per cup: 0g
Fat per cup: 0g
Protein per cup: 1g
✦ **Sodium per cup: 10mg**

Tomato Sauce
❖

2 pounds tomatoes, roughly chopped or 44 ounces canned tomatoes (2 large cans)
1 small onion, chopped
1 garlic clove, minced
1 tablespoon tomato paste
2 cups chicken stock (1 cup if using canned tomatoes)
4 leaves fresh basil, snipped, or 1 teaspoon dried basil

⅔ teaspoon sugar
½ teaspoon salt if using fresh tomatoes (omit if
    using canned)

1. Combine all the ingredients in a medium-size saucepan and boil, uncovered, until reduced by half.
2. Puree the mixture in a food processor or blender, and
   strain to remove the seeds and skins if desired. The
   sauce may be frozen if you wish.

Yield: about 3 cups
✦ **Calories per cup: 96**
  Carbohydrate per cup: 21g
✦ **Cholesterol per cup: 00g**

Dietary fiber per cup: 0g
Fat per cup: 1g
Protein per cup: 4g
Sodium per cup: 380mg

Chunky Homestyle Ketchup

❖

Making your own low-sugar ketchup is infinitely easier—
to say nothing of better—than you might expect! Supermarket tomatoes and farmstand "seconds" are good can-
didates here—no need to waste the vine-ripened
beauties. This ketchup makes good giving and will keep
up to two months in the refrigerator.

2 pounds tomatoes
1 shallot, minced
1 garlic clove, minced
1 bay leaf
1 6-ounce can tomato paste
⅛ teaspoon cayenne pepper
½ teaspoon paprika
1 teaspoon salt
2 tablespoons sugar
⅓ cup balsamic vinegar
2 teaspoons cornstarch

1. Quarter the tomatoes and put them into a 2½-quart saucepan. Cover and bring to a boil over medium heat. When a boil is reached, lower heat, and add the shallot, garlic, and bay leaf. Simmer 45 minutes, stirring occasionally.
2. Discard the bay leaf. Puree the tomatoes in a food processor or food mill, then strain the puree through a coarse strainer, pressing the juices from the solids with the back of a wooden spoon. Return the puree to the saucepan.
3. Add the tomato paste, cayenne, paprika, salt, and sugar. Reserve 2 tablespoons of the vinegar, and add remaining vinegar to the puree. Stir. Simmer, uncovered, for 15 minutes.
4. Meanwhile, dissolve the cornstarch in the reserved vinegar. Stir it into the puree and simmer 5 minutes or until thickened. Refrigerate.

Note: Ketchup will thicken on chilling, so don't be alarmed if it's a bit runny when it's hot.

Yield: 4 cups
✦ Calories per tablespoon: 7
Carbohydrate per tablespoon: 2g
✦ Cholesterol per tablespoon: 0mg

Dietary fiber per tablespoon: 0g
Fat per tablespoon: 0g
Protein per tablespoon: 0g
Sodium per tablespoon: 40mg

❖ Focus: When Sugar ❖ Becomes a Bitter Pill

We've all heard we should eat more carbohydrates; sugar is a carbohydrate, therefore, if weight is no problem, what's wrong with cookies and candy? Research shows heart disease occurs most often in persons who have a high blood cholesterol level coupled with a high blood triglyceride (a kind of fat) level. Sugar may stimulate the body to produce triglycerides particularly when caloric intake is higher than needed and carbohydrate intake is also high. Limiting sugars, therefore, and maintaining ideal body weight are important for a healthy heart.

❖ Recipe Index ❖

Looking for a meatless entree or an interesting salad? This index by category will help you find the recipe you need without wading through the individual menus.

APPETIZERS
Beef Sticks, Grilled with Horseradish Sauce, 12
Cherrystones, Roasted Oregano, 13
Crudités, with Chili-Coriander Dip, 11
Onions, Sweet and Sour, 10
Shrimp, Grilled, 240
Tartlets, Shiitake and Pine Nut, 5
Wontons, Steamed Crabmeat, 7

BREADS
Banana with Wheat Germ, 292
Bread Sticks, Whole Wheat, 322
Cornbread Loaf, Moist, 334
Muffins, Whole Wheat Oatmeal, 302
Rolls, Cheese, Garden Goodness, 180

CONDIMENTS, STOCKS, AND STAPLES
Broth, Enriched, Quick, Commercial, 104
Creole Spice Mix, 252
Ketchup, Chunky Homestyle, 352
Mayonnaise, Chinese, 310
Relish, Tomato, 32
Salsa, Fresh Herb, 270
Sauce, Tomato, 351
Stock, Beef, 348
Stock, Chicken, 347
Stock, Fish, 350

DESSERTS
Apple Slices, Baked with Bourbon Sauce, 79
Banana Bread with Wheat Germ, 292
Bananas Creole, 68
Cake, Lemon Mousse with Raspberry Sauce, 25
Cappucino Cream, 100
Chiffon, Spiced Rum Pumpkin, 280
Cookies, Oatmeal Softies, 343
Custard, Mocha, 230
Fruit, Fresh and Cheese, 304
Fruits, Tropical with Apricot Cream, 154
Honeyed Lemon Frost, 203

Mousse, Iced Fruit, 50
Oranges, Glazed Ginger, 89
Parfait, Strawberry, 324
Peaches and Nectarines in Minted Orange Sauce, 34
Pears, Meringue Poached, 58
Pot de Crème, Orange, 259
Sherbet, Strawberry-Buttermilk, 195
Strawberries with Strawberry Cream, 312
Sorbet, Pineapple, 173
Tarts, Nutted Fall Fruit, 40

FISH
Cod, Curried with Couscous, 288
Codfish, Crumbed with Lemon Mustard Sauce, 97
Halibut, with Nutted Confetti, 115
Mussels in Black Bean Sauce, 264
Salmon Fillets, Dry-Fried, 188
Salmon Steaks with Green Sauce, 165
Shrimp and Crab Gumbo, 251
Shrimp and Lobster Patties, Grilled, 151
Shrimp, Grilled, 240
Shrimp, Spicy and Cashew Stir-Fry, 171
Swordfish, Pan-blackened, 157
Swordfish, Poached with Lemon Dill Sauce, 30

MEATLESS ENTREES
Angel Hair Pasta with Chèvre, 241
Black Bean Soup, 340
Eggplant and Spinach Cheese Strata, 141
Eggs Imposter, 176
Frittata, Vegetable with Two Cheeses, 257
Lasagne, Vegetable with Spinach Noodles and Three
    Cheeses, 234
Minestrone Soup, 332
Pasta, Red Pepper with Vegetables and Herb Vinaigrette, 189
0
MEATS
Beef, Filet of with Lobster Sauce, 84
Flank Steak, Grilled Stuffed, 132
Ham and Bean Salad, 300
Lamb, Loin of, Persillade, Roasted, 47
Lamb Medallions in Phyllo with Green Peppercorn Stuffing,
    22
Pork Medallions with Cider and Apples, 38
Pork Tenderloin, Grilled Ginger-Lime, 55
Veal and Artichoke Ragout, 276
Veal, Loin Chop, Grilled, 64
Veal, Medallions with Mushrooms and Marsala, 73
Veal, Pan-seared Lemon, 119

PASTAS

Angel Hair with Chèvre, 241
Angel Hair with Ham and Peas in "Cream" Sauce, 198
Buckwheat, Salad, with Spinach and Scallops, 214
Fettucine, Basil with Mussels in Red Wine Sauce, 207
Lasagne, Vegetable with Spinach Noodles and Three
    Cheeses, 234
Noodles, Chinese, 285
Poppy Seed, 122
Raviolis, Seafood with Tomato Cream Sauce, 222
Red Pepper with Vegetables and Herb Vinaigrette, 189

POULTRY

Chicken and Broccoli Salad, 308
Chicken Breast with Spinach and Feta, 103
Chicken Breasts with Green Peppercorn Sauce, 314
Chicken, Chinese Steamed with Mushrooms and Broccoli,
    284
Chicken Paillard with Fresh Herb Salsa, 270
Tabouli Salad with Shredded Chicken, 328
Turkey Breast with Port and Mushrooms, 126

SALADS AND SALAD DRESSINGS

Apple, 342
Apple, Walnut, and Roquefort, 279
Avocado-Pear with Hot Lime Dressing, 131
Beet, Hot and Parsnip on Beet Greens, 137
Bibb Lettuce with Balsamic Dressing, 229
Buckwheat Pasta with Spinach and Scallops, 214
Buttermilk Dressing, 335
Chicken and Broccoli, 308
Corn and Tomato with Blue Cheese Dressing, 153
Cucumber, Shredded, 211
Green, Tossed with Shredded Radishes, 72
Greens, Mixed with Honey-Tarragon Dressing, 117
Ham and Bean, 300
Mediterranean, 201
Mushroom, Hot with Red Pepper Jelly Dressing, 20
Romaine Lettuce with Garlic Vinaigrette, 238
Sesame-Chive Dressing, 258
Tabouli with Shredded Chicken, 328
Tahini Dressing, 291
Three-Green with Champagne-Orange Vinaigrette and
    Melted Goat Cheese, 193
Tossed with Creamy Herbed Dressing, 144
Tossed with Raspberry Vinaigrette, 254
Vegetable, Grilled, 53
Watercress, Endive, and Grapefruit with Poppy Seed
    Dressing, 82

SOUPS

VEGETABLES, STARCHES, AND GRAINS

❖ Index ❖